Here's How to Write Well

SECOND EDITION

Elizabeth McMahan
Illinois State University

Robert Funk
Eastern Illinois University

Longman

NEW YORK • SAN FRANCISCO • BOSTON
LONDON • TORONTO • SYDNEY • TOKYO • SINGAPORE • MADRID
MEXICO CITY • MUNICH • PARIS • CAPE TOWN • HONG KONG • MONTREAL

Vice President and Publisher: Eben W. Ludlow
Marketing Manager: Carlise Paulson
Project Coordination, Text Design, and Electronic Page Makeup:
    UG / GGS Information Services, Inc.
Cover Design Manager: Wendy Fredericks
Cover Designer: Kay Petronio
Cover Illustration: © Ben Killen Rosenberg/Artville
Senior Manufacturing Manager: Dennis J. Para
Printer and Binder: R. R. Donnelley—Harrisonburg
Cover Printer: Coral Graphic Services, Inc.

For permission to use copyrighted material, grateful acknowledgment is
made to the copyright holders on p. 268, which are hereby made part of
this copyright page.

Library of Congress Cataloging-in-Publication Data
McMahan, Elizabeth.
    Here's how to write well / Elizabeth McMahan, Robert Funk.—2nd ed.
    p. cm.
    Includes index.
    ISBN 0-205-33733-3
    1. English language—Rhetoric. 2. English language—Grammar. 3.
    Report writing. I. Title.

PE1408 .M39475 2001
808'.042—dc21

2001022590

Please visit our website at http://www.ablongman.com

ISBN 0-205-33733-3
  2 3 4 5 6 7 8 9 10—DOH—04 03 02

Brief
Contents

Detailed

Contents

Chapter **2**

Addressing Your Readers   18

Chapter **3**

Chapter 4

Composing Effective Paragraphs 51

Chapter 5

Polishing Your Sentences   71

Chapter **6**

The Revising and Editing Process   95

Chapter **7**

Chapter **8**

Chapter **9**

Using Your Sources

PART III *How to Make Your Writing Clear and Correct* **181**

Chapter **11**

Reviewing the Basics of Grammar 183

Chapter **12**

Punctuating for Clarity and Effectiveness 190

Chapter **13**

Working with Verbs   220

Preface

This book demonstrates in plain, straightforward language how to become a capable writer. The conversational tone in no way compromises the integrity of the instruction, but it does make the material more accessible—pleasant to read and easy to understand. *Here's How to Write Well* is organized into three parts.

PART I, HOW TO PUT A PAPER TOGETHER, provides a guided tour of the writing process—from gathering, sorting, and organizing ideas to drafting, revising, and editing the final version. Chapter 3 presents strategies for handling writing assignments in six commonly used rhetorical modes. The discussion of each mode includes ideas for developing the content, sample outlines illustrating how to organize the material, warnings about possible pitfalls, and appealing paper topics to inspire good writing. Next comes advice on composing and developing paragraphs (Chapter 4), on crafting and polishing sentences (Chapter 5), and on revising and editing final drafts (Chapter 6), all complete with handy checklists. Chapter 7 focuses on thinking critically and logically.

PART II, HOW TO WRITE A RESEARCH PAPER, constitutes a concise but thorough guide for completing a research paper. Three chapters provide detailed instruction for finding and writing from sources—including electronic sources—and for using two systems of documentation—MLA and APA.

PART III, HOW TO MAKE YOUR WRITING CLEAR AND CORRECT, is a handbook explaining the rules of punctuation, grammatical correctness, and usage—all the information writers need to complete the revising and editing stages. These explanations depend only lightly on grammar to make them as easy as possible to understand. The occasional exercises allow anyone in need of extra help to practice the tricky parts. The final chapter, a glossary of usage, provides advice about a number of words and phrases that writers typically find confusing.

Throughout the text, boldfaced **TIP!**s emphasize important concepts and reinforce learning. A number of collaborative activities enable students to work together and learn from each other.

This second edition offers several valuable additions. A new chapter, "Reviewing the Basics of Grammar," examines the parts of speech and briefly explains the structure and uses of phrases and clauses. The instruction on devising and using a thesis has been amplified. The section on research writing now offers a sample working outline with notecards and a complete outline for the sample research paper. The advice on computer-assisted writing has been expanded with topics drawing on the Internet in Chapter 3, an update of the discussion for employing and documenting electronic sources in researched writing, as well as suggestions for utilizing the computer in the planning process.

This still slender book—presented in clear, concise, informal language—contains few frills but all the essentials. Anyone who wants to become a proficient writer will find ample help within its covers.

A cknowledgments

Our sincere thanks to those who have helped with the polishing and production of the text: our astute reviewer, Ellen O'Keefe/Franklin Institute of Boston; our esteemed editor, Eben Ludlow; his peerless assistant, Grace Trudo; and our assiduous production editor, Terri O'Prey. We are, as always, especially grateful to our exemplary consulting editor, Susie Day, for her excellent advice.

—Elizabeth McMahan
—Robert Funk

I

How to Put a
Paper Together

1

The Planning Process

Don't let anybody kid you: writing well requires effort. But as our friend Charlie Harris says, "I hate to write, but I love to have written." That's it, exactly. Writing can be most rewarding—if you do a good job.

The Need for Good Writing Skills

The rewards are more than psychological. Writing well is one of the most useful skills you can develop—essential even—and extremely valuable to prospective employers. You will improve your chances of landing and keeping a good job if you can write clearly, correctly, and convincingly. Let's face it. You need to be able to write. This book can help you learn.

Allow Plenty of Time

Because of all the thinking that goes into good writing, the process always takes longer than you think it possibly could. So plan ahead. Get started early and you'll have a chance to get your paper done in time to let it cool a day—well, at least a few hours—before revising and proofreading. Otherwise, you'll be pulling an all-nighter, for sure, and your work will probably show it.

TIP! Remember Mark Twain's Rule: writing always takes twice as long as you think it's going to.

W *riting Seldom Goes Step-by-Step*

Be advised that although we're going to describe writing as a step-by-step process, it's really a lot messier than that. And everybody's process is a little different. Experienced writers, for instance, often revise as they go. But other writers—especially those who have to struggle just to get their ideas down on paper—save the revising for later. Some people plunge straight into a first draft with no planning whatsoever and then keep doing drafts until they come up with something suitable. Others devise a plan of some sort before they begin. Whatever works for you is what you should do.

So, bear in mind that we're simplifying the writing process as we explain it. We're going to straighten it out, tidy it up, and take it in steps to make it easy to understand.

T *hink Before You Write*

Before beginning a first draft, you need to consider three things:

- *Your purpose:* Why am I writing?
- *Your readers:* Who am I writing for?
- *Your main point:* What am I writing about?

All of these questions are important, and your answer to one will often affect your response to the others.

TIP! Try to keep your purpose, your readers, and your main point in mind as you write.

Ponder Your Purpose

Ask yourself, "Why am I exerting all this energy and straining my brain to write this paper?" An honest reply might be that someone told you to, but that's not a useful answer.

Think beyond that immediate response to find a better reason. What do you hope to accomplish? Are you writing to provide information? Do you hope to persuade your readers to take some course of action or to change their minds on some issue?

(You may, of course, be writing in a journal as an aid to learning or just to keep track of your life, but you don't need our help there.)

Your purpose affects your whole approach to writing: how you begin, whether you state or imply your main idea, how you organize the material, what details you choose, how you end, as well as what words you select. If your purpose, say, is to explain how to follow a process, you'll want to state your thesis clearly up front, arrange your ideas step-by-step, include easily visualized details, warn about any possible pitfalls at the end, and write the whole thing in easy-to-understand language.

If, on the other hand, your purpose is to entertain with an account of your disastrous visit to Alaska in midwinter, you'll leave your thesis unstated, arrange the details to build up to the worst fiasco, conclude with a vow never to travel again, and use humorous slang and metaphorical language.

TIP! Determine your purpose early on and stay focused on it as you continue planning and writing.

Consider Your Audience

You can't hope to accomplish your purpose without also thinking about who's going to read this piece of writing. Your audience may be a single person—your instructor, a coworker, your boss, your senator, perhaps. Or you may at some time want to reach a more diverse audience—your city council, the urban planning commission, the readers of your local newspaper, or maybe the readership of *Time* magazine, the *Chicago Tribune,* or an interest group on the Internet. If, for instance, you're writing to explain the hazards of mixing household cleaning products, it makes a huge difference whether you're doing it for a college home economics instructor or a fifth-grade health class. Or, say you're writing to persuade your readers that physician-assisted suicide should be legalized. Consider how different your tactics would need to be depending upon whether you were addressing the Knights of Columbus or the American Civil Liberties Union.

TIP! Think about your readers as you decide what material to present—and in exactly what words to present it.

C *ome Up with a Working Thesis*

Keep both your purpose and your audience in mind as you think about finding a *thesis*—that is, *your main idea, the point you intend to make.* We think it helps to have it clearly thought out— and down on paper—early in the planning process. You'll be able to use it as you gather information and construct your paper.

Gain Unity with Your Thesis

All your major ideas will relate to this thesis, and your supporting details will relate to those main ideas. As a result, your whole paper will be effectively unified. Of course, as you proceed with the planning and the actual drafting, you can narrow the thesis, expand it, or even change the focus as new ideas occur to you. If you do depart from your original thesis in the process, don't forget to go back and check each paragraph to be sure you haven't drifted away from your main idea as the paper evolved.

Start with a Topic

First you'll choose (or be assigned) a topic or subject to write about. In composition class you may be allowed to choose your topic. In history class you are more likely to be told the topic. On the job, unless you're the boss, you'll probably be told what to write about. But whether assigned or chosen, a *topic is not a thesis*—until you turn it into one.

Narrow the Topic

Let's assume that in your horticulture class, you've been assigned a three to four page paper on the topic of home gardening. Since you aren't interested in growing flowers, you narrow the topic to home vegetable gardening. That's still a subject more suited to a book than a short essay. How about organic vegetable gardening? Better, but four pages isn't much—only six or seven paragraphs, plus a brief introduction and conclusion. You need to narrow the topic still more. What about the problem of insects eating the tender plants? Should the gardener try to control them with insecticides or find other methods? How about focusing on methods of fighting bugs organically? Now, that sounds promising.

Try *Freewriting* to Reel Out Ideas

If this narrowing down doesn't come naturally, you can try this technique for your horticulture paper. Just scrawl your topic at the top of a piece of paper (or the top of your computer screen) and then start writing down all the ideas that come to mind as you think about this topic. Pay no attention to spelling, punctuation, or organization—not for nothing is this technique called *free*writing. After you've written for ten minutes or so, read over the pages looking for one idea that sounds suitable as a possible thesis. If all the ideas seem too broad, choose the most promising one and do another round of freewriting. Keep writing and choosing until you discover a thesis idea that pleases you.

W*riting Exercise 1.1*

Select one of the following broad topics and freewrite until you find a suitable thesis idea for a paper of about 700 words. Then write the idea in a single sentence.

Parenting	Soap operas
Science	Movies
Teen pregnancy	Politics
Violence	Fashion
Sports	TV shows

Make a Point in Your Thesis

Once you have narrowed your idea, you need to find an approach that will allow you to make a point about the topic. So, ask yourself, what *about* fighting bugs organically? Clearly, the point here is to get rid of the voracious bugs without using hazardous chemicals. So, your working thesis might read something like this:

> Fighting bugs organically allows home gardeners to avoid the dangers of pesticides.

You make your point by writing a complete sentence—with both a subject and a verb. The subject of the thesis statement is your topic. The verb states the point you're going to make about the topic. Notice the difference between topics and thesis statements in the following examples:

NOT A THESIS: Romance

NOT A THESIS: Romance and losing it after marriage

THESIS:	Several simple strategies can help keep romance alive for married couples with young children.
NOT A THESIS:	Drug abuse
NOT A THESIS:	Drug abuse and abusing prescriptions
THESIS:	Serious drug abuse can occur even with legal prescriptions.
NOT A THESIS:	Air pollution
NOT A THESIS:	Air pollution and the internal combustion engine
THESIS:	The popularity of gas-guzzling sports utility vehicles contributes significantly to air pollution.
NOT A THESIS:	High school football
NOT A THESIS:	High school football and raising academic requirements
THESIS:	High schools should require all football players to maintain a C average to be on the team.

TIP! Before beginning a first draft, write out your thesis in a single clear sentence with a subject and verb.

Say Something Solid

A verb won't save your thesis if the point isn't worth making. You want your essay to be interesting, informative, persuasive, and insightful. You do not want it to be obvious, predictable, shallow, or boring. If you can't tell whether your idea is worth writing about, ask somebody—better yet, ask several people. Be especially wary of a thesis that has the ring of a greeting card message : "Happiness is a warm puppy." Think twice about ideas you've heard all your life that may or may not be true: "Playing sports builds character." And try not to bore your readers by telling them something they already know: "Illegal drugs cause a huge problem in our society."

Positioning Your Thesis

In most writing—especially for college classes—you'll do well to state your thesis in the opening paragraph. Your readers can more easily follow the ideas if they know where the paper is going. In narrative and descriptive writing, of course, where conveying ideas is not the point, it is better to leave your thesis unstated. You should have in mind—and perhaps on paper—what you hope to accomplish as well as how the story or description will develop. But announcing your purpose in advance will take the edge off for your readers.

C hanging Your Thesis in Mid-Writing

Keep in mind that the main idea of your paper can change during the writing process. As British author E. M. Forster once observed, "How do I know what I think until I see what I say?" If you come up with a better idea or a different approach as you write, be prepared to shift gears and go with the new insight. Word processors allow changes—even major changes—to occur easily with a few keystrokes. So, don't become locked into the main idea you began with. Let your thesis evolve when it makes sense to do so.

Starting Without a Thesis

Some writers, in fact, plunge right in writing in order to discover what they have to say. They just begin putting down ideas about the topic until they have completed a first draft, a discovery draft. Then they begin revising and keep on revising—adding ideas, taking out ideas, rearranging ideas—until they have a finished product. This method strikes us as less efficient than planning ahead, but if you suffer from writer's block, you might want to give it a try.

D *iscussion Exercise 1.2*

With a small group of classmates, discuss the following sentences one by one. Some are workable thesis sentences for an essay of two to three typed pages, double-spaced with one-inch margins. But some need to be made more specific. Identify the successful ones, and figure out what's wrong with the losers.

Then, writing individually, turn each unsatisfactory sentence into a reasonably good thesis. When finished, compare results as a group.

1. Many Americans spend so much time in front of the TV set that they never really experience their own lives.

2. Personal freedom and independence carry with them responsibilities and consequences.

3. Making a lemon pie is easy.

4. I think that college students and teachers would be happier with education if people didn't enroll in college before the age of twenty-five.

5. My dog and my boyfriend are much alike.
6. Thousands of Americans go through the vicious cycle of eating until they are overweight and then dieting until they reduce, only to gain the pounds back again.
7. I learned not to worry when I was sixteen.
8. The perfect omelet is fluffy, light, delicately browned, and even attainable if the cook follows five practical guidelines.
9. The purpose of this paper is to compare and contrast the Catholic schools and the public schools.
10. The prevailing views on capital punishment are quite controversial.

D *eveloping Details: Invention Techniques*

Once you have established your thesis, your purpose, and your audience, you need to get your mind in gear and come up with plenty of ideas to use in developing your essay. Here are some strategies that will get you started.

Brainstorming a List

Because you want to come up with as many details as possible, start thinking about your topic, and jot down every idea that comes to mind. Don't be selective at this point. You can eliminate useless or irrelevant material during the arranging stage that follows. You'll probably end up with a jumbled list something like the one generating ideas for gardening without pesticides shown in Figure 1.1.

Clustering to Find Ideas

If you aren't a linear thinker, you may want to work out your brainstorming in clusters rather than jotting your ideas down in a list. The process is the same. Write your topic or thesis in the middle of a page, draw a circle around it, start thinking, and let your ideas radiate out from there, using the same gardening material illustrated in Figure 1.2.

Freewriting to Find Ideas

If freewriting worked for you in narrowing your subject, you can use it again to generate material. This time, write your thesis

Fighting Bugs Without Pesticides

Birds eat insects
Some insects eat other insects! (Good
  ones eat bad ones, hopefully)
Can buy good insects from mail order catalogs
Soapy water kills some bugs - or drives
  them away - doesn't hurt plants
Garlic water does too - real strong!
Slugs like beer - love to drown themselves
  in it
Praying mantises eat caterpillars + mites
Ladybugs devour tons of aphids.
Can pick bugs off by hand (drown them
  in a jar) but take lots of time!
Milky spore disease kills Japanese
  beetles (according to article)
Bacillus thuringiensus kills cabbage worms
  (same article)
Reflection from aluminum foil drives
  aphids nuts.
Green lacewings eat mealy bugs.

FIGURE 1.1 *Brainstorming List*

at the top and continue writing as you think about that idea. Continue for ten minutes at least. Then, using a highlighter, mark the lines containing information that you might want to incorporate into your paper. Finally, on a separate sheet, record everything that's useful, and you'll have a list of ideas to choose from when you organize.

In Chapter 3 you'll find detailed advice and a number of strategies for developing details.

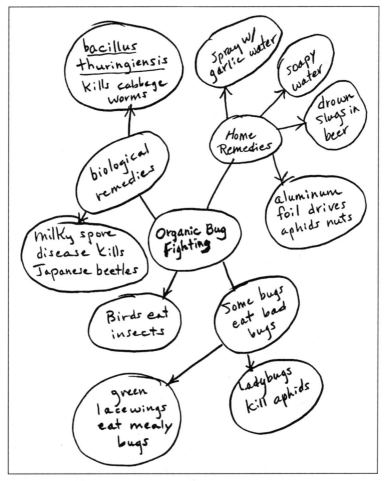

FIGURE 1.2   *Clustering Ideas*

Exploring Ideas on a Computer

Most of the invention techniques discussed in this chapter can be done on the computer. You may find that you can brainstorm or freewrite more quickly and easily on a keyboard. To increase your concentration, turn down the brightness on the monitor so you can write without seeing the screen. When you've finished, turn the brightness back up and view your freewriting on screen; then use the boldface or italic codes to highlight points and details that seem valuable. As you develop more material, review it periodically and highlight the important points; then transfer these items to a separate file for later use. If you have a draw or paint program, use it to do some visual planning such as clustering.

Invention Exercise 1.3

Using the thesis that you devised in Exercise 1.1, develop details for that thesis by brainstorming, clustering, or freewriting. Consider using all three techniques if you have trouble coming up with enough material to support the thesis.

Prewriting Checklist

Here's a list of questions that will help direct your thinking as you transform your brainstorming, freewriting, or clustering into an essay. Write out your response to each question.

1. What's my topic?
2. What's the main point I want to make about the topic?
3. Who is my primary audience? That is, what group of readers do I want to reach?
4. What's my specific purpose in regard to those readers?
5. What kinds of evidence am I going to use?

Your responses will probably turn out something like these:

1. Topic: needle exchange programs to reduce spread of AIDS
2. Main point: Needle exchange programs are an effective and relatively inexpensive means of reducing the spread of HIV among drug users.
3. Primary audience: readers who doubt or are unsure about value and usefulness of needle exchanges.
4. Specific purpose: to get doubters to reconsider their opinions—to understand why needle exchanges are effective, not detrimental.
5. Evidence: mainly reasons and explanations, but also summaries of several studies I've read about needle exchanges—a couple of quotations from columnist Clarence Page, who has written on this issue recently.

B ringing Order Out of Chaos: Outlining

Finally, it's time to work out a plan—to arrange all this material into a sequence your readers can easily follow. You'll need at least three or four main ideas to serve as the major points in your outline. In your paper about organic gardening, those major points will be methods of controlling insect pests.

Sorting Out Main Ideas and Supporting Details

Examine the ideas you have generated, looking for patterns of similarity. Try first to determine which are the major ideas. These are the ones for which you can find *supporting details*—that is, the points and examples that explain, identify, illustrate, or qualify a major idea.

In the brainstorming list in Figure 1.1, for instance, "Some insects eat garden pests" is clearly a major idea. There are several examples to support it—praying mantises, ladybugs, and green lacewings; there are also the specific insects they control and the fact that all these useful insects can be purchased by mail. That's plenty for one paragraph.

You may detect several supporting details that are similar but need to have a major heading added. Notice in the list that these items all share a common trait:

Putting out beer for slugs

Laying down aluminum foil to kill aphids

Squirting soapy water or garlic water on plants

These methods all use products usually found in the kitchen. By adding a heading, you can group these three under, "Try safe and easy household remedies."

Two other items on the list clearly belong together: milky spore disease and *Bacillus thuringiensis*. (You discover such unusual remedies by reading articles or inquiring at your favorite garden store.) Since these biological techniques work by introducing diseases fatal to insects but harmless to plants and people, you might head this section, "Introduce insect diseases to destroy pests."

Only two items in the brainstorming list remain unused: picking insects off by hand and encouraging birds to come to the garden. Probably picking bugs off by hand is too tiresome to be a practical suggestion. And enticing birds may hurt more than help. Birds eat bugs indiscriminately—the ladybugs along with the aphids—and are exceptionally fond of many succulent garden vegetables as well. You decide to let the idea of attracting birds go and mention in your conclusion that if all else fails, the fanatical gardener can always pick off the beastly bugs one by one.

Arranging Your Major Points

After you finish choosing your main ideas and supporting details, the last step before the actual drafting involves deciding in what order to present the ideas. Since there is no chronology (time order) involved in presenting the material, you want to begin with an interesting point to grab your readers' attention. Most importantly, you need to end with your strongest point to leave your audience feeling they have read something worthwhile.

With this pest control outline, you could almost flip a coin. But with the household remedies being the most practical and the most entertaining to describe, you might want to begin there. Save the section on importing natural enemies for the end, since it sounds like a dramatic and sure-fire solution. A sample scratch outline using this material appears on the next page in Figure 1.3.

NOTE: In the next chapter you'll find a lot more help with organizing material and several more sample outlines.

Outlining on a Computer

Using a computer to create an outline allows you to experiment with different ways of organizing your ideas. If you put the main headings in large, bold letters, they will keep the larger structure of your paper in view as you fill in subheadings and subpoints. You can add new points simply by moving the cursor and typing; you can shift details from one subheading to another by marking a line and hitting a few keys. Whole sections within your on-screen outline can be cut, renumbered, or rearranged.

If you did your prewriting on the computer, you can use the cut and paste functions to move key phrases and sentences from your freewriting or brainstorming into an informal outline. Some computer programs let you go back and forth between screens or windows, a feature that makes it easier to turn prewriting into an outline. Many word processors also have an outline feature that sets the levels within your outline for you; you can then use the outliner's collapse and expand functions to view your work at different levels of detail.

Collaborative Exercise 1.4

The following outline illustrates a number of weaknesses—supporting points that don't really support, minor points that pose as major points, major points that lack supporting points, and so on. With two or three

Thesis: Fighting bugs organically allows home
gardeners to avoid dangers of pesticides.

Intro.
— Need to keep chemicals out of vegetables

(1) Try safe, easy household remedies.
— set out trays of beer to attract + drown slugs.
— spray soapy water or garlic water on plants.
— spread shiny aluminum foil under plants to
disorient aphids, driving them to their doom.

(2) Introduce insect diseases.
— milky spore disease kills Japanese beetles.
— bacillus thuringiensis is death to cabbage worms.
— both remedies available at garden stores.
— both harmless to plants and humans.

(3) Bring in natural enemies.
— praying mantises eat caterpillars + mites.
— ladybugs eat their weight in aphids.
— green lacewings feed on mealybugs.
— all can be ordered by mail.

Conclusion
— If all else fails, pick bugs off by hand.

FIGURE 1.3 *Scratch Outline*

classmates, discuss this sorry example until the group has revealed all its
shortcomings; then, still working together, revise the material by adding,
omitting, and rearranging ideas as necessary to produce what everyone
agrees is a good outline.

Thesis: Studying in a dorm is impossible for anyone who lacks
unswerving discipline.

1. Phones ringing and stereos playing
2. Friends drop by and keep me from studying
   a. Card playing and bull sessions
   b. Watching TV more fun than studying

3. Neighbors are forever partying
    a. Loud music, talking, and laughing distract me.
4. Studying is really hard for me
    a. I fall asleep.
    b. Chemistry 101 is beyond me.

Outlining Exercise 1.5

Look over the material you generated in Exercise 1.3, and construct an outline for a short paper on that topic.

2

Addressing Your Readers

In the previous chapter we explained that all the choices you make about your writing—from selecting a topic to deciding how much material to include and how to arrange it—are determined by your purpose and your audience. You also need to consider how your readers will respond to the words you choose.

W *rite Naturally as You Speak*

As a writer, how do you want to come across to your readers? Do you want to sound like an expert, lecturing the uninformed? Or like an old friend, informally discussing your thoughts and opinions? Do you want to seem serious or playful, warm or distant, excited or detached? The approach you choose determines the *voice* that your readers will hear when they read your writing.

Lewis Lapham, editor of *Harper's* magazine, complains that "few writers learn to speak in the human voice, that most of them make use of alien codes (academic, political, literary, bureaucratic, technical)." Many people think they're supposed to sound grand and impressive when they write, so they try to produce a form of language they would never use in speaking.

Use First Person

You should strive for a human voice when you write— preferably your own. Those "alien codes" that Lapham speaks of are usually stuffy and pretentious and often sound like this:

> One can appreciate the health benefits of high school athletics for the ones who participate as well as the entertainment value for the ones who observe.

Put that sentence into plain English and you get:

> I think high school athletics can be healthful for the players and enjoyable for the fans.

Good writers usually prefer *I* or *we* instead of *one,* and many address their readers as *you.* On rare occasions the use of *one* is still required—in scientific writing, for instance, and in some theses and dissertations. We'll explain later how to handle *one* gracefully, just in case you're backed into a corner and have to write on a very formal level. You should also know that the first person will make your writing sound too familiar and chummy for some readers; college professors and business publications may prefer that you use the first person sparingly. The key is to know your audience and their expectations.

TIP! **Avoid the Indefinite *you.***
The words *you* and *your* should always refer to the readers. You may draw an unexpected laugh if you're explaining how to prune a tree and write, "Grasp your diseased limb firmly and saw it off above the joint."

Revising Exercise 2.1

Translate these sentences into clear, straightforward English. You may have to guess at the meaning sometimes, but do your best. We'll rewrite the first one to help you start.

1. One could conclude that the primary cause of her poverty was the number of offspring she possesses.
   Translation: I think that she's poor because she has too many children.
2. This writer's report enjoyed a not unfavorable reception by the management.
3. The unacceptability of one's lifestyle can result in the termination of one's employment in some companies.
4. In colonial times, you had to depend on wood for fuel.
5. It was with no little enthusiasm that one's peers inflicted various contusions and lacerations on members of the opposing affinity group.
6. It is the feeling of this committee that the established priorities in management–employee relations are in need of realignment.

A*djust Your Tone*

You may sometimes want to make your audience angry— about injustice, poverty, bigotry—but you always want to avoid making them angry at you. You need to adopt a tone that will appeal to your readers. *Tone* means the attitude a writer conveys toward the subject matter and the audience. The language you use will tell your readers if you're serious, humorous, interested, bored, cynical, confident, defensive, irritated, enthusiastic, and so on. You have to understand that your writing will have a tone, whether you consciously think about it or not. So you might as well think about it.

The English language offers you a number of ways of saying the same message, depending on tone. You can word the simplest request to express subtle variations in your meaning:

Lend me ten dollars.

Please send me ten dollars.

Can you spare ten dollars?

I need ten dollars. I'll pay you back tomorrow.

I'd like you to give me ten dollars.

The tone you use should reflect your understanding of the needs and feelings of your readers. It's difficult to make generalizations about tone, but you should avoid talking down to your readers by stating the obvious or talking over their heads by using words and phrases they won't understand. You also don't want to be falsely enthusiastic: readers can usually tell when you're not sincere. Also resist the temptation to be dogmatic, abusive, or overly sarcastic. Mark Twain never published a line or even mailed a letter until his gentle wife Olivia had approved it. His famous letter to the gas company shows you why:

Hartford
February 12, 1891

Dear Sirs:

Some day you will move me almost to the verge of irritation by your chuckled-headed goddam fashion of shutting your goddam gas off without giving notice to your goddam parishioners. Several times you have come within an ace of smothering half of this household in their beds and blowing up the other half by this idiotic, not to say criminal, custom of yours. And it has happened again to-day. Haven't you a telephone?

Ys

S L Clemens

Needless to say, Livy didn't let this one pass. Twain revised his correspondence daily as his rage subsided, until he finally produced a temperate version that wouldn't invite a libel suit. Try to do the same with your own writing.

TIP! **Imagine your readers reacting to what you've written.** If you think your readers might get the wrong impression or have the wrong reaction, edit your tone accordingly.

C *hoose an Appropriate Level of Language*

The tone of your writing will reflect just how formal you want to be. As always, audience and purpose will dictate the level of language that you decide to use. Although these levels overlap, you have three main forms to choose from: *formal, informal,* and *familiar.* You need different levels of language for different writing occasions, just as you sometimes need formal attire for banquets and weddings, informal clothes for dates and shopping, and your grubbies for around the house.

The level of language that you choose will depend on your relationship with the topic and the audience. If you're writing to a close friend or family member about something personal, you'll probably use familiar language. For less chummy or intimate writing, you'll use informal or formal language. Figure 2.1 provides an illustration of these language levels.

Formal Writing

You use formal language when your purpose is serious and you want to keep some distance between yourself and your audience. Many textbooks (although not this one) are written in formal English, as are most scholarly articles and books and some magazines. Business writing still observes many of the conventions of formal usage, but nowadays the use of *I* or *we* has re-

Formal:	One should not admit defeat too quickly.
	I shall not admit defeat too quickly.
Informal:	We should not give up too quickly
	I'll not give up too quickly.
Familiar:	I'm not throwing in the towel too quick.

Formal	*Informal*	*Familiar* (slang)
automobile	car	wheels
comprehend	understand	dig
depart	leave	split
residence	home	crib
odious	offensive	gross
debilitated	exhausted	wasted
morose	sad	bummed out

FIGURE 2.1   *Levels of Language for All Occasions*

placed the strictly formal third-person approach. Here are the main features of formal writing:

1. No contractions or slang
2. Third-person approach *(one, he, she, it, they);* do not address the readers directly as *you.*
3. No sentence fragments
4. A serious or neutral tone

TIP!   Use formal language when you want to downplay your personal involvement and emphasize the factual content of your writing.

Exercise on Tone 2.2

Rewrite each sentence to make the tone consistent and more appropriate for the subject. We'll show you how with the first one.

1. Many students who matriculate in a curriculum leading toward medical school really dig biology.
   Revised: Many premedical students like to major in biology.
2. People who want to improve physically can undertake several schemes to shed poundage and acquire robustness.
3. I think Desdemona is such a wimp; she just lies down and dies.

4. When running for office, a candidate can always try to make the other guy look like a dufus.
5. The very people who bug one the most are often those who most want to please one.
6. We must suppose, then, that the figures cited are OK.
7. You can't help expressing yourself, unless one resides in a vacuum.
8. If you want to hold the attention of your reader, you should cultivate a bitchin' style.
9. Scientists have recommended that one strategy for alleviating the threat of global warming is to cut way back on car fumes.
10. The governor explained his reform proposal at length, but the audience was clearly tuned out and just didn't get it.

Informal Writing

The formality or informality of language is a matter of degree. Little writing is exclusively formal or completely informal. Most of the writing you'll be called on to do will probably be informal, although some teachers and bosses may insist on a more formal approach. Here are the guidelines for informal language:

1. Use contractions, if you want to.
2. Use slang *only* if it's appropriate for your audience.
3. Write in the first person; address your readers as *you*, if you wish.
4. Use an occasional sentence fragment for stylistic effect.
5. Adopt any tone that's appropriate for the purpose and audience.

Familiar Writing

This is the language found in personal letters, journals, and diaries. You use it when you feel close to your readers and can assume they will understand the context of your writing. It also comes in handy for reproducing the feel of an actual person's speech in an essay that is otherwise more formal. In this kind of writing contractions are expected, slang is fine, the first person *(I)* and second person *(you)* are typical, sentences fragments are acceptable, and the tone is often light or even humorous.

TIP! Use a familiar tone only when you are completely sure that your readers will enjoy and approve of this style of writing.

Colloquialisms and Slang

Colloquialisms are expressions used in conversation and found primarily in familiar writing. You might talk about "hanging out" with your friends or "getting even" with someone who "ripped you off," but you would probably *write* that you "spent time" with your friends and "retaliated" against someone who "cheated" you. Colloquialisms also include shortened versions of words, like *prof* for *professor, lab* for *laboratory, grads* for *graduates.* Called clipped forms, these give a conversational tone to informal prose but are not appropriate for more formal writing.

Slang is extremely informal language; it is often imprecise and understandable only to a certain age group or social set. Terms like *geek, wimp, dis,* and *phat* and phrases like *schizzed out* and *book it* can be lively and colorful, but they go out of style quickly. You run the risk of not being understood or of not being taken seriously if you use slang and colloquialisms in your writing. Some readers will object to its use on any level.

W*riting Exercise 2.3*

Compose a brief paragraph in which you try to persuade the members of your household that they should conserve electricity or gasoline or natural gas. Then rewrite the paragraph twice more, choosing a suitable level of language to address each of the groups below. You will end up with three paragraphs. Be prepared to explain the differences in your three versions.

1. The Lost Souls Motorcycle Club
2. The local chapter of the American Association of University Women (AAUW)

U *se Jargon Carefully*

The term *jargon* has several meanings. Sir Arthur Quiller-Couch defined the term in his famous essay "On Jargon" as vague and "woolly" speech or writing that consists of abstract words, elegant variations, and "circumlocution rather than short straight speech." This kind of language, which is used to make thoughts and ideas sound more important than they are, is almost always ineffective because it sets up a barrier to communication with the reader.

Jargon can also refer to the technical vocabulary used within a trade, profession, or field of interest. This language is understood perfectly well by members of that specialized group but not by outsiders. Computer users mean something entirely different by *bit, mouse, crash, drive, disk, boot,* and *virus* than nonusers do.

Consider your audience and your purpose. If you know your readers will be familiar with the jargon, go ahead and use it. But the kind of jargon you should try to avoid includes those pretentious phrases that creep into the language from all sides—phrases like "increased propensity to actualize" (meaning "apt to happen"), "employee repositioning" (meaning "demoting and firing workers"), and "sociologically compatible behavioral parameters" (meaning who knows what).

W*riting Exercise 2.4*

Think of some group you belong to or some activity you engage in; make a list of its specialized words and phrases. Then write a paragraph to a general audience in which you define several of these terms. For instance, you might explain the basic shots in tennis—serve, ground stroke, volley, approach shot, lob, passing shot—for people who don't know what these terms mean.

U *se Gender-Free Language*

In considering your audience, keep in mind that many of your readers may be displeased by gender-biased language—that is, words and phrases that unfairly ignore one sex or inaccurately call attention to gender. Fortunately, it's fairly easy to avoid sexist language. Here are some pointers to follow as you write and revise:

- Don't use the words *man* and *mankind* to refer to both men and women. Use the words *person, individual, human being, humankind, humanity,* or *the human race* instead. This advice also applies to words containing *man* or *men:*

INSTEAD OF	USE
chairman	chairperson, moderator, chair
clergyman	minister, pastor
congressman	representative, legislator, member of Congress
fireman	firefighter
foreman	supervisor
mailman	mail carrier, postal worker
manpower	personnel, workers, staff
policeman	police officer
salesman	salesperson, sales representative
weatherman	weather forecaster, meteorologist
workman	worker, laborer

- Use parallel terms when referring to members of both sexes. If the males are *men,* then the females should be *women,* not *girls.* If you write about *ladies,* then also write about *gentlemen.*
- Don't mention gender when it's not necessary. Avoid such phrases as *male nurse, woman engineer, lady doctor, female architect.*
- Don't use the pronouns *he, him,* or *his* to refer to a singular noun that includes both genders. Instead of writing

> Every writer should be careful with the pronouns he chooses.

use the plural:

> All writers should be aware of the pronouns *they* choose.

or use *he or she,* if you can do it only once or twice:

> Every writer should be careful with the pronouns *he or she* chooses.

or eliminate the pronouns:

> Every writer should be careful when choosing pronouns.

> **Gendered Language Exercise 2.5**

See if you can eliminate all the gendered language from the following sentences without changing the meaning or causing awkwardness. We'll rewrite the first one for you.

1. Man must work in order to eat.
   Revised: People must work in order to eat.
   Humans must work in order to eat.
2. Anyone with a brain in his head can see the dangers of using atomic reactors.
3. A home owner can pay his taxes by mail or at the county courthouse.
4. The gregarious dog is man's best friend, but the aloof cat keeps his distance.
5. Girls outnumber the men on campus by almost two to one.
6. Gertie's mother is a computer repairman for the university.
7. The lady surgeon who performed Adrian's bypass operation got her medical degree from the University of Toronto.
8. The hippopotamus is happiest when he is half submerged in mud.
9. American pioneers loaded up their wagons and moved their wives and children westward.
10. "As long as man is on earth, he's likely to cause problems. But the man at General Electric will keep trying to find answers." (advertisement for GE)

A void Biased Language

You should avoid any derogatory language that is directed at a group, race, religion, or nationality. Identify all groups of people by their accepted proper names, and take care to avoid assigning stereotypical physical or behavioral characteristics to members of a particular group. Also, be aware that usage changes and that certain descriptive terms for groups of people may acquire unfavorable connotations. As a matter of respect to your readers, be sensitive to these details, and always use the terms that groups choose for themselves.

To Say It or Not to Say It: Euphemisms

There may be times when you want to soften your language if you're writing about an unpleasant or emotionally loaded subject. In such cases you can employ linguistic smokescreens called *euphemisms,* most of which are quite innocent. Rather than bluntly saying, "He died of cancer," you can say, "He passed away following a lingering illness." It takes the shudder out and cloaks the whole grim business of dying in a soothing phrase. Undertakers (or "funeral directors," as they prefer to be called) sometimes carry euphemism to grotesque extremes, like calling the room where the body lies the "slumber chamber." And in Victorian times, people would refer to the "white meat" of the chicken (instead of the "breast") and to the "second joint" (instead of the "thigh").

Such delicacy is quaint and amusing, but some people use euphemisms to evade the truth and conceal their meaning. In political discourse, this kind of language is called *doublespeak.* The CIA, for example, substitutes the meaningless phrase "terminate with extreme prejudice" for the blunt word "murder." The Pentagon refers to lethal weapons as "antipersonnel implements" and civilian deaths are glossed over as "unintended military consequences." Such transparent attempts to make human slaughter sound inoffensive are far from innocent.

This deceptive misuse of language has become widespread. Killing masses of people is called "ethnic cleansing." Police officers don't shoot to kill; they aim "to neutralize the adversary." The Air Force didn't lie to Congress about the B-1 bomber; they just "inadvertently disclosed incorrect information." An accident at a nuclear power plant is an "abnormal evolution" and an explosion is an "energetic disassembly." When the patient dies on the operating table, it's a "therapeutic misadventure" or "a negative patient-care outcome"; a death in the emergency room is "an adverse occurrence." Such euphemisms are deliberately misleading and border on being unethical.

You have to decide if innocent euphemisms are appropriate for your readers. Certainly you should never use deceptive ones. In most cases, your readers will probably want you to be honest and direct.

Euphemism Exercise 2.6

Translate these euphemisms into more direct language.

1. employee downsizing
2. preowned automobile
3. chemical dependency
4. adult entertainment
5. intelligence gathering
6. correctional facility
7. misspoke
8. at-risk students
9. information specialists
10. revenue enhancement
11. substandard housing
12. encore telecast

3

Useful Strategies for Developing Ideas

Experienced writers employ a number of strategies for developing their ideas, usually without ever consciously thinking about how they're doing it. You may find your own planning and drafting easier if you become familiar with some of these techniques. Usually you'll combine several strategies within one paper. For instance, you may include a narrative or a description or both while writing the explanation of a process.

We're going to present the basic strategies one by one here because that's the only way to explain them clearly. After each explanation, we'll ask you to write an essay focusing primarily on that strategy to give you practice in using it.

S trategies for Narratives

A *narrative* is simply a story, and *narration* involves telling a story. We use narrative frequently, both in everyday speech and in writing, because stories provide convincing examples, especially those about personal experiences. Stories also can be quite engaging, if skillfully told.

TIP! **Use a narrative when you want to illustrate a point or in your introduction to catch your readers' attention.**

Organizing a Narrative

Since a narrative recounts an event or an experience, you can simply arrange the details in the order in which they happened—that is, in *chronological order*. Sometimes, though, a *flashback* is effective. A jump into the past can reinforce a mood, explain someone's motivation, or give background to help readers understand the event. How do you decide whether such out-of-sequence material is a useful flashback or a tiresome digression? Keep your purpose firmly in mind. Ask yourself how much the proposed addition contributes to that goal, and give it space in proportion to its contribution.

Get your story straight by outlining before you begin—or else straighten it out when you revise. Eliminate any dull, unnecessary, or repetitious material, and then work hard to make it interesting by coming up with just the right examples and illustrations. All good writing is full of specific details, but a narrative will positively fall flat without them.

Developing a Narrative

The process of deciding which details to include or exclude is critical to successful narrative writing. Give a lot of thought to these choices. No one wants to hear about the syllabus of your college philosophy course when the main point of the story has to do with the unusual way you disposed of the textbook when the class was over.

As in all good writing you'll want to make a point of some sort in your narrative, but avoid just tacking on a moral at the end. Neither does your point have to involve weighty revelations about the Meaning of Life or the Human Experience. Your purpose can be to tell an amusing, entertaining, exciting, unusual, or puzzling story. This kind of narrative can have a worthwhile point too. Just keep in mind that when you're describing a peaceful stroll on a perfect fall day, you may choose to ignore the squashed squirrel in the gutter.

TIP! **In writing a narrative essay, do not state your thesis in the introduction.**

Put your thesis or purpose on your outline; then leave the main point implied in the paper itself. You don't want to take the edge off.

Pitfalls of Narrative Writing

Narratives are the easiest kind of writing to organize but probably the most difficult to write well. Ask someone reliable, preferably a classmate, to read your draft and help you figure out what needs improvement. It's hard to be objective about your own writing—hard to see what needs adding and what needs taking out.

With your helper, go over the following questions, and take notes recording any changes that should be made.

1. Is the point of the narrative clear? Can the reader tell why I'm telling this story?
2. Are the events in order? Any gaps? Any flashbacks?
3. Are there enough details? Are these details specific and interesting? If not, which ones need improving?
4. Are there any details that are boring or unnecessary and should come out?

Topics for Narrative Writing

Before you begin, think about who your audience is and what point you want to make in this narrative but refrain from including that point in the introduction. After completing your first draft, find someone to help you evaluate what you've written and plan your strategies for revision.

1. I learned _____ the hard way.
2. Think of a conflict situation between two people: teacher/student, parent/child, employer/employee, man/woman. Narrate the conflict first as though you were one person and then as though you were the other.
3. Write an account of your initiation into some element of the adult world that you were unaware of as a child: violence, hypocrisy, prejudice, sexuality, and so forth.
4. Write the story that your older relatives most often tell about something you did as a child.
5. Tell about the first time you remember being punished at school (or at home).
6. Recount a situation in which you fortunately or mistakenly followed someone else's judgment rather than your own.
7. Narrate an experience that led you to a new realization about yourself (or someone else).
8. Tell the story of a tough ethical decision you once had to make and of what happened afterward.

9. Write a narrative to support or disprove some familiar proverb, like "Honesty is the best policy," "Nice guys finish last," or "Home is where the heart is."
10. To get some ideas for writing a narrative, visit a Web site like the StoryTellers Challenge *(http://storytellerschallenge.com)*, where you'll find topics in the form of "challenges." Or look at the "Story of the Week" page at *www.storyteller.net*; it might spark some ideas.

S *trategies for Descriptions*

Seldom will a description form the basis of an entire essay, unless you're writing for practice or pleasure. But you will probably use description in virtually everything you write—especially if you write creatively and interestingly.

Organizing a Description

Writing specialists point out that most descriptions are organized spatially—top to bottom, left to right, near to far, back to front, and so on. True, you can describe your cat from nose to tail. But where do you include the texture of the fur, the stripes or spots, the color of the paws, the way the cat moves? And what about the meow?

Good description involves working a number of carefully chosen details into some sort of spatial arrangement. There's no convenient way (like presenting details in chronological order) that will work with description. You have to tailor the arrangement of details to suit your subject.

Developing a Description

First, consider your purpose. Do you want to arouse an emotional response in your readers? Or are you trying to convey a word picture, without emotion but sharp and clear as a photograph? Your choice of words and details will differ according to the effect you want.

Before you begin to write, look—really *look*—at what you plan to describe. Maybe you'll want to smell and taste and touch it as well. Then try to record your sense impressions—the exact shapes, the lights and shades, the textures, the tastes, the sounds, the smells. Don't include everything, of course, or you may overwhelm your readers. Carefully select the details that suit your purpose in order to give your readers an image of what you're describing. Then, as you revise what you've written, you can search for the precise words to let them see what you envision.

TIP! Try to put a picture in the reader's mind.

Notice in the following passage how Annie Dillard, through her selection of details and choice of words, allows us to both see and hear the ocean:

> The white beach was a havoc of lava boulders black as clinkers, sleek with spray, and lambent as brass in the sinking sun. To our left a dozen sea lions were body-surfing in the long green combers that rose, translucent, half a mile offshore. When the combers broke, the shoreline boulders rolled. I could feel the roar in the rough rock on which I sat; I could hear the grate inside each long backsweeping sea, the rumble of a rolled million rocks muffled in splashes and the seethe before the next wave's heave.
>
> —"Innocence in the Galapagos"

Pitfalls of Descriptive Writing

Remember that good descriptive details can clarify and enliven almost any kind of writing, but they are the very essence of descriptive writing. To include too few is fatal. Using tired, colorless words will also kill a description. Search your mind for lively verbs and choice descriptive words.

Topics for Descriptive Writing

This assignment is designed to exercise your descriptive skills. You are not expected to produce a fully developed essay with a point, unless you happen to be so inspired.

1. Describe as thoroughly as possible two of the following: how soft rain feels, how hard wind feels, how modeling clay feels, how whipped cream tastes, how a snake moves, how a cat leaps, how your dog greets you—or how a vampire looks, or a werewolf, or a visitor from outer space.
2. With as much sensory detail as possible, describe a food you hate or love.
3. Describe something you know more about than most people.
4. Describe a place (like a classroom, a coffee shop, the local pool hall, a jail cell, a hospital room, your grandmother's

kitchen, a professor's office), and try to convey how you feel about it through your use of specific details. Avoid making an explicit statement of your feelings.

5. Describe a place in which you feel at peace—or one in which you feel ill at ease.

6. Describe a memorable vacation you took. Assume that your readers have not visited this place. Use the Internet to refresh your memory and check the details for your description. If you vacationed in Nova Scotia, for example, you could browse the province's official tourism site at *www.explore.gov.ns.ca*.

S *trategies for Explaining a Process*

One of the most practical kinds of writing tells readers how to do something. Being able to provide an accurate, step-by-step explanation of how something is done or will be done or how something works is an essential skill.

Organizing Process Writing

Chronological structure, step-by-step, is usually the best way to explain a process. No flashbacks here. If you suddenly remember a detail that you should have included earlier, you need to go back and insert that point where it belongs. You know how frustrating it is when someone giving you directions says at the end, "Oh, wait a minute! I forgot to tell you to hang a left at the courthouse." A scratch outline will let you avoid such discouraging mishaps in writing.

Be careful to start at the actual beginning. Mention any necessary preparation, any gathering of supplies, any tips on how to get started. If, for instance, you're going to explain how to bathe a large reluctant dog, you'll first want to suggest putting on old clothes or a bathing suit and proceed from there. Your outline might look something like this:

Sample Process Outline

Thesis: How to wash a dog without losing your temper or frightening the washee.

1. What to wear
   a. In summer—old clothes or bathing suit
   b. In winter—next to nothing in the shower

2. Gathering the implements
   a. Mild soap or dog shampoo
   b. Lots of old towels
   c. Hand-held hairdryer, if winter
3. Where to do it
   a. In summer—on driveway or patio to avoid killing grass with soap
   b. In winter—in bathtub with shower curtain drawn
   c. If no shower curtain, wait till summer
4. Reassuring the animal
   a. Dog thinks you plot a drowning
   b. Talk continually in soothing tones
5. The actual washing
   a. Wet entire dog, apply soap or shampoo, work up lather
   b. Keep soap out of eyes and ears
   c. Don't forget the underside and tail
   d. Rinse very thoroughly—then stand back
6. Drying the dog
   a. Dog will shake, like it or not
   b. Rub damp-dry with towels
   c. If winter, finish with hairdryer

You might conclude that having a shiny, fragrant, flealess dog makes all this tribulation worthwhile. Or you might instead conclude that dog owners in their right minds who can afford the fee should pack the beast off to the groomer and let the experts do it.

There are, of course, other sorts of process papers that do not lend themselves to this easy chronological organization—topics like "How to choose a personal computer" or "How to care for an aquarium." For such subjects, you must fall back on classification, which is covered later in this chapter.

Developing Process Writing

The process paper, although easy to organize, is difficult to make interesting. You might begin with a brief narrative introduction recounting your first failed attempt to wash your Labrador retriever. Best to leave out the swearing, but include as many descriptive words and lively verbs as you can without making the whole thing sound grotesque.

You may assume that if you're describing a technical process, such as how to clean a carburetor or how to replace a hard drive, your readers will follow out of a desire for enlightenment. There's no obligation to entertain. But instead, you must be doubly sure to identify all parts and to explain each and every step clearly in language your reader will be able to understand. Define any terms that you suspect your readers may not know.

Make your word choice precise and concrete. If you're explaining how to change a light switch, don't say, "Strip a *short* piece of wire"; say, "Strip *one inch* of wire." If you're telling how to repair a toaster, label the parts (*A, B, C, D*) to help your reader visualize what fits where.

Include reasons whenever possible—especially if knowing the reason helps to understand the process. After you tell your reader to mix the dry yeast with lukewarm water, mention that cold water won't activate the yeast and hot water will kill it, and either way, the bread won't rise.

If your process has any foreseeable mishaps, like a wet, shaggy dog shaking in the bathtub, you should warn your readers in advance to pull the shower curtain. If a dangerous mistake is possible, use italics or capital letters: "Before sticking your fingers in the fuse box, TURN OFF THE ELECTRICITY BY PULLING OUT THE MAIN FUSE."

TIPS!   Don't forget the getting ready part.
Include all the necessary steps—in order.
Warn about any possible mishaps.

Pitfalls of Process Writing

The problems you encounter in process writing often have their roots in understanding your audience. Give careful consideration to how much—or how little—your readers know before deciding where to start your explanations. You need to back up far enough so that you don't lose them at the outset.

Your best bet is to enlist the help of someone whose knowledge of the process is about the same as that of your intended audience. Ask this person to read your draft and respond to these questions:

1. Have I chosen the right starting point? Did I give too much background information? Too little?
2. Have I defined enough terms? If not, which ones need clarifying?
3. Have I been specific enough in the details? Was the explanation unclear at any point? If so, where? How can I make it easier to follow?

Topics for Process Writing

Before you begin, think about who your audience is and how much (or how little) they already know about your topic.

1. How to train an animal (dog, parrot, turtle, cat, or such).
2. How to get rid of a bad habit: nail biting, smoking, interrupting others, procrastination, habitual lateness.
3. Find out and explain how some simple, familiar thing works (for example: soap, can opener, ballpoint pen, automatic pencil sharpener).
4. Think of some established process that could use improvement (registration, income tax, or courtship, for example). Describe how a preferable substitute system would work.
5. Think of an everyday operation that you'd like to have automated. Describe in detail how a fantasy machine would perform this function.
6. Using a health Web site, like the Mayo Clinic Health Oasis (*www.mayohealth.org*), gather information on diabetes, breast cancer, Alzheimer's, arthritis, AIDS, or any other chronic illness. Write a paper explaining the symptoms of the disease, options for treatment, and the outlook for new drugs and therapies.

S trategies for Classifying and Analyzing

We classify and analyze things all the time with no struggle at all. We classify political candidates into Republican, Democrat, Socialist, or Independent. We classify doughnuts into plain-glazed, chocolate-covered, and jelly-filled. We analyze whenever we try to figure out a friend's behavior or decide the best way to store the potatoes. If you're an English major, you might classify people into those who like Tolstoy, those who like murder mysteries, those who like spy novels, and those who like Harlequin romances. If you then try to figure out why some readers choose Tolstoy while others favor romance novels, you're analyzing.

For much of the writing you'll be doing in your life, classification provides an effective means of organizing. Also, breaking a subject down into categories facilitates critical thinking by enabling you to examine and analyze the relationship of the parts.

Organizing Classification and Analysis Writing

To make an outline using classification, you devise a way to separate the material into categories—preferably into orderly, meaningful categories. For instance, in a paper for your child psychology class, you might classify various methods of disciplining five-year-olds this way: (1) scolding, (2) calling time-outs, (3) withdrawing privileges, and (4) spanking.

In deciding how to arrange your points, there are lots of choices: easiest to hardest, least effective to most useful, earliest to most recent, top to bottom, least complicated to most complex, smallest to largest, or even least annoying to most annoying. The trick is to find some reasonable kind of logical division that suits your material.

The following outline shows how journalist Florence King organized her analysis of a stereotype, the "Good Ole Boy."

Sample Classification Outline

Thesis: The Good Ole Boy is a Southern WASP type easy to recognize but difficult to pin down.

Introduction
1. Physical characteristics
   a. Middle-aged, jowlish, beer belly
   b. Big buckle, white socks, ten-gallon hat
2. Dominant types
   a. Pearl, the playful masher
   b. Calhoun, the kindly fascist
3. Typical attitudes
   a. A lover of little dinky females
   b. Always searching for the oversexed Melanie
   c. A worshiper at Johnny's Cash 'n' Carry Tavern
Conclusion

Developing Classification and Analysis Writing

Usually you will announce what you are classifying or analyzing in your introduction: four methods of disciplining five-year-olds, three unfair government subsidy programs, six signs of a troubled marriage, three types of stress, and so on. Each section could be a single paragraph or several, but the major sections should be fairly equal in length. If you write 150 words about one type of stress, you should use about the same number of words on each of the other two.

If the material is complex, you can do your readers a favor by using headings. Under each heading, include similar information and present it in the same order. For instance, in writing about three kinds of stress, you might give the first type a heading, like *Stress on the Job*, followed by a description, followed by examples. Then you would present the material about the other two kinds of stress in the same way. This parallel development helps readers to process the information more easily and clarifies the distinctions between categories.

Pitfalls of Classification Writing

Here are a couple of things to watch out for when you work with classification.

1. *Be careful not to shift the basis of your division.*
   If that sounds confusing, look at the following skimpy outline, and you'll understand what we mean.

   ### Types of Aardvarks

   A. The fuzzy aardvark
   B. The hairless aardvark
   C. The friendly aardvark

   The first two categories of aardvarks are based on physical characteristics, while the last type shifts to personality. You see the worry this causes: Can a hairless aardvark be friendly? Are fuzzy aardvarks ill-tempered? How much hair does a friendly aardvark have?

2. *Be careful not to shift the rank of your division.*
   This simple outline will show you what can go wrong.

   ### Types of Recorded Music

   A. Classical
   B. Easy listening
   C. Marilyn Manson

   Although Marilyn Manson represents a type of music quite distinct from classical or easy listening, the third category is not parallel, not equal in rank, to the first two. It's too narrow. It should be heavy metal, with Marilyn Manson used as an example.

TIP! Check your outline for shifts in categories.

Topics for Classification and Analysis Writing

Before you begin, think about who your audience is and what point you want to make. Analyze your material thoughtfully.

1. If you've ever been a salesperson, receptionist, or food server, analyze and classify your clientele.
2. Interview ten people to discover their attitudes toward the death penalty. Classify, then analyze their responses.
3. What types of TV shows are the most popular this season? Analyze the appeal of each type.
4. Study a magazine advertisement or an ad campaign (a series of related ads, like the Joe Camel cigarette ads). What emotions or beliefs is this advertising designed to appeal to?
5. Divide into types and analyze any of these subjects: neighborhoods, marriages, laughter, prisoners, automobiles, intelligence, dreams, teachers, students, tennis players, drinkers, pet owners, jokes, novels, bicycles.
6. Write an essay classifying several different methods for managing money that you see among your friends and family. Give specific examples to identify each type of money manager that you know. To develop this topic, locate some sites on the Internet that give advice and information about managing finances; see what kinds of problems and approaches they mention.

S *trategies for Comparing and Contrasting*

One of the most common methods of development involves focusing on similarities and differences—or perhaps on one or the other—in order to make a point. Sometimes writers use a comparison to clarify. An effective way, for instance, to explain impressionism in literature is to compare it with impressionism in painting, which is visual and thus easier to grasp. Frequently writers employ a comparison to persuade, as many have done by paralleling the failure of prohibition in the 1920s with the ineffectiveness of the current war on drugs.

When focusing on differences, writers often seek to show that one category is somehow better than the other. You could, for example, establish a useful contrast between two products, focusing on their differences, in order to recommend one as a better buy than the other. You could contrast the campaign promises of two candidates to establish which would be the better choice for mayor. Or you could humorously contrast the differences between toads and snakes in order to contend that toads make better pets than snakes.

Organizing a Comparison or Contrast

Whether focusing on differences or similarities, you have two ways of organizing a piece of comparison or contrast writing.

Using *Block* Organization

Especially handy for responding to essay examinations, this simple method of organization also serves perfectly to show how something has changed or developed: your earliest views about AIDS compared with your views now; Americans' attitudes toward Communism in the fifties compared with attitudes today; Henry James's early novels compared with his later ones. In general, here's how to organize using the block plan:

1. State your purpose.
2. Present your points for the first part of the comparison.
3. Provide a transition.
   (for contrasts: *on the other hand, but, however, yet, in contrast, contrary to, nevertheless, nonetheless*)
   (for similarities: *similarly, also, likewise, in the same way, in a similar manner*)
4. Present similar points for the second part of the comparison.
5. Draw your conclusions.

If, for example, you were going to write a paper comparing the relative merits of airbeds versus waterbeds for people contemplating a purchase, your block outline might look like the one below.

Sample Block Comparison or Contrast Outline

Thesis: Airbeds have several major advantages over waterbeds but cost a great deal more.

Introduction
A. Features of a waterbed
   1. Fills with a hose
   2. Adjusting for comfort tricky
   3. Needs an electric heater
   4. Extremely heavy when full of water
   5. Reasonable in cost

  B. Transition
  C. Features of an airbed
    1. Inflates with a button
    2. Adjusting for comfort easy
    3. No need for a heater
    4. Light because just full of air
    5. Expensive to buy
Conclusion

Using *Point-by-Point* Organization

A more precise way of showing a contrast involves setting it up point by point. This arrangement sharpens the contrast, but it also requires more planning because you have to thoroughly classify your material. You choose as your major points of comparison those ideas that best illustrate the similarities or differences. For instance, say you decide to write an essay contrasting married life without children and married life with children. After thinking of several important ways that parenthood alters lifestyle, you might come up with an outline like this one.

Sample Point-by-Point Comparison or Contrast Outline

Thesis: Having children causes life changes that bring major increases in responsibilities.
  1. Sleep—and lack of
    a. Before kids
    b. After kids
  2. Household chores
    a. Before kids
    b. After kids
  3. Expenses—present and future
    a. Before kids
    b. After kids
  4. Leisure time activities
    a. Before kids
    b. After kids
  5. Romance in the marriage
    a. Before kids
    b. After kids
Conclusion: Parenthood involves sacrifices as well as joys.

You could, of course, use exactly this same material in writing an essay in block organization. The choice depends on which arrangement best suits your purpose.

Developing a Comparison or Contrast

The introduction of your essay should disclose the subject and set it in context. Here's a summary of the purposes mentioned earlier for using comparison and contrast:

1. to clarify (explaining the unfamiliar by comparing with the familiar)
2. to persuade (showing that one element is better than another)
3. to inform (comparing past and present or by showing differences between similar elements)

You may want to mention one of these purposes in your opening paragraph. For example, here's an introduction written by a student in a paper focusing on differences between similar events—in this case, two concerts by Elton John:

> Time changes everything, or so we are told. Over a period of time our looks, opinions, and viewpoints change. When I was a kid, I was a rabid fan of Elton John. I idolized Captain Fantastic when I saw him perform at McCormick Place in June of 1976. Still a devoted admirer, I recently attended another concert and was surprised by the differences in the two performances.
>
> —Debbie Brown

Using the block pattern, Debbie then went on in the body of her paper to describe her response to the first concert; then, after making a transition, she described her response to the second one, concluding with this paragraph, summarizing her changed impressions:

> As his third encore, he gave us "Your Song." I stood on that hillside, tears streaming down my face, once again listening to my favorite singer performing my favorite song. By now my initial disappointment at discovering that Captain Fantastic had turned into Reg Dwight was totally gone. Idolizing had changed to respect. Yes, time changes many things—but not everything.

Notice that the first sentence of her introduction is, "Time changes everything, or so we are told." She neatly echoes that line in her final sentence, giving her essay a satisfying closure.

Pitfalls of Comparison and Contrast Writing

You can avoid one major pitfall by presenting the material in each category in the same order. Here are a couple of other mistakes to avoid.

1. *Don't use too many transitional words.*
   Point-by-point comparison and contrast writing naturally involves a lot of shifting back and forth between ideas. But you won't need to signal each one with a transitional word because your reader will become familiar with the pattern and will be expecting the shifts. If you use too many transitional words, your reader will become annoyed at being forcibly led rather than guided.
2. *Don't apologize in your conclusion.*
   After presenting a strong case for the superiority of one item over another, you may get to the conclusion and panic. You're tempted to write, "Of course, this is just my opinion; others might disagree." Don't do it. This modesty undercuts the effectiveness of your paper.

Topics for Comparison and Contrast Writing

Before you begin, think about your purpose, who your audience is, and what point you want to make.

1. Discuss one or more illusions that are presented as reality on television, and compare the illusion with the reality as you know it.
2. Compare and/or contrast: two lifestyles you have experienced, two novels, two films, a film and the book it was based on, two television characters, two cars you have driven, two sports you have played.
3. A group of extraterrestrial beings visits Earth. On their planet people are neither male nor female: each person is both. Using one of these beings as a first-person narrator, explain how their society is different from ours.
4. Write about a situation in which you expected one thing and got another—in other words, the expectation and the reality were different. Consider: your first day of school, your college roommate, your first date, your high school prom, your wedding day, dining in an expensive restaurant.
5. Find a typical magazine for men and one for women. Discuss three or four major differences that set these publications apart.
6. Visit two similar Web sites—two museums, two zoos, two cooking sites, or two music sites, for example. After exploring both of them, write a comparison and contrast article explaining which site is more interesting and worthwhile.

S trategies for Explaining Causes and Effects

Human beings are naturally curious. We want to know why. Why won't the lawnmower start? Why does the computer keep giving me that error message when I've done nothing wrong? Why are some people better at math than others? Why did Celine Dion retire? This common human impulse to understand why things happen provides a powerful motive for reading and writing.

A lot of the writing done in college courses requires cause and effect thinking. Students are frequently asked to explain: the causes of the Civil War, the origins of prejudice, the consequences of divorce on children, the effects of sleep deprivation on learning. As a bonus, once you learn to analyze causes and effects, you'll become good at problem solving—a useful skill both on the job and in everyday life.

Organizing Cause and Effect Writing

When you develop a piece of writing by analyzing causes, you are explaining to your readers why something happened. If you go on to explore the effects, you are analyzing what happened—the consequences. For example, if your topic is divorce and you write "Why Teenage Marriages Fail," that's primarily a cause paper. But if you write "What Divorce Does to Young Children," that's primarily an effect paper. You'll probably stick to one purpose in a single essay, but you might take up both causes and effects if you have the time and the assignment allows you to.

Focusing on Causes

Begin by describing a condition or result or problem (like having claustrophobia, failing your philosophy course, having your car's engine overheat), and then explain as fully as possible the causes or reasons.

Sometimes you may be able to use chronological organization. If, for instance, the problem is your claustrophobia, you could trace its development from the earliest cause at age five (getting locked in a broom closet), through another incident at age eleven (getting locked in a restroom), to the latest trauma at age twenty (getting locked in a stairwell).

More likely, though, your organization will fall into some logical pattern based on the relative importance of the causes—

from least significant to most vital, from the most subtle to the most obvious, from local to nationwide. The following sample outline is arranged from the most understandable causes (poor reading and writing skills) to the least defensible one (missing class).

Sample Outline Focusing on Causes

Thesis: I failed Philosophy 101 for several reasons, mostly due to my own shortcomings.

A. I couldn't do the reading.
  1. Abstract material is especially hard for me.
  2. I couldn't follow the textbook.
B. I wasn't good at writing either.
  1. I couldn't express the complicated ideas asked for on exams.
  2. I put writing the papers off for so long that every one was turned in late.
C. I was intimidated by the class discussion.
  1. Usually I could not answer when called on because I did not understand the ideas.
  2. Because I felt so stupid, I never asked questions that might have helped me.
D. The class met at 8 A.M., so I often slept through it.
Conclusion: Because this class is required, I resolve to work harder next time.

Focusing on Effects

You can start with some condition or event and explain the consequences. For example, you might begin by describing the breakup with your girlfriend and then go on to show how it affected you. Again, you can present the effects as they happened. At first you were depressed; then you began to spend more time with your friends. You also had more time to study, so your grades improved. Finally, you began to date again and found a much better girlfriend.

More likely, though, you'll want to sort your ideas into some logical arrangement that has more to do with the importance of the effects than simply with chronology, as we suggested above. In the following outline, the effects are classified into negative and positive. Because the writer wants to emphasize the positive effects, she puts them last.

Sample Outline Focusing on Effects

Thesis: My family has adjusted well to having Mom become a college student.

Introduction: After ten years as a housewife, I have gone back to college, amid a chorus of whining.

A. Negative effects
   1. My husband feels a bit intimidated.
   2. The children's clothes don't always get ironed.
   3. The house is not as clean as it used to be.
   4. I no longer have time to read for pleasure.

B. Positive effects
   1. My husband is learning to know our children by sharing their care.
   2. The kids are learning to accept personal and family responsibilities.
   3. I enjoy a rewarding sense of accomplishment and have been freed from some boring housework.

Conclusion: The family has risen to the challenge, has accepted the changes, and now takes pride in my good grades.

Developing Cause and Effect Writing

Since people are naturally curious about causes and effects, a good introduction will stimulate your readers to ask "Why?" For instance, if you're writing about what causes a hangover, you could begin by saying, "When you take two aspirins with a glass of water to cure a hangover, the water probably does you more good than the aspirin." Then you go on to explain in detail how alcohol dehydrates the cells causing headache, dry mouth, and general malaise.

Another good way to begin is by making a prediction. Then in the body of the paper, you discuss the reasons that allow you to make such a statement. For example, you might begin an essay by declaring, "If you put radial tires on your car, you will probably save thirty-five dollars on gas next winter." Your readers will want to know how radial tires save gas, so you tell them.

In your conclusion, you can use any of the standard strategies—advise the reader, predict the future, or issue a call for action. Another strategy that works well in some cause and effect papers involves suggesting larger areas that your subject might branch into, leaving your reader with something additional to think about. If you're explaining how agricultural chemicals get into the grain fed to animals, for instance, you could close with an observation on the probable contamination also of drinking water and soil by herbicides and pesticides.

Pitfalls of Cause and Effect Writing

An explanation of causes and effects won't be successful if your readers find your thinking fuzzy or flawed.

1. *Avoid oversimplifying.*
   Most conditions and events are complex, involving multiple causes and numerous effects. In a short essay, you may have to focus on only the primary reasons, so be sure to let your readers know that's what you're doing.
2. *Be sure your causes are valid.*
   Just because you catch a cold after forgetting your sweater on a cold day doesn't mean that getting chilled caused the cold. More likely, someone sneezed on you. Before writing on causes, study *Jumping to Conclusions* in the section on logic in Chapter 7 (pp. 111–112).
3. *Don't confuse the words* effect *and* affect.
   Check these terms in Chapter 15 if you have a problem keeping these words straight.

Topics for Cause and Effect Writing

Before you begin, think about who your audience is and what point you want to make. After completing your outline, examine the logic of your causal analysis.

1. Discuss the probable causes of any situation, practice, law, or custom that strikes you as unfair.
2. Imagine that a close friend tells you that she/he is homosexual. The friend is the same sex as you. What are your reactions? Why would you have these reactions?
3. All school attendance has just been declared voluntary. How will this change the schools?
4. Explain the causes (or effects) of any drastic change of opinion, attitude, or behavior you've undergone in your life.
5. Write a paper in which you explain what causes some natural phenomenon (for example, rain, dew, blue sky, twinkling stars, sweat, hiccups, the phases of the moon).

6. Does playing video games shape values and affect personality? Brainstorm to jump-start your own thinking; then gather more information and ideas by browsing the Internet. Look at sites where video games are advertised and played, as well as those where other points of view might be provided, such as sites created by parent-teacher associations.

4

Composing
Effective
Paragraphs

Your writing will be made up of paragraphs: first, an effective introduction; then several interesting, unified, well-developed body paragraphs; and finally, a forceful, emphatic conclusion. Since the body paragraphs are the heart of any piece of writing, let's begin with them.

U nderstanding the Basic Paragraph

If you are doing academic, business, or technical writing, the paragraphs that constitute the body of your paper should each have a topic sentence supported by plenty of concrete details. The average paragraph runs from about 100 to 150 words—somewhat longer for formal writing, considerably shorter in newspaper and magazine stories where the small type in narrow columns requires frequent breaks to avoid eye strain and make for easier reading.

Use a Topic Sentence

Every paragraph is going to be about something: It will describe something, question something, demand something, reject something, define something, explain something. That "something" can be identified in a topic sentence. Although narratives and descriptions may not include an explicit topic sentence, most informative writing does.

When writing reports, position papers, academic essays, summaries, and examinations, you will almost always place the topic sentence first. Like the thesis sentence for an essay, a topic sentence states the controlling idea for the paragraph. The ideas and details within the paragraph will support, elaborate, interpret, illustrate, or justify that idea. As you develop your thoughts in a paragraph, be sure that all the points and details pertain to the idea stated in the topic sentence. If, for instance, you decide to write a paragraph about the undeserved good reputation of dogs, you might begin with this topic sentence: "Far from being our best friends, dogs are slow-witted, servile, useless beasts that seldom deserve their board and keep." Then you trot out examples of slavish spaniels and doltish Great Danes you have known in order to convince your readers that dogs are more trouble than they're worth. But if you observe, "Cats are pretty contemptible, too," you need a new paragraph or a new topic sentence. Otherwise, toss that comment out as being beside the point, the point being whatever idea you committed yourself to in the topic sentence.

Build on the Topic Sentence

The topic sentence states the main idea in each paragraph. You build on that idea by supplying facts, figures, examples, reasons, explanations, and specific details that relate to the topic sentence. A building strategy that works for some writers is based on the theory that each sentence in a paragraph stems directly from the sentence before it and in some way responds to it. Thus, adding material in a paragraph becomes a matter of expectation and response: each sentence responds to the one before it as well as providing the expectation (or idea) that the next sentence will relate to.

Let's look at a paragraph that begins with the following topic sentence:

> The new McDonald's system was predicated on careful attention to detail.

As a reader, what do you expect from that sentence? You'll probably want to know about that "attention to detail," right? So if the next sentence were something like

> The McDonald brothers began their business in Chicago.

you might feel a slight confusion or a momentary letdown because you were expecting something else. As a matter of fact, the next sentence in the original paragraph does pick up on the expectation about attention to detail:

The McDonald brothers shortened the spindles on their Multi-Mixers so that shakes and malts could be made directly in paper cups.

Now, what do you expect from that sentence? You may want to know why that detail is important. So the writer explains with this next sentence:

There would be no metal mixing containers to wash, no wasted ingredients, no wasted motion.

The writer then adds a series of similar details, as you might expect, like this:

They developed dispensers that put the same amount of catsup or mustard on every bun. They installed a bank of infrared lamps to keep French fries hot. They used disposable paper goods instead of glassware and china. They installed a microphone to amplify the customer's voice and reduce misunderstandings about what was being ordered.

After this series of examples, what do you expect next? You probably want to know what all this attention to detail adds up to, so the writer concludes with these statements that sum up the significance of the paragraph and bring it to a close:

By 1952 the McDonald brothers' employees, all men dressed neatly in white, were said to be capable of serving the customer a hamburger, a beverage, French fries, and ice cream in twenty seconds. Word of their proficiency began to spread through the restaurant industry.

—Philip Langdon, "Burgers! Shakes!"
Atlantic Monthly

TIP! Stay focused on the main idea expressed in your topic sentence.

Make sure that whatever you put in a paragraph helps your readers to understand that main idea.

Writing Exercise 4.1

Choose one of the topic sentences below and write a paragraph of about 150 words using the "expectation and response" strategy for paragraph development explained in the preceding section. Feel free to alter and adapt the topic sentence to fit your interests and experience.

1. My "bargain" used car caused me no end of trouble in my first week of ownership.
2. When I offered to build a fire at our campsite, I thought I could have it roaring in about five minutes.
3. I know that claustrophobia is all in the mind, but I still feel panic coming on when I'm in a closed space. [Substitute your own favorite phobia.]
4. If I'm having trouble getting started writing, I go through a few familiar rituals.
5. Since I am by nature a night person, having to get up at six in the morning brings out the worst in me.

D eveloping the Ideas Fully

Adequate and interesting development of material is crucial to writing effective paragraphs. Most experienced writers make their ideas clear and convincing by providing support for every observation or generalization. This supporting material may appear as descriptive details, factual items, illustrations and examples, or a combination of these varied modes of development.

Use Descriptive Details

Descriptive details are usually intended to convey an impression—how something looked, smelled, tasted. They are especially effective in recounting personal experiences or eyewitness accounts, as in the following vivid picture of the plight of Chicago's poor during the Great Depression of the 1930s.

There is not a garbage dump in Chicago which is not deliberately haunted by the hungry. Last summer in the hot weather when the smell was sickening and the flies were thick, there were a hundred people a day coming to the dumps, falling on the heap of refuse as soon as the truck had pulled out and digging in it with sticks and hands. They would devour all the pulp that was left on the old slices of watermelon and cantaloupe till the rinds were as thin as paper; and they would take away and wash and cook discarded onions, turnips, and potatoes. Meat is a more difficult matter, but they salvage a good deal of that, too. The best is the butcher's meat which has been frozen and hasn't spoiled. In the case of the other meat, there are usually bad parts that have to be cut out or they scald it and sprinkle it with soda to kill the taste and the smell.

—Edmund Wilson

Supply Factual Information

You can use facts and figures, if you have them, in developing your ideas. Note how the author of the following paragraph uses factual details to support the topic sentence at the beginning:

No one change led to the virtual demise of the train robbery. A combination of stronger steel cars, modern law-enforcement techniques, and improved methods of transferring wealth made robbing trains too risky and unrewarding. Other forms of illegal activity in the 20th century occupied men (and a few women) who might have preyed on passenger trains fifty years ago. Bootlegging liquor, for example, seemed to be the 1930s equivalent of blowing up express cars.

—John P. Hankey

This next paragraph is developed primarily by citing statistics:

The linguist Michael Krauss says that as many as 3,000 languages, comprising half of all the words on earth, are doomed to silence in the next century. According to Krauss, who keeps count of dead and dying languages, 210 of the original 300 or more languages once spoken in the United States and Canada remain in use or in memory; 175 are spoken in the United States, including Alaska, and of these all but 20, perhaps fewer, cannot survive much longer. Only 250 languages in the entire world have at least a million speakers, considered the necessary safety level as globalization homogenizes every nation, every village, no matter how remote. Only languages with state sponsorship seem likely to survive: Spanish, French, English, Italian, etc. What of the more than 800 languages of Papua New Guinea? The 410 of Nigeria? The more than 300 in India?

—Earl Shorris

Provide Illustrations and Examples

Most of the time writers use illustrations and examples to flesh out paragraphs. Here is a paragraph that supports the claim in its topic sentence with one main example:

The history of medicine is replete with accounts of drugs or modes of treatment that were in use for many years before it was recognized that they did more harm than good. For centuries, for example, doctors believed that drawing blood from patients was essential for rapid recovery from virtually every illness. Then, midway through the 19th century, it was discovered that bleeding served to weaken the patient. King Charles II's death is believed to have been caused in part by administered bleedings. George Washington's death was also hastened by the severe loss of blood resulting from this treatment.

—Norman Cousins

In this next example the writer develops his paragraph by naming and describing the tests referred to in the topic sentence:

Neurologists have a host of clinical tests that let them observe what a brain-damaged patient can and cannot do. They stroke his sole to test for a spinal reflex known as Babinski's sign or have her stand with her feet together and eyes closed to see if the ability to maintain posture is compromised. They ask him to repeat a set of seven random digits forward and four in reverse order, to spell *world* backward, to remember three specific words such as *barn* and *handsome* and *job* after a spell of unrelated conversations. A new laboratory technique . . . uses radioactively labeled oxygen or glucose that essentially lights up specific and different areas of the brain being used when a person speaks words or see words or hears words, revealing the organic location for areas of behavioral malfunction.

—Floyd Skloot

Be Specific and Concrete

Abstract words like *democracy, truth, justice, liberty,* and other familiar terms mean different things to different people. And sometimes they convey little meaning at all. Consider the following paragraph which purports to explain what a "democratic" education can do for a child:

A democratic plan of education includes more than the mere transmission of the social heritage and an attempt to reproduce existing institutions in a static form. The purpose of democratic education is the development of well-integrated individuals who can live successfully in an ever-changing dynamic culture. The democratic school is also required to indoctrinate individuals with the democratic tradition which, in turn, is based on the agitative liberties of the individual and the needs of society.

If you can divine meaning from this paragraph, it's a vague, shadowy sort of understanding that can't be pinned down precisely because of the numerous abstract words: *democratic, social heritage, well-integrated, dynamic culture.* And what *agitative liberties* are, only the writer knows. He doesn't provide a hint. The entire passage contains not a single concrete example to help us grasp the ideas.

You can't avoid abstractions entirely, of course, but try to follow abstract words with concrete illustrations. For example, if you say that motorcycle riding can be *dangerous* (an abstract concept), mention the crushed noses, the dislocated limbs, the splintered teeth, the broken bones. Or provide some statistics about the high cost of insurance for motorcyclists and the frequency and severity of their accidents.

Revising Exercise 4.2

Rewrite the following paragraph about first dates, adding specific details and concrete examples that will bring the material to life. Be as creative as you wish. Feel free to alter wording. Use first person (*I, me, my*) if that approach works best.

> A first date is always a risky occasion, with endless possibilities for disaster and disappointment. Sometimes both people realize at the very beginning of the date that it is a mistake. At other times they get to know each other a little before they see that their interests and personalities don't fit well at all. And frequently, only at the end of the date does the mismatch become clear.

Writing Exercise 4.3

Think of a concept or an idea that is hard to explain to someone else. It might be a scientific principle, a belief about love or friendship, a political term, a formula for success. Write a paragraph about this concept, using examples and concrete details to help you clarify your thinking. Show your paragraph to several classmates; ask them if they understand what you mean. If they have trouble understanding, ask them to help you decide what changes or additions are needed to make your explanation clear.

K *eeping Your Readers with You: Unity and Coherence*

As you are constructing paragraphs and putting them together to make a paper, remember that you want your readers to understand what you've written and to understand it easily on the first reading. You don't want them to get lost when you move from one idea to the next or when you change the direction of your ideas. The things you do to make your writing *unified* and *coherent*, to make it hang together, are fairly simple; yet they can often mean the difference between a first-rate paper and a merely passable one.

Maintain Coherence Within Paragraphs

The first principle for writing a coherent paragraph is to make sure the sentences follow one another in a clear, logical sequence. Using the "expectation and response" strategy that we described earlier in this chapter will do a lot to insure that your thoughts flow smoothly. But there still may be places where you need to provide signposts to guide your readers through your prose.

Repeat Key Words.   One way to achieve coherence in a paragraph is to repeat key terms. Most of this repetition occurs naturally as you write, but being aware of the process will help you when you revise. In the following paragraph, observe how the sentences are held together by repeating the key term *addict* and the pronouns that refer to it (all italicized so you can notice them):

> What to do about drug *addiction?* I give you two statistics. England with a population of over 55 million has 1,800 *addicts*. The United States with over 200 million has nearly 500,000 *addicts*. What are the English doing right that we are doing wrong? They have turned the problem over to the doctors. An *addict* is required to register with a physician who gives *him* at controlled intervals a prescription so that *he* can buy *his* drug. The *addict* is content. Best of all, society is safe. The Mafia is out of the game. The police are unbribed, and the *addict* will not mug an old lady in order to get the money for *his* next fix.
>
> —Gore Vidal

Supply Connectors and Transitions.   You can also use certain words and phrases to indicate the connections between details and ideas. These include coordinating conjunctions—*and , but, or, for, nor, yet, so*—to link words, phrases, clauses; subordinating conjunctions, such as *if, although, when, because, since, unless,* which mark different levels of importance among ideas; conjunctive adverbs, such as *however, thus, therefore, indeed, furthermore,* and *consequently*; and transitional phrases like *for example, in addition, on the other hand,* and *in fact.*

Figure 4.1 (pp. 60–61) lists the most common shifts in thought that writers make (such as moving to a new point, adding an example, providing a contrast) and then offers a wide selection of words and phrases to fit each shift. Take note of the different types of transition illustrated; then tuck in a bookmark in case you get stuck and need a transition to help you over a rough spot.

In the following paragraph, biologist Stephen Jay Gould achieves coherence by skillfully blending transitional words and phrases, which we've italicized, with a series of repeated key terms *(brain, body, animal, large, small)*, which we've put in boldface type:

> I don't wish to deny that the flattened, minuscule head of the **large bodied** "Stegosaurus" houses **little brain** from our subjective, top-heavy perspective, *but* I do wish to assert that we should not expect more of the beast. *First of all,* **large animals** have relatively **smaller brains** than related, **small animals.** The correlation on **brain** size among kindred **animals** (all reptiles, all mammals, *for example*) is remarkably regular. *As* we move from **small** to **large animals,** from mice to elephants *or* small lizards to Komodo dragons, **brain** size increases, *but* not so fast as **body** size. *In other words,* **bodies** grow faster than **brains,** *and* **large animals** have low ratios of **brain** weight to **body** weight. *In fact,* **brains** grow only about two-thirds as fast as **bodies.** *Since* we have no reason to believe that **large animals** are consistently stupider than their **smaller** relatives, we must conclude that **large animals** require relatively less **brain** to do as well as **smaller animals.** *If* we do not recognize this relationship, we are likely to underestimate the mental power of very **large animals,** dinosaurs in particular.
>
> —"Were Dinosaurs Dumb?"
> *The Panda's Thumb*

Try Rhetorical Questions and Short Sentences

In the paragraph about drug addiction, quoted above, Gore Vidal uses two rhetorical questions: one to get the paragraph started ("What to do about drug addiction?") and one to move

To move to the next major point:

too	*moreover*	*next*
in the first place	*second*	*third*
again	*besides*	*in addition*
further	*likewise*	*also*
furthermore	*beyond this*	*admittedly*
like		

Examples: We *also* can see that the quality of most television programs is abysmal.

Furthermore, the commercials constantly assault our taste and insult our intelligence.

To add an example:

for example	*for instance*	*such as*
that is	*in the following manner*	*namely*
in this case	*in the same manner*	*as an illustration*
at the same time	*in addition*	

Examples: The daytime game shows, *for instance*, openly appeal to human greed.

Soap operas, *in the same manner*, pander to many of our baser instincts.

To emphasize a point:

especially	*without doubt*	*primarily*
chiefly	*actually*	*otherwise*
after all	*as a matter of fact*	*in fact*
without question	*even more*	*more important*

Examples: The constant violence depicted on television, *in fact*, poses a danger to society.

Even more offensive are deodorant commercials, *without question* the most tasteless on TV.

FIGURE 4.1   *Useful Transitional Terms*

the discussion along ("What are the English doing right that we are doing wrong?"). This technique of posing a question that you intend to answer can be very effective for leading your readers into the next point, but you probably can't get away with it too often in a short paper. You must have other devices in stock.

Like the rhetorical question, the short-sentence transition must not be used often, but it comes in handy when you need it. You simply state briefly and clearly what you intend to discuss next, like this:

To contrast a point:

but	*still*	*on the other hand*
on the contrary	*nevertheless*	*contrary to*
however	*nonetheless*	*conversely*
yet	*although*	*in contrast*
neither		

Examples: We abhor violence, *yet* we cannot approve of censorship.

Although commercials may enrage or sicken us, they do, *after all*, pay the bills.

To qualify a point:

in some cases	*admittedly*	*of course*
granted that	*no doubt*	*certainly*

Examples: There are, *of course*, fine educational programs on public television and some cable networks.

Admittedly, these shows enrich our culture; *in some cases*, they are inspiring and enlightening.

To conclude or sum up a point:

consequently	*therefore*	*so*
accordingly	*then*	*as a result*
hence	*in sum*	*in conclusion*
in other words	*thus*	*before*
in short	*finally*	*at last*

Examples: Soap operas *thus* contribute to the subtle erosion of moral values.

Commercials, *therefore*, are not worth the sacrifice of our integrity.

Television, *in short*, costs more than society should be willing to pay.

FIGURE 4.1   *Useful Transitional Terms (continued)*

Europeans think more highly of Americans now than they ever did. *Let me try to explain why.* [Italics added.]

—Anthony Burgess

Molly Ivins uses both a question and a short sentence (together with several transitional expressions) to move her readers along in this paragraph:

While we're meditating on Christmas gifts, let us consider who got coal and switches this year. According to the Center on Budget and Policy Priorities, 93 percent of all the entitlement reductions passed by Congress in the last two years were in cuts for programs for poor people. *This is an appropriately Dickensian plot for the season, don't you think?* Ninety-three percent of everything that's been done to balance the budget in this way is being taken out of the pittance of low-income people. *Of course, not all the news is bad.* CEO Michael Ovitz, for example, will receive at least $95 million in compensation for leaving the Disney Company after sixteen months of what is widely regarded as an unsatisfactory performance. [Italics added.]

—"Early Christmas for Aerospace Giants"

Exercise on Transitions 4.4

In the paragraph below, we have removed the transitional terms and have inserted blanks in their place. Read each sentence carefully to determine which word or phrase from Figure 4.1 best conveys the meaning of the transition needed. Write your choice in the blank. Notice the punctuation so that you can tell when to use a capital letter.

The federal government deregulated the Savings and Loan business; _____, greedy money managers defrauded the taxpayers out of billions of dollars. The fleeced taxpayers were outraged, _____ they were helpless. The news media revealed the scandal; _____ Congress reacted with shock. Some people suggested, _____, that Congress had known about the thievery for some time. Several congressmen were clearly implicated; _____, two or three were known to have accepted huge campaign contributions from failed Savings and Loans. First, Congress promised a thorough investigation. _____, they set up committees to gather evidence. The taxpayers waited to see the rich managers brought to justice. _____ they hoped that some of the money would be recovered. _____ few of the guilty were even brought to trial, _____ getting the lost money back proved nearly impossible. _____, the American people are now saddled with this huge new debt, _____ the already staggering national debt. We taxpayers will have to shoulder this financial burden for years to come. _____, we might as well face up to it.

Provide Transitions Between Paragraphs

You may sometimes need signposts for your readers when you change paragraphs. The indention for a new paragraph provides a visual clue that you are moving on to another main idea, but indention alone isn't always helpful. Often you can use those same devices that you use when your thought changes direction or you want to add another example within the same paragraph: transitional expressions, rhetorical questions, and short transitional sentences. For instance, here are the opening sentences from several paragraphs of an essay entitled "Fighting Back" by Stanton Wormley, Jr. (the transitional words and phrases have been italicized).

In the spring of 1970, I was an 18-year-old private at Fort Jackson, South Carolina.

Afterward, I was angrily confronted by a young black streetwise soldier named Morris.

Nevertheless, that question—Why didn't I fight back?—haunted me long after the incident had been forgotten by everyone else.

And we American men buy that attitude—*especially* those of us who are members of minority groups.

I suppose there are *still* situations in which immediate, violent retaliation is necessary.

Once in a great while, past events are repeated, granting people a chance either to redeem themselves or to relive their mistakes.

As I walked away, I was filled with a feeling of exultation.

Writing Exercise 4.5

Stanton Wormley's organization and transitions are so effective that you can probably follow the development of his argument, even though you don't have the complete text of the article. Write a paragraph in which you summarize Wormley's main ideas.

Use Echo Transitions. An *echo transition* gives you a subtle way to move smoothly from one paragraph to the next. You manage this artful transition by "echoing" the last idea in one paragraph at the beginning of the next. You create the echo by repeating the same word or by using a word meaning the same thing, which thus "echoes" the idea. It's a neat technique and not difficult to perform once you see how it works. Here's an example from Stanton Wormley's essay:

> Fighting back, on the other hand, is active and defiant. It involves the adoption of *an attitude* that one's retribution is morally justified—or even, at times, morally obligatory.
> And we American men buy *that attitude*—especially those of us who are members of minority groups. [Italics added.]

You can see how the repetition of the word *attitude* in the opening sentence of the new paragraph forms a link to the previous paragraph and at the same time leads into Wormley's next idea: explaining how and why *that attitude* appeals to minority males.

You don't have to repeat the very same word. You can, instead, use a synonym or a related phrase, as in this next example, which gives you the final sentence from a paragraph by Frederick Lewis Allen about the big Red scare in the twenties, followed by the opening sentence of the next paragraph which explains the reasons for the scare. The transitional words are italicized in our examples.

> It was an era of lawless and disorderly defense of law and order, of unconstitutional defense of the Constitution, of suspicion and civil conflict—in a very literal sense, *a reign of terror.*
> For this *national panic* there was a degree of justification.

Finally, notice the easy transition from a paragraph describing the deafening noises of a large city to the next paragraph suggesting possible relief:

> Reveille is celebrated in New York these frantic days by the commencement of *pneumatic drills.*
> The only way to escape *the din of the asphalt bashers* is to move out or up.
>
> —Horace Sutton

Pneumatic drills are, of course, one kind of *asphalt basher.*

Exercise on Coherence 4.6

Locate an essay, article, or chapter of a book that uses a variety of strategies for achieving unity and coherence. Identify each of the strategies—transitional expressions, repeated words, rhetorical questions, short sentences, echo transitions—and comment on their effectiveness.

C *omposing Special Paragraphs*

Not all of your paragraphs are going to conform to the advice we've been giving you about the content and organization of typical paragraphs. Most notably, introductions and conclusions have special requirements that you need to consider.

Advice About Introductions

You can draft the introduction to a paper at any point during the writing process. Some people like to write it first as a way of getting started; others wait till last so they can tailor it to fit the rest of the essay. Regardless of when you write the introduction, remember that because your audience reads it first, it should make a favorable impression.

State Your Thesis. Although getting your readers' attention is an important element of most introductions, the chief function is to let readers know what you're writing about. You will not always need a straightforward announcement of your central idea, but the more formal the writing, the more likely you are to need a clear thesis statement. In the following introduction the writer comes straight to the point:

> Today in the United States there is one profession in which conflict of interest is not merely ignored but loudly defended as a necessary concomitant of the free-enterprise system. That is in medicine, particularly in surgery.
>
> —George Crile, Jr.

This is point-blank as introductions go. Normally, you take several sentences to work up to your main idea, giving a little background information or making some fairly broad remarks about your subject, then narrowing the focus to the specific idea in your thesis. This method is used in the following introduction (thesis statements are italicized throughout this section):

> To her, tight jeans and no bra mean she's in style. To him, they mean she wants to have sex. So it goes among adolescents in Los Angeles, according to a survey by four researchers at UCLA. Despite unisex hair salons, the women's movement, and other signs of equality between the sexes, *boys still read more sexual come-ons into girls' behavior than girls intend.*
>
> —*Psychology Today*

The article then presents other examples of dress and behavior that are often misinterpreted, just as the introduction promises.

Catch Your Readers' Attention. Unless you are writing for readers that already have a professional interest in the topic of your paper, you need an introduction that will catch their attention and encourage them to continue reading. One good way involves putting a picture in their minds, as the writer does in this introduction:

> You know the couch potato: the flabby muscles and a generous waistline, one hand on the remote control and the other in a bag of chips. Medical research now has confirmed the aptness of this depiction. *Long hours in front of the tube and obesity, it turns out, go together like Monday Night Football and beer nuts.*
>
> —Elizabeth Stark

Find Fascinating Facts. Another way to hook your readers is to begin with some eye-opening facts and figures, as in this introduction:

> Every two-and-a-half minutes someone in the United States is robbed at gunpoint, and every forty minutes someone else is murdered with a gun. The weapons find their way into the hands of the criminals in a manner that almost nobody understands. Made in factories owned and operated by the most secretive industry in the country, the guns move through various markets and delivery systems, all of them obscure. Each year police seize about 250,000 handguns and long guns (rifles and shotguns) from the people they arrest. *Given the number of guns that the manufacturers produce each year (2.5 million long guns and 4 million handguns) the supply-and-demand equation works against the hope of an orderly society.*
>
> —Steven Brill, *Harper's*

Select a Quotation. Sometimes a relevant and interesting quotation provides an effective way to introduce your main idea. In the following introduction from an essay on crime statistics, the author uses dialogue from a popular film to set up his main idea:

> One of the great comedic scenes of modern times takes place in the 1977 Woody Allen movie *Annie Hall*, in which Allen and Diane Keaton play an embattled couple who tell their shrinks how often they have sex. "Constantly!" says Keaton's character. "I'd say three times a week." On the other hand, says Allen's character: "Hardly ever. Maybe three times a week." In the language of shrinks, that

kind of situation is known as "desire discrepancy": the two sides agree on the numbers, but extrapolate entirely different conclusions. *The same thing applies to the way we look at crime-related issues in Canada.*

—Anthony Wilson-Smith, *Maclean's*

Try a Definition. Another useful way to get started is by defining your subject, like this:

> Tennyson called it a "flying game." Benjamin Franklin termed it a "sudden and terrible mischief." In Roman mythology, the god Jupiter used spiky thunderbolts as letters to the editor when he chose to show displeasure with the poor mortals below. *By whatever name, lightning is a spectacular natural event.*

—Michael Cluston

Avoid Mindless Generalizations. In your effort to begin with a general observation and narrow that down to a thesis statement, you want to avoid obvious generalizations like these:

Life can be very interesting.

People are funny sometimes.

If you begin with such clichéd comments, your readers may never get beyond the opening sentence.

TIP! Don't expect to write the perfect introduction on the first try. Refine your introduction and your thesis as you work through your draft and your revisions.

R*evising Exercise 4.7*

Find a paper you have written recently, and look at the introduction. How can you improve it? Write ~~two~~ one more versions of the introduction, using the strategies described in this chapter.

Advice About Conclusions

Like introductions, conclusions ought to be forceful and to the point. Work especially hard on your last paragraph. Its effectiveness will influence the way your readers react to the whole paper. If you trail off at the end, they will sigh and feel let down.

Avoid any sort of apology or hedging at this point. You want an impressive ending.

Echo Your Thesis Statement. What you want in a conclusion is a tidy ending that reinforces the point you set out to make in the beginning. An echo of your thesis statement can be perfect. Consider the conclusion of the article on misinterpreting sexual signals (the introduction appeared on page 65):

> The young people's ethnic backgrounds, ages, and previous dating and sexual experiences had almost no effect on their reactions. The girls' "relatively less-sexualized view of social relationships," the psychologists suggest, "may reflect some discomfort with the demands of the dating scene"; women do, after all, have more to lose from sexual activity, facing risks of pregnancy and/or a bad reputation. The girls in the study were more likely than the boys to agree with the statement, "Sometimes I wish that guys and girls could just be friends without worrying about sexual relationships."
>
> —*Psychology Today*

The quotation at the end echoes the thesis idea ("boys still read more sexual come-ons into girls' behavior than the girls intend"), restating it in different terms and giving the article a neat unity.

Summarize Your Main Points. If your essay is long and complex, your readers may appreciate a summary of the major ideas. You want to be careful, however, not to write an ending that sounds forced and simply repeats your introduction. It's a good idea to combine your summary with another strategy. For example, the professional author of an essay on the problems of young black males in America's inner cities concludes by combining a review of her main points with a general call for action:

> If black youths are given real opportunities for education, if they are provided with meaningful jobs, if they have adequate income to care for their families, if they have hope for future mobility, then they will contribute their fair share to the larger community. We have the knowledge, the technology, and the resources to improve life chances for young black males. What we need is the compassion, commitment, and consensus to create a human environment for all youth in this country.
>
> —Jewelle Taylor Gibbs

Suggest Solutions. If you're writing an analysis or a persuasive piece, a useful closing strategy involves offering suggestions—possible solutions for problems discussed in the paper. This approach is valid only if you can come up with some sound ideas for solving the problems. Here is the conclusion of the article about containing the proliferation of guns in the United States (the introduction is on page 66):

> All these small steps toward sanity are possible if we force the people who profit from America's free-wheeling gun traffic to be open, accountable, and fully responsible to law-enforcement needs. If we're going to continue to allow the RGs or the Smith and Wessons to make guns at all for civilian use, we ought to at least demand that they become partners in the effort to curb the carnage their weapons cause. When we think of people murdered or robbed at gunpoint, we have to start thinking of brand names.
>
> —Steven Brill

Offer Encouragement. Especially in process writing, in which you are explaining how to do something, it's constructive to close with a few words of encouragement. Tell your readers how delicious they will find the cheesecake if they follow your instructions carefully. Or tell them how rewarding they will find growing their own tomatoes, as the writer does in this conclusion:

> When you shop for tomato seeds or plants this season, consider trying at least one new variety. There are hundreds to choose from and if you keep looking, one of them may find a home in your garden. Even if you find nothing to match your favorite, you'll have fun, and the pleasure of gardening is not just in the eating.
>
> —Mark Kane

Speculate on the Future. Think about the long-term implications of what you have said in your paper. You might want to conclude by warning of hazards or by suggesting possible benefits. In the next example, the writer does both, concluding his argument about crime in Canada (the introduction is on pages 66–67):

> No one is saying the war on crime is over, or ever will be. But it's possible to look at the upside. Despite all the forecasts that Canada's increasingly multicultural composition would lead to more conflict and unrest, there's little statistical evidence of that. It also wouldn't hurt to give cops some credit: maybe, contrary to the

old line, there *is* one around more often than not when you need one. Finally, what happens if everyone keeps insisting the statistics are wrong, and we're descending into chaos? Who's best served if law-abiding people become so scared of life on the streets that they stay off them? Let that happen, and the bad guys *will* win.

—Anthony Wilson-Smith

Conclusions aren't really all that difficult. Often they turn out weak because we write them last, when our energy and inspiration are lagging.

TIP! Treat your conclusion like your introduction: Think about it off and on while you are writing—during coffee breaks or whenever you pause to let your mind rest.

Revising Exercise 4.8

The following conclusion is flat and doesn't leave much of an impression on the reader. Use one of the strategies just discussed to put more punch in this ending. Even though you didn't write the essay, you should be able to improve this concluding paragraph. Work especially hard in crafting the final sentence.

College is a big change for thousands of students every year. As I have indicated, these students are expected to be fairly mature; they must develop independence and self-discipline; and they have to take more difficult tests and compete for grades. Almost everyone finds college more difficult than high school.

Writing Exercise 4.9

Using any of the strategies just described, write ~~two~~ one additional conclusions for a paper that you have written recently. Show these alternate endings to several friends or classmates, and ask them which one seems the most effective for your paper and if they have any suggestions for improvement.

5

Polishing Your Sentences

In order to perfect your paragraphs, you need to revise your sentences—to make them more clear perhaps, more vivid, more concise, more interesting, more forceful. Before any paragraph can be effective, the sentences within that paragraph must be both coherent and readable.

S *entence Combining: Coordination and Subordination*

One way to improve coherence is through skillful sentence combining, which involves placing ideas within each sentence according to their importance so that the readers' attention stays focused on your major points.

Perhaps you've noticed that when little children talk, they tend to string simple sentences together, like this:

> We got hats and balloons and Buffy got presents and Angie was late and we had cake with candles and ice cream and I blew my balloon up big and . . .

So it goes, on and on and on, with little variety, few modifiers, and no distinction between important events and passing details. That's *coordination*—linking ideas together—in its most primitive form. We learn to read and write with a similar simplicity. But by the time we progress to the third grade, we become sophisticated and start putting sentences together in patterns which depend upon subordination.

Clauses Versus Phrases

Subordination involves tucking less important ideas into dependent (or subordinate) clauses and small details into phrases. Then, major ideas are elevated into independent (or main) clauses, where they receive proper emphasis. If you're hazy about the difference between phrases and clauses, remember that a clause has both a subject and a verb, whereas a phrase has only one or the other. Notice the difference:

PHRASES:	having lost my head
	to lose my head
	after losing my head
CLAUSES:	after I lost my head (dependent)
	I lost my head (independent)
	that I lost my head (dependent)

An independent clause can be a complete sentence all by itself. Because a dependent clause begins with a subordinating word (see list on page 208), it must be attached to an independent clause in order to form a complete sentence.

H *ow Sentence Combining Works*

Most of this subordinating—this stashing of details into phrases and clauses—we do automatically as we speak and write. But it helps to understand the process when you revise and want to combine ideas to improve your sentence structure. Here's how it's done.

Subordinating in a Phrase

Say you want to incorporate the following ideas into a single sentence:

Garfield is a cat.

Garfield is orange.

Garfield is striped.

Garfield weighs fifteen pounds.

Garfield is incorrigible.

Garfield is a glutton.

Garfield is a cartoon character.

You could combine several of those details into a phrase this way:

> Garfield, an orange-striped, fifteen-pound cartoon cat, is an incorrigible glutton.

You have subordinated the color, stripes, weight, and cartoon status of the cat in one fell swoop. But suppose you wanted to stress Garfield's being a cartoon cat rather than his gluttony. The sentence might come out this way:

> Garfield, an incorrigibly gluttonous, fifteen-pound, orange-striped cat, is a cartoon character.

Same details, but see the difference in emphasis? Because English is a language depending on word order for meaning, the way you put a sentence together affects the sense as well as the style. In the first example, the key positions in the sentence are these:

subject	verb	complement
Garfield	is	incorrigible glutton

In the second one

subject	verb	complement
Garfield	is	cartoon character

Subordinating in a Clause

Of course, a clause can also become the less important element in a sentence if you make it a subordinate clause, like this:

> Garfield, who weighs fifteen pounds, is an orange-striped, incorrigibly gluttonous cartoon cat.

Or, you could do it this way:

> Because he is an incorrigible glutton, Garfield, the orange-striped cartoon cat, weighs fifteen pounds.

But you would not want to arrange the ideas this way:

> Because he is an incorrigible glutton, Garfield, who weighs fifteen pounds, is an orange-striped cartoon cat.

That's called upside-down subordination, and you can see why. It makes no sense to say that because the cat eats too much he has orange stripes and appears in a cartoon.

TIP!   When combining ideas, be sure to get your important
ideas into the main clauses, not the subordinate clauses.

W *hen to Use Sentence Combining*

1. *If you are writing a lot of short choppy sentences, consider combining some.*

   For example:

   > Maria became a doctor. She didn't become a regular doctor. She
   > became a medical missionary.

   Combined:

   > Rather than becoming a regular doctor, Maria became a medical
   > missionary.

2. *If you notice needless repetition of a word or phrase, consider combining.*

   For example:

   > Dierdre judges all her friends severely. Dierdre always judges
   > according to her own rigid standards.

   Combined:

   > Dierdre always judges all her friends severely according to her
   > own rigid standards.

3. *When a sentence begins with "This is" or "It is," you may want to
   combine that sentence with the one ahead of it.*

   For example:

   > To Michael, his car establishes his place in society. It is a sleek,
   > shiny, luxurious Jaguar.

   Combined:

   > To Michael, his car—a sleek, shiny, luxurious Jaguar—estab-
   > lishes his place in society.

| *S* *entence Combining Exercise 5.1*

Look at the last paper you wrote. Did you find a fair number of short
choppy sentences? If so, this exercise may help you become more fluent.

If you need this practice, combine each group below into one easily understood sentence by subordinating the less important ideas. We'll do the first one to show you the idea.

1. Fido is a dog.

   Fido belongs to me.

   Fido needs a bath.

   Fido has muddy paws.

   Fido has fleas.

   (Combined) My dog Fido, who has muddy paws and fleas, needs a bath.

   (Combined) Because he has fleas and muddy paws, my dog Fido needs a bath.

2. Uncle Zou is coming to visit.

   He lives in Edmonton.

   He drives a city bus there.

   He is coming on the early train.

   He will stay with us a week.

3. My garden is in the backyard.

   Rabbits ate the lettuce.

   Worms got the tomatoes.

   The cucumbers got trampled.

   Somebody stepped on them.

4. I get off work at 4:30.

   I pick up the kids.

   The kids are at daycare.

   I fix dinner.

   I wash the dishes.

   I fall asleep in front of the TV.

5. All the characters in this bestseller are stereotypes.

   Some of these stereotypes are the Idealistic Young Man, the Disillusioned Older Man, the Scheming Siren, and the Neglected Wife.

Sentence Combining Exercise 5.2

If you are a fairly fluent writer who wants to practice sentence combining to avoid wordiness and improve your sentence structure, try the following exercise. Combine the following pairs of sentences, all of which were written by students in one of our classes in writing about literature.

1. Flowers serve an important role in Cather's "Paul's Case." Therefore, they are worthy of closer examination.

2. The boy's illusion is conveyed even more clearly through Joyce's description of the girl. Joyce describes her as turning a silver bracelet on her wrist.

3. Edna was so happy that she shouted for joy. Learning to swim was a big achievement for Edna.

4. The similarities between Dr. Sloper and Morris Townsend are numerous. They can be seen throughout the book.

5. Dr. Sloper warns his daughter about the dangers of marrying Morris. He does this because he sees so many of his own weak points in his daughter's suitor.

Sentence Combining Exercise 5.3

Find the last paper you wrote and read through it slowly, paragraph by paragraph. Look for short sentences, needlessly repeated words or phrases, and sentences beginning with "This is" or "It is." If you find any of these signals, combine sentences to improve your style.

Cut Out Unnecessary Words

Try to make your writing clean, clear, and concise. We don't mean to deprive you of effective stylistic flourishes, but ineffective stylistic flourishes have to go. So does just plain lazy wordiness. It's far easier to be verbose than to be concise. As Pascal wrote, "I have made this letter longer than usual because I lack the time to make it shorter." And as Hugh Henry Breckenridge tellingly observed, "In order to speak short on any subject, think long." Nothing will annoy your readers more than having to plow through a cluttered paragraph because you neglected to spend time cleaning it up.

You must diligently prune your prose. Sentences like the following may cause even a gentle reader to contemplate justifiable homicide:

It is believed by a number of persons in this country that the young people of today do not assume as much responsibility for their actions as it might be hoped that they would. (34 words)

You can say the same thing more clearly with fewer words:

Many people believe that young people today assume too little responsibility for their actions. (14 words)

Exercise on Conciseness 5.4

If you have trouble saying things succinctly, practice by tidying the following wordy sentences. Keep the same meaning but eliminate the extra words. We'll revise the first one.

1. The male-gendered style used on-line in ListServe communications is characterized by an adversarial attitude.

   (revised) The male style used in communications on ListServe is adversarial.

2. It is my desire to be called Ishmael.

3. In my opinion there are many diverse elements about this problem that one probably ought to at least think about before arriving at an opinion on the matter.

4. The obnoxious child was seldom corrected or reprimanded because its baffled and adoring parents thought its objectionable behavior was normal and acceptable.

5. There came a time when, based on what I had been reading, I arrived at the feeling that the food we buy at the supermarkets to eat is sometimes, perhaps often, bad for us.

U se Mostly Active Voice

If your writing is somewhat lifeless, the passive voice may be part of the problem. In the passive (which always involves some form of the verb *to be* plus a past participle) the subject is acted upon instead of doing the acting. Notice the difference between active and passive:

(active)　　　The guard fed the prisoner.

(passive)　　　The prisoner was fed by the guard.

As you can see, it takes more words to express an idea with a passive verb—unless you leave out the performer of the action. Thus a passive sentence like this one,

A decision on the matter has been made by the court.

takes longer to read and process than the active version,

The court decided the matter.

The Devious Passive

Notice that the passive allows us to leave out information. You don't have to mention who fed the prisoner, you can just say, "The prisoner was fed." That's not a misleading sentence because probably nobody was perishing to know who fed the prisoner anyway. But consider the same sentence with the verb changed:

(passive)   The prisoner was beaten.

Now we want to know *by whom*? By the sheriff? By one of the deputies? By a guard? By a fellow prisoner? There's no way to tell from the passive construction. As Richard Gambino, an authority on doublespeak, observes, "The effect of the habitual use of the passive is to create a world where events have lives, wills, motives, and actions of their own without any human being responsible for them."

The Appropriate Passive

Notice, it's the *habitual* use of the passive that is questionable. We don't mean that you should never employ the passive voice. Sometimes it can be the best way to convey information. You would likely choose the passive to announce that "The President was elected by a comfortable majority," rather than using the active voice: "A comfortable majority elected the President."

The passive is also a good choice when you want to stress the action or the receiver of the action:

(passive)   The city hall was damaged by an earthquake.

(passive)   My bicycle was demolished by a truck.

(passive)   The candidate's credibility has been questioned by the media.

Revising Exercise 5.5

If you have trouble distinguishing active from passive—or if you suspect that you use the passive too much—rewrite the following passive sentences in the active voice. We'll do the first one to get you going.

1. Let our daily bread be given to us on this day.
   (revised) Give us this day our daily bread.
2. The whistle was blown by the referee.
3. It was believed by the police that the child was kidnapped.
4. The day that he discovered sex was never forgotten by Cosmo.
5. Some basic human rights were violated by the officers.
6. Bribes were accepted frequently by the city engineer.

P *ractice the Passive*

Despite all these warnings against habitual use of the passive, we are aware that writers in a number of jobs and in some academic disciplines are expected—even required—to use the passive voice. If you are taking courses in education, corrections, or any of the hard sciences (chemistry, biology, physics, and the like), you must learn to write gracefully in the passive voice. It can be done, but you may need to practice to get the hang of it.

Proceeding from the pen of an accomplished writer, the passive voice is not in the least objectionable. Jessica Mitford, for one, employs the passive so skillfully that you never notice its presence:

> Today, family members who might wish to be in attendance would certainly be dissuaded by the funeral director.

That sentence is not noticeably improved by making it active voice:

> Today, the funeral director would certainly dissuade family members who might wish to be in attendance.

In order to help you perfect your use of the passive, we have collected some useful and fairly simple sentences as models. If you'd like to learn to use the passive skillfully, try working out the following exercise.

S *entence Modeling Exercise 5.6*

Copy each sentence carefully. Then, choosing subject matter from your academic major, write five sentences imitating the passive structure of each of the originals. Pretending to be agriculture majors, we'll do the first one to show you how it's done.

1. Certain things were not mentioned.   (Jane O'Reilly)
   (Imitations)
      Synthetic fertilizers were not invented.
      Pesticides were not advised.
      Crop rotation was not used.
      Early harvesting was not recommended.
      Organic methods were not tried.
2. The SKIP option can be used in input and output statements.
   (J.S. Roper)
3. The poor are slated to take the brunt of the federal budget cuts.
   (Barbara Ehrenreich)
4. The emphasis is generally put on the right to speak. (Walter Lipp-
   mann)
5. All others are excluded by law from the preparation room. (Jessica
   Mitford)
6. Every dollar earned was wrestled from the earth, carved, blasted,
   crushed, melted down, and skimmed off. (Will Ferguson)

B *e Specific and Vivid*

Paul Roberts once wrote that most subjects—except sex—are basically boring, so it's up to the writer to make the topic interesting. Since you can't write about sex all the time, you need to incorporate some of the following suggestions aimed at keeping your readers awake.

Choose Action Verbs

One way to liven up your writing is to use lively, specific words whenever possible. You can't always avoid the lifeless *to be* verb (*am, is, are, was, were, been, being*), but when given a chance, you can toss in an action verb. James Thurber writes of a "world made up of gadgets that *whir* and *whine* and *whiz* and *shriek* and sometimes *explode*." (Our italics.) The force of the verbs conveys the feeling of anxiety produced by machine-age living.

George Orwell describes a dog that "came *bounding* among us with a loud volley of barks, and *leapt* round us *wagging* its whole body with glee." (Our italics.) The italicized words and the descriptive detail about the barking allow us to visualize the excitement of the dog.

Thomas Heggen, in *Mister Roberts,* writes, "Surely an artillery shell fired at Hanover *ripples* the air here. Surely a bomb dropped on Okinawa *trembles* these bulkheads." (Our italics.) These verbs and the specific place names produce precisely the effect he wants: the suggestion of being touched, but only barely touched, by events far away.

There are, of course, other stylistic elements combining to make the above examples effective. But if your writing is colorless and vague, consider adding specific details and substituting more descriptive verbs for these limp ones: *is, are, was, were, has, have, had, get, go, come, make.* If you've written, "We all got into the truck," try "All four of us piled into Billy Bob's rusty pickup." You can, of course, overdo the use of forceful verbs and specific details, but most writers err in the other direction.

TIP!   Avoid the overworked words *terrible, wonderful, very.* Find more precise terms, like *inept, skillful, excellent.*

Find the Exact Word

Mark Twain once observed that the difference between the right word and almost the right word is the difference between the lightning and the lightning bug. Our language is full of synonyms; but synonyms have different shades of meaning. Don't write *ambiguous* if you really mean *ambivalent.* Don't write *sensuous* if you really mean *sensual.* Don't write *forceful* when you mean *forcible.* Especially, be careful not to confuse words that sound alike but mean something entirely different. Don't write *apprise* if you really mean *appraise.* Don't write *disinterested* if you really mean *uninterested.* Don't write *elicit* when you mean *illicit.*

Dust Off Your Dictionary

Any desk-size dictionary can enlighten you on these distinctions. But in order to get reliable help from your dictionary, you should first learn how to use it. Nobody has ever standardized the format for dictionaries, so they arrange their material in slightly different ways.

Many people believe that the first meaning listed for a word will be the one they want. Not necessarily true. The first meaning will often be the oldest meaning and thus the least used. The same is true of alternative spellings. Lots of people think the first spelling is preferred. But unless some usage label is inserted (like "also" or "variation of"), all spellings listed are equally acceptable.

The only way to find out how your dictionary handles these matters is to force yourself to read the "Explanatory Notes" at the beginning. It's not lively reading, to be sure, but it can be rewarding. You'll find out, for instance, that in most dictionaries the principal parts of verbs, degrees of adjectives, and plurals of nouns are not listed unless irregular. You'll find, if you persevere, explanations of various usage labels, which warn you about words that may not be acceptable in standard English (archaic, slang, substandard, etc.).

You may also, if you have an inquiring mind, discover interesting material in the back (or sometimes in the front) that you never suspected was there. Many dictionaries include lists of abbreviations, proofreader's marks, signs and symbols; rules for spelling, punctuation, and capitalization; and occasionally a list of all the colleges (with locations) in the United States and Canada. One dictionary even offers lists of common first names and of words that rhyme.

TIP! Good writers keep a dictionary handy and consult it often.

If the only thing you ever do with your dictionary is use it to prop up books, that may be part of your problem.

Trot Out Your Thesaurus

A thesaurus, which is a dictionary of synonyms, comes in handy for locating just the right word. Your word-processing program probably has one that's quick to consult. It may not be as good as the kind that comes in book form, but it's better than none and a sight easier to use.

If you need a synonym, either because you think the word you've used is not the precise word or because you've used it three times already, call up that word on your word processor's thesaurus or look it up in the book version that you keep on your desk. Sometimes we use both if the electronic one fails to offer enough choices. Did you notice that we've used a form of the word *use* four times already in this paragraph? That's a signal to consult a thesaurus.

We just called up *use* on our popular word-processing program and found seven words—*employ, utilize, exercise, manipulate, apply, exploit, operate*—and only the first two fit our meaning. The word *consult*, which we thought up ourselves, wasn't even listed. So, we checked our pocketbook-size thesaurus and found almost a full page of synonyms arranged according to meaning and part of speech (verb, adjective, adverb, etc.), with a *See* at the end citing four other words we could look up to find additional meanings. Clearly, you need a back-up for your electronic thesaurus if you want to discover all your verbal options.

TIP! **Synonyms are not always interchangeable.**
Never choose an unfamiliar word from your thesaurus. Look it up in your dictionary first.

E *xercise Your Imagination: Figures of Speech*

Try to come up with a few lively figures of speech—analogies and other imaginative comparisons—to add interest and clarity to your writing. Ralph Waldo Emerson once remarked that "New York is a sucked orange." Now there's an observation full of meaning, phrased with great economy. Maya Angelou writes that some social changes "have been as violent as electrical storms, while others creep slowly like sorghum syrup."

Such comparisons are a form of analogy, a useful method of comparing something *abstract* (like the quality of life in a city) to something *concrete* and visual (like a sucked orange). Here's an apt analogy from Sharon Begley: "The immune system is notorious for falling apart like a dishwasher past its warranty."

When Dorothy Parker declares, "His voice was as intimate as the rustle of sheets," her *simile* (a comparison stated with *like* or *as*) is more interesting than just telling us that the man was speaking seductively. Notice how forcefully Barbara Ehrenreich conveys the hazards of smoking when she asserts that the "medical case against smoking is as airtight as a steel casket." And Margaret Atwood gives a vivid action image when she writes, "She came whizzing down the stairs, thrown like a dart."

Brigid Brophy uses a *metaphor* (an implied comparison) to assert her belief that monogamy is too confining: "At present, monogamy is the corset into which we try to fit every married couple—a process which has on so many occasions split the seams that we have had to modify the corset."

Make Your Metaphors Meaningful

In writing expository prose (the kind we're focusing on in this text), your figures of speech should clarify your meaning—unlike metaphoric language in poetry, which often conceals meaning. Part of the pleasure of poetry involves puzzling out the meaning. Not so in expository prose. The cardinal rule here is Thou Shalt Not Puzzle Thy Readers. Better no metaphors at all than one that is confusing or mixed up. A *mixed metaphor* runs two metaphors together in an illogical way, like this gem: "The wheels of justice are coming apart at the seams." Just try to visualize that image, and you'll see why it's a mistake. Lapses like that may bring, not admiration for your fine turn of phrase, but an unwanted chuckle from your bemused readers.

Avoid Clichés

Be sure your figures of speech really *are* lively. Don't settle for the first phrase that comes to mind, as it will likely be a *cliché*—an expression people pick up because it sounds good and then tend to use over and over until it loses its force, like these chestnuts:

bottom line	ballpark figure
burning questions	high and mighty
crystal clear	last but not least
few and far between	pretty as a picture
first and foremost	untimely death
at this point in time	have a nice day

TIP! The simple word "fine" is preferable to the tarnished phrase "worth its weight in gold."

Revising Exercise 5.7

To limber up your imagination, rewrite the following correct but lackluster sentences. Add details and substitute action verbs and descriptive words wherever appropriate. Here's how we would revise the first one.

1. She was up late last night trying to finish typing her term paper.

   (revised) Selina sat hunched over her typewriter, pecking away doggedly until three o'clock in the morning, trying to finish her term paper.

2. Alec left his office, walked to a store, and made a purchase.
3. The person I went out with last night was a character.
4. She came into the room, took off her shoes, and sat down.
5. Some person had removed the article I needed from the magazine in the library.

R*evising Exercise 5.8*

Drag out your last paper, and revise the word choice as you go through it, sentence by sentence, replacing or eliminating overworked, tired words with more precise, colorful language.

C *onstructing Impressive Sentences*

Another way to make your prose effective involves writing an occasional forceful or unusual sentence. If every sentence built to a climax, the technique would lose its effectiveness, so don't work at it too hard. But in a key position—such as at the beginning or end of a paragraph or as the last line in your essay—a carefully constructed sentence is worth the time it takes to compose it.

Save the Clincher for the End: Periodic Structure

Most of the time we don't deliberate about our sentence structure. We string ideas together, automatically subordinating the less important ones, until we come to the end of the thought, where we put a period and start in on the next one. These everyday sentences—like the one we just wrote—are called *cumulative* and constitute the bulk of our writing. If, however, you need a Sunday-best sentence, you either consciously plan it or rearrange it when you revise. You want to order the details to build to a big finish, so you don't disclose your main idea until just before the period where it gains emphasis. These sentences are called *periodic*. Notice the difference in these examples:

cumulative: Sylvester made the honor roll while holding down a part-time job and playing the lead in *Hamlet*.

periodic: While holding down a part-time job and playing the lead in *Hamlet*, Sylvester made the honor roll.

cumulative: Our first consideration is the preservation of our envi-
                ronment, even though preventing pollution costs
                money.

periodic: Even though preventing pollution costs money, our first
                consideration is the preservation of our environment.

If you have a feel for prose, you probably already write periodic
sentences when you need them without being aware that you're
doing it. If, on the other hand, you're not long on style, you can
develop some by cinching up a few of your sentences. Here are a
few more useful strategies.

Try a Short One for Variety, Emphasis, or Transition

The short-short sentence is easier to handle than the periodic
sentence and is remarkably effective—as long as you don't
overdo it. Often short-short sentences appear at the beginning or
at the end of a paragraph, since these are the most emphatic positions. But you can lob one in anytime if you want to vary your
sentence structure. Remember, though, not to overdo it. You can't
use short-short sentences often or you'll lose the effect; your writing will merely seem choppy.

Notice the emphasis achieved in the following examples by
the brief sentence preceding or following one of normal length:

This is our hope. This is the faith with which I return to the South to
hew out of the mountain of despair a stone of hope.

—Dr. Martin Luther King, Jr.

Webster's dictionaries and the endless multiplication of handbooks
and courses in English composition represent a desperate effort to
prevent class distinction from revealing itself in language. And, of
course, it has failed.

—John Hurt Fisher

What, therefore is the prognosis of our terminally ill planet? It is
gloomy.

—Helen Caldicott

The short sentence also functions effectively as a transitional
device between paragraphs (our italics):

Economics, foreign policy, the split in the party as it relates to racial
equality, and some resulting questions of political style all require a
special word. *To these matters I now turn.*

—John Kenneth Galbraith

Experiment with the Dash

Since the end of a sentence is an emphatic position, you can use a dash there to good advantage, as Woodrow Wilson did in this warning:

> I have seen their destruction, as will come upon these again—utter destruction and contempt.

The dash can be used to tack on an afterthought, but you'll find it more impressive for reinforcing a point or for elaboration, like this:

> Hollywood offered the public yet another marvel—talking films.

> This was the year of the big spectaculars—Biblical extravaganzas spiced with sex and filmed in glorious Technicolor.

The dash, like the short sentence, can't retain its effect if overused. In fact, a flurry of dashes produces an unfortunate, adolescent style.

TIP! For emphasis, use dashes and short sentences sparingly.

U *se Parallel Structure*

Another way to keep your ideas clear and make your sentences impressive is to use parallel structure. This technique depends upon deliberate repetition—sometimes of the same words, always of the same grammatical structures (phrases, clauses). Virginia Woolf repeats the same adverb *(well)*, changing the verb each time to achieve this elegant sentence:

> One cannot think well, love well, sleep well, if one has not dined well.

Mark Twain, in a less elevated tone, repeats independent clauses:

> It was marvelous, it was dizzying, it was dazzling.

For Everyday Writing

While parallel structure lends itself particularly well to emphatic sentences, the technique is fundamental to all good writing. If you by chance put together a sentence involving two similar elements or a series of them, your readers expect these similar parts to be balanced using parallel structure. Whenever you join parts of a sentence with a coordinating conjunction *(and, but, or, for, nor, yet, so)*, you need to make those parts parallel.

Consider the problem caused by lack of parallelism in this first simple example:

Clyde likes *to smoke* and *drinking.*

Your readers expect those italicized parts to sound and look alike—to be parallel in construction, like this:

Clyde likes to *smoke* and *drink.*

Or you could revise it this way:

Clyde likes *smoking* and *drinking.*

Let's look at a more typical example, the kind of sentence you might write in a first draft and should make parallel in structure when you revise:

Politicians today face the difficult tasks of *solving urban problems* and *how to find the money* without raising taxes.

You need to match the two parts connected by *and.* The easiest way is to make *how to find* sound and look like *solving*—that is, use *finding:*

Politicians face the difficult task of *solving urban problems* and *finding the money* without raising taxes.

For Sunday-Best Sentences

Once you become adept at constructing parallel sentences, you'll find the technique perfect for composing splendid climactic sentences—the kind you need to summarize key points, to conclude paragraphs, and to bring your essays to a resounding finish. Martin Luther King, Jr. learned from the Bible how to repeat parallel phrases with ringing effect:

With this faith we will be able to work together, to pray together, to struggle together, to go to jail together, to stand up for freedom together, knowing that we will be free one day.

Here is Thomas Jefferson expressing righteous outrage in the Declaration of Independence:

He [King George III] has plundered our seas, ravaged our coasts, burnt our towns, and destroyed the lives of our people.

Parallel structure also provides the most effective way to compress a number of ideas into a single sentence with perfect clarity and easy readability. Notice how many ideas T. E. Kalem packs into this nicely balanced comment on one of George Bernard Shaw's plays:

> Shaw steadily sounds his pet themes: the chicanery of politics, the corruptive power of money, the degrading stench of poverty, the servile dependencies of marriage and family, the charlatanism of medicine, the fossilization of learning, the tyranny of the state, the stupidity of the military, and the bigoted, sanctimonious zeal of the church.

TIP! There's no better strategy than parallel structure to deliver so many ideas so clearly in so readable a way.

You can also use parallel structure to good effect in separate sentences by repeating key words in the same grammatical structure. Because the technique involves building to a climax, you can't use it often, but the effect is impressive when well done. Notice how Pastor Martin Niemoeller, a Lutheran minister, achieves eloquence by using simple, parallel sentences to explain how he ended up in a Nazi concentration camp during World War II:

> In Germany, the Nazis first came for the Communists, and I didn't speak up because I wasn't a Communist. Then they came for the Jews, and I didn't speak up because I wasn't a Jew. Then they came for the trade unionists, and I didn't speak up because I wasn't a trade unionist. Then they came for the Catholics, and I didn't speak up because I was a Protestant. Then they came for me, and by that time there was no one left to speak for me.

Revising Exercise 5.9

The following sentences were written by students whose grasp of parallel structure was less than perfect. We want you to restore the parallelism. Don't aim for impressive or emphatic sentences in this exercise. Just try to produce good, clear, everyday sentences.

First, read each sentence and decide which parts need to be made parallel. Look for elements in series or connected by coordinating conjunctions (*and, but, or, for, nor, yet, so*). Then change the part that's irregular so that it matches the other part or parts.

Often you can find several equally good ways to revise such sentences. Here's how we would do the first one:

1. The plan is not workable; it delegates too much power to the states and because it is unconstitutional.

That sentence consists of three clauses in series. All three should be parallel. The first two are independent:

The plan is not workable

it delegates too much power to the states

Fine so far. The clauses don't have to be precisely parallel as long as the basic structure is the same. The trouble comes with the third clause, which is not independent but dependent (beginning with the subordinating word *because*):

because it is unconstitutional.

Probably the easiest way to revise the sentence is to make all three clauses independent by dropping the subordinating word *because:*

The plan is not workable, it delegates too much power to the states, and it is unconstitutional.

Or you could make the last two clauses both dependent, like this:

The plan is not workable because it delegates too much power to the states and because it is unconstitutional.

Now have a go at revising these sentences:

2. The final step involves making a ninety-degree kick-turn and to start the pattern over from the beginning.

3. European trains are frequent, punctual, having easy connections, and travel at high speeds.

4. In the movies college men are portrayed as single, driving a nice car, well-off financially, good looks, and wearing cool clothes.

5. Progressive education aims to teach children to be open-minded, thinking with logic, know how to make wise choices, having self-discipline, and self-control.

6. This proposal would alert society to the fact that rape is a prevalent crime and also only a few convictions are made each year.

| **R**evising *Exercise 5.10* |

Look at that last paper again. Do you find any sentences that are out of kilter—that need parallel structure? If so, whip them into shape.

Have you written an emphatic closing sentence? If not, write an impressive sentence using parallel structure.

Use Repetition Wisely

Deliberate repetition, such as you observed in many of those impressive parallel sentences, can be one of your most effective rhetorical devices. But needless repetition will probably irritate your readers because they can tell it stems from lack of thought and inadequate revision, as in this student's sentence:

> Walking up to the door, I came upon the skeleton head of a cow placed next to the door.

That's too many *to the door* phrases. Just changing the first one solves the problem:

> Walking up to the house, I came upon the skeleton head of a cow placed next to the door.

You need to eliminate any word or phrase that's been needlessly used twice:

> Clarence found the challenge of trying to make the honor roll a great challenge.

When you revise, just eliminate the first challenge:

> Clarence found trying to make the honor roll a great challenge.

Deliberate repetition can be powerful, as you saw in many of the examples of parallel sentences. Another way to achieve the same clarity and emphasis is to repeat a key term deliberately, as Katherine Anne Porter does in this sentence describing the execution of Sacco and Vanzetti (our italics):

> They were put to death in the electric chair at Charleston Prison at *midnight*, a desolate dark *midnight*, a *night* for perpetual mourning.

You see the difference between well-executed deliberate repetition and careless repeating of the same word. Porter's *midnight* tolls like a bell reinforcing the darkness of the deed.

TIP! A deliberately repeated word or phrase can reinforce a key idea.

S *traightening Out Screwed-Up Sentences*

Some sentence problems are impossible to categorize as other than messed up. And these are the worst kind because the sentences make no sense and are likely to drive readers to drink—or induce them to quit reading.

The Confusion of Mixed Constructions

The sorry sentences known, for want of a better term, as *mixed constructions* apparently result when a writer begins to say something one way, loses track in the middle, and finishes another way because the brain is faster than the fingers. That's our guess, anyway. The people who write them are more surprised than anyone when confronted with these prodigies.

These are the kinds of sentences that make readers do a double take. We shake our heads, rub our eyes, and read them again, hoping for a better connection next time. But we never get it from mix-ups like these:

> When students have no time for study or moral training also breeds a decadent society.

> The first planned crime will tell how well a boy has learned whether or not he is caught to become a juvenile delinquent.

Now those are pretty hopeless cases. They need to be scrapped. You'll lose more time trying to revise sentences like these than you will by backing off and starting a different way. Take that last example. It needs a totally new beginning, perhaps like this:

> Whether or not he is caught in his first planned crime may determine whether a boy will become a juvenile delinquent.

Occasionally a screwed-up sentence can be easily revised, like this one:

> When frequently opening and closing the oven door, it can cause a soufflé to fall.

All you need to do to correct that one is scratch out the *when*, the *it*, and the comma:

> Frequently opening and closing the oven door can cause a soufflé to fall.

Nobody will hold you accountable if you accidentally write a mixed-up sentence in a first draft, but it's your job to catch and correct the problem when you revise.

The Problem of Faulty Predication

We can describe what goes wrong in a sentence to produce faulty predication: the subject doesn't match the predicate—the part that follows the verb. Apparently the writer loses track of the subject when supplying the predicate, so that the sentence ends up not quite making sense, like this:

> The excuse for earning money offers Paul the job of ushering at Carnegie Hall.

Everybody knows that *excuses* don't *offer jobs,* so the statement has a lapse in logic.

Some faulty predication problems are easy to fix, like this one:

> Your first big city is an event that changes your whole outlook if you grew up in a small town.

Clearly, a *big city* is not an *event,* but we can set this one to rights just by adding a new subject:

> Your first trip to a big city is an event that changes your whole outlook if you grew up in a small town.

TIP! **Pay close attention to meaning as you revise to be sure every sentence makes perfect sense.**

R*evising Exercise 5.11*

Straighten out the following sentences, written by students. Some are mixed constructions; some suffer from faulty predication. If a sentence can't be easily revised, consider backing off and beginning a different way.

1. The Rites of Spring Festival has been postponed because of too many students are sick with the flu.
2. Illegal parking is towed away at the owner's expense.
3. In time of crisis must be handled with cool judgment.
4. The second qualification for my ideal roommate would have to be easygoing.
5. Whether a person makes the choice to go to college or not has both its problems and rewards.
6. Miss Brill tries to convince herself that she really is a significant contribution to society.
7. By no means is the novel to glorifying war.
8. No matter if she is loved or not, did not matter any more.
9. Mrs. Pontellier carried herself in a way that people thought she would only be the mother of strong, gallant sons.

10. The importance of remaining married is essential in Edna's society.

11. Containers breeding mosquitoes may be carriers of disease.

12. The school busing controversy was intended to correct inequalities in educational opportunities.

6

The Revising and Editing Process

A common myth about writing is that good writers get it right the first time. The truth is that good writers almost never say what they want to on the first try; they nearly always plan on revising. Teacher and writer Anne Lamott says that every piece of writing should go through at least three drafts. The first draft she calls "the down draft—you just get it down"; the second draft is "the up draft—you fix it up"; and the last draft is "the dental draft, where you check every tooth, to see if it's loose or cramped or decayed, or even, God help us, healthy."

We agree that these drafts are essential, but we call them the rough draft, the revision draft, and the editing draft. If you don't work through those last two, you won't achieve the best results, no matter how good you think your first draft is.

R evising Your First Draft

Revision involves more than just tidying up your prose. The process of correcting your spelling, punctuation, and mechanics is called *editing,* but your paper is not ready for that yet. First you need *re-vision*—seeing again—to discover ways of making your writing more effective.

TIP! Schedule your time so that you are able to put the rough draft aside at least overnight before attempting to revise it.

While a draft is still warm from the writing, you cannot look at it objectively. And looking at it objectively is the basis of productive revision. Your fondness for a well-turned sentence should not prevent you from cutting it when, in the cold light of morning, you realize that it doesn't relate to your thesis.

Revise from the Top Down

Not all revising is the same. One kind of revision involves large-scale changes, ones that significantly affect the content and structure of your paper. Such changes might include enlarging or narrowing your thesis, adding more examples or cutting irrelevant ones, and reorganizing points to improve logic or gain emphasis. A second kind of revision focuses on improving style: checking paragraph unity, strengthening transitions, combining and refining sentences, finding more effective words, adjusting tone. We recommend that you take a top-down approach to revising by starting with the large-scale issues and working down to the smaller elements.

Tackling the simple problems first may seem reasonable, but you will find that dealing with a major difficulty may eliminate some minor problems at the same time—or change the way you approach them. If you try to do the fine-tuning and polishing first, you may also burn up valuable time and energy and never get around to the main problems.

TIP! Distinguish between larger problems (like content and organization) and smaller ones (like sentence structure and word choice). Work on the large problems first.

Outline the Draft

To be sure that your discussion is unified and complete, you should briefly outline your rough draft. This kind of after-the-fact outlining is not a waste of time, as it allows you to detect flaws in your organization and to review the development of your main ideas at the same time. First, write down your thesis statement; then add the topic sentence of each paragraph along with your important supporting ideas. Don't bother with complete sentences; short phrases are easier to check and evaluate.

After completing this scratch outline, you should use it to check your paper for unity and completeness by considering these points:

1. Make sure that the topic sentence in every paragraph relates directly to your thesis.
2. Consider whether your support is adequate. Sometimes a paragraph can be developed with a single extensive example, but more often you will want at least three or four examples, details, or reasons. If you fail to find adequate support for a topic sentence, perhaps you need to rethink it, omit it, or combine it with another main idea.
3. Examine your supporting details to see if any are irrelevant or overlapping and need to be cut.
4. Look at the order of your paragraphs and the order of the supporting details in each paragraph. Your sentences and paragraphs should follow one after the other with no breaks and no confusion.
5. Make sure you have tied your sentences and paragraphs together with transitional hooks and signposts. For a handy list of transitional terms, see Chapter 4, Figure 4.1 (pp. 60–61).

Add Headings to Highlight Your Points

Writers are using headings in all kinds of publications these days to highlight main ideas and to indicate shifts in topics, making the text easier to follow. Headings have always been appropriate in technical writing and business reports. Textbook authors also use them to focus attention on key concepts, provide greater clarity, and make the material easy to review. You'll notice headings in newspaper and magazine articles. Whenever you present complex material that your readers might have difficulty following, consider inserting meaningful headings to signal your major points.

Word-processing programs make using headings a snap. With a single command, you can center them. Or you can set them flush left and boldface them. You can also indent material to set it off and thus call attention to it. If you glance at the formatting of this book, you'll see a number of options for breaking up blocks of type, adding emphasis, and thus achieving greater readability. You can perform every one of them with your word processor.

Remember, though, the essential factor in making a text easy to follow is having it clearly and logically organized. All the formatting in the world is not going to save a paper that is not unified or lacks continuity.

Revise for Style

Once you are satisfied that your ideas are developed fully and proceed smoothly and logically, you need to consider the shape of each sentence. Is any phrasing wordy or repetitious? Does the writing sound natural and interesting? Are the sentences forceful and varied? Rewrite those sentences that carry key ideas to make them elegant and emphatic. Work particularly hard on the opening and closing sentences—especially that last one. Don't let your otherwise fine essay trail off limply at the end because you ran out of steam.

Now is also the time to look up word meanings and use your thesaurus, if necessary, to find just the right words. Also make sure that the tone and language level are suitable for your purpose and audience. (See Chapter 2 for guidance about tone and language levels, Chapter 5 for specific direction about words and sentences, and Chapter 7 for a brief review of logic.)

Get Feedback: Peer Review

Writers routinely seek the help of potential readers to find out what is working and what is not working in their drafts. Even professional writers ask for suggestions from editors, reviewers, teachers, and friends. In college, your composition instructor may divide your class into small groups to review one another's papers and provide suggestions for improvement. In the workplace, much of the writing you do will be passed around, with various writers adding their sections and making suggestions about yours.

Someone else can often see places where you *thought* you were being clear but were actually filling in details in your head, not on the page. You can help people who are reviewing your paper by assuring them that you want honest critical responses. Here are some guidelines to follow when asking for help with your revision:

1. *Specify the kind of help you want.*
   If you already know that the spelling needs to be checked, then ask your readers to ignore those errors and focus on other elements in the draft. If you want suggestions about the thesis or the introduction or the tone or the organization or the examples or the style, then ask questions about those features.

2. *Ask productive questions.*
   Be sure to pose questions that require more than a yes or no answer. Ask readers to tell you in detail what *they* see. You can use the questions in the Revising Checklist (Figure 6.1, p. 101) to help you in soliciting feedback.
3. *Don't get defensive.*
   Listen carefully to what your reviewers have to say, and interrupt only when you don't understand their comments. Above all, don't argue with your readers. If something confused them, it confused them. You want to see the writing through *their* eyes, not browbeat them into seeing it the way you do.
4. *Make your own decisions.*
   Remember that this is your paper; you're responsible for accepting or rejecting the feedback that you get. If you don't agree with the suggestions that are offered, then don't follow them. But also keep in mind that your peer reviewers are likely to be more objective about your writing than you are.

R *evising on a Word Processor*

Revision is much easier if you are using a word processor. Probably the biggest advantage of word processing is that it helps you to see that writing is *changeable.* You can consider every word, sentence, or paragraph as just one possible choice among many. Because you can delete, move, and save the text in different files, the word processor invites you to explore alternatives. You can try a change and see how it reads; if the revision flops, you can easily restore the original draft.

Computer software can also help with sentence-level revisions. Many word-processing programs have spell checkers that identify questionable spellings and suggest possible correctly spelled alternatives. Of course, a spell checker does not understand your text and can't determine if its suggestions are appropriate or even plausible, but it can focus your attention on words that you may need to change. Other programs, called *text analyzers* or *style checkers,* will give you information about word choice, sentence length, and other features of style. These programs can only point out *possible* problems, such as a long sentence or a weak verb; you have to decide whether the verb is effective or the sentence really is too long.

Avoid Computer Pitfalls

There are some disadvantages to revising on a computer. Early versions of your essay are lost as you revise. In most cases, this loss is no problem, but if you make big changes, you need to stop and print out old drafts as you go. They may contain work that can be retrieved later and used elsewhere. We encourage you to print your rough draft even when you know it's due for a major rewrite.

In addition, certain problems are easier to see on a printed copy than on the computer screen. For example, you see more paragraphs at a time on the page. On the screen, you may not notice that you've used the same transitional phrase at the beginning of several paragraphs, or that the paragraph lengths are wildly unbalanced. And when you revise sentences on the screen, you are much more likely to neglect to delete the old version or perhaps a word or two of it, leaving you with a garbled sentence.

A final caution about revising on computers: instructors expect clean, neat, correct final copy when papers are done on word processors. Some allow for tidy corrections done in ink, but others insist on a new printout when you find an error. Your instructor may be righteously indignant over a misspelling that should have been flagged by the spell-checker, attributing the error to your laziness or haste.

S *etting a Revision Agenda*

Your revision will be easier and more efficient if you establish some priorities to guide your rethinking, rearranging, and rewriting. Not all revisions require the same amount of time and energy. You need to consider how much time you have and how effective your first draft is. If you have left enough time for your writing to evolve, you may not need a wholesale revision. On the other hand, a hurried first draft will need more thorough reworking.

The list of questions in Figure 6.1 will help you to set up your own revising agenda. This checklist focuses on general questions first and takes up smaller matters later.

1. Does the paper meet the assignment and make the point I set out to make?
2. Is the thesis clear and intelligent?
3. Is the main idea of each paragraph directly related to the thesis?
4. Are the paragraphs fully developed with examples and details?
5. Do the ideas flow coherently? Are the transitions easy to follow?
6. Are the sentences clear and effectively structured?
7. Does the introduction capture the reader's attention and make the main point of the paper clear?
8. Does the conclusion provide intelligent closure for the paper?

FIGURE 6.1 *Revising Checklist*

E *diting the Final Draft*

After you've finished your revisions, you must force yourself—or someone completely trustworthy—to read the paper yet one more time to pick up any careless mistakes or typos. Jessica Mitford rightly says that "failure to proofread is like preparing a magnificent dinner and forgetting to set the table." So, be polite—proofread and then correct any errors. This correcting is called the editing process.

Careless errors can be unintentionally funny, like these from the real-life job applications of people who apparently didn't edit their copy:

I am a rabid typist and have a proven ability to track down and correct erors.

I was instrumental in ruining the entire operation of a Midwest chain store.

Thank you for your consideration. I hope to hear from you shorty.

Do you suppose any of those applicants got the job?

Many careless errors are just plain witless and annoying—like repeating a word needlessly ("and and") or leaving off an -s and producing an illiteracy:

The protester were arrested and herded off to jail.

Such errors do nothing to encourage your readers to admire the brilliance of your ideas—no matter how keen they are. So watch the little things. Don't write "probable" for "probably," or "use to" for "used to" or "you're" for "your" or "then" for "than."

1. Make sure that each sentence really is a sentence, not a fragment—especially those beginning with *because, since, which, that, although, as, when,* or *what* and those beginning with words ending in *-ing*.
2. Make sure that independent clauses joined by *indeed, moreover, however, nevertheless, thus,* and *hence* have a semicolon before those words, not just a comma.
3. Make sure that every modifying phrase or clause is close to the word it modifies.
4. Check your manuscript form to be sure it's acceptable: Have you skipped three lines between the title and the first line of the essay? Did you double-space throughout? Did you leave at least one-inch margins on all sides, including top and bottom? Did you prepare a title sheet, if requested to do so? Did you clip the pages together?

FIGURE 6.2 *Editing Checklist*

Check possessives to be sure the apostrophes are there—or not there in the case of "its." Figure 6.2 gives you some other points to keep in mind as you edit your draft.

Proofreading Advice

Most of us have difficulty proofreading our own writing because we know what we wanted to say and thus don't notice that we haven't said it flawlessly. We become caught up in the content and fail to see the errors. If you have this trouble, try reading the sentences from the bottom of the page to the top, out of order, so that you can't become interested in what you're saying because it won't make sense. Try to read slowly, word by word. Figure 6.3 gives you a list of points to check for when you proofread.

Pay no attention to content. Read only for errors to make certain that you have

1. No words left out or carelessly repeated
2. No words misspelled—or carelessly spelled (*use to* for *used to*)
3. No plurals left off
4. No apostrophes omitted in possessives or in contractions
5. No periods, dashes, commas, colons, or quotation marks left out
6. No confusion of *to/too, their/they're/there, its/it's, then/than, your/you're*

FIGURE 6.3 *Proofreading Checklist*

A Word of Encouragement About Spelling

In the past people were considerably more relaxed about correct spelling than we are today. William Shakespeare, demonstrating his boundless creativity, spelled his own last name at least thirteen different ways. John Donne wrote "sun," "sonne," or "sunne," just as it struck his fancy. But along about the 18th century, Dr. Samuel Johnson decided orthography was out of hand. He took it upon himself to establish a standard for the less learned and brought out his famous dictionary. Of course, the language refused to hold still—even for the stern-minded Dr. Johnson—and his followers have been trying to make it do so ever since.

Today educated people are expected to be able to spell according to the accepted standard. Nobody encourages a lot of creativity in this area. So, if you didn't learn to spell back in grade school, you may need help.

Use Your Spell Checker, If You Have One. Help with spelling is easy to come by if you write on a word processor. You just need to run your handy spell checker after you finish revising and make the necessary corrections. But remember that your spell checker won't flag those troublesome words that are easy to confuse—*its/it's, to/too/two, then/than, there/they're/their, altogether/all together, choose/chose, effect/affect,* and all those other pesky soundalike words—because you're not misspelling them. You're just using the wrong one. So, you still need to proofread carefully in case you've accidentally typed the wrong word.

Keep a List and Study It. If you have serious trouble with spelling, you need to keep a list of the words you get wrong and learn how to spell them. Start now. Add to it whenever you discover you've misspelled a word. If you keep adding the same word—especially an easy, often-used word, like "writing" or "coming"—make a point of *remembering* that you can't spell it so you can look it up or choose a synonym that you *can* spell.

Find a Friend to Help. If you're fortunate enough to have a friend or relative who can spell, you are in luck. Beg or bribe this gifted individual to check your papers for misspelled words.

7

Thinking Critically and Logically

The most important element in the writing process is the critical thinking that produces what you write. Most of the knowledge and many of the insights you use in writing are acquired through reading. As you read, you'll be exposed to ideas, theories, and opinions as well as facts. Reading, discussing, and synthesizing all this new information constitutes a large part of becoming educated.

Cultivate a Questioning Attitude

The educational process bogs down if you don't keep an open mind. You shouldn't reject a new idea just because it conflicts with an opinion you presently treasure. Because you've heard and accepted a statement all your life doesn't make that statement true. As Mark Twain observed in his *Notebook*, "One of the proofs of immortality is that myriads have believed it. They also believed that the world was flat."

You should be willing to consider new ideas, examine them, think about them critically, and decide on the basis of the available evidence what is and is not valid. You'll be bombarded by facts and opinions from all sides. Much of what we read and observe is designed to sway our opinions or sell us something—or both. Just consider the barrage of messages we are subjected to daily from advertising alone—in magazines and newspapers, on television, at the movies, on billboards and matchbooks—even on clothing. Not to mention all the misinformation that flows from

Washington, DC. In order to avoid being manipulated or deceived, you must try to distinguish the truth from the tripe. Truth may be mighty, but it doesn't always prevail.

TIP! **Adopt a questioning mindset.**
Look for the unstated assumption that often underlies apparently objective statements.

Be Suspicious of Slogans

As you form the habit of questioning statements, the first ones to examine are the ones that come in the form of *epigrams* or *slogans*. These prepackaged ideas are neat and tidy, easy to remember, pleasant to the ear. We've been brought up on them and have Ben Franklin to thank for a sizable number, like "A stitch in time saves nine" and "Early to bed, early to rise, makes a man healthy, wealthy, and wise." Epigrams usually state a simple truth, but often they cleverly disguise opinion as fact. For instance, you've heard that "Home is where the heart is," but George Bernard Shaw rewrote that one as, "Home is the girl's prison and the woman's workhouse." Clearly, the truth of either statement is debatable and may lie somewhere in between.

A slogan is a catch phrase or motto designed to rally people to vote for a certain party, buy a certain product, or agree with a certain group. During the Spanish-American war a popular slogan was "My country, right or wrong!" Those same sentiments were voiced again during the Vietnam conflict as "America—love it or leave it!" Both are ringing, patriotic-sounding phrases, for sure, but not the least bit logical. Good citizens do not encourage their country in doing wrong. They want their country doing right. Slogans may sound inspiring, but don't mistake them for reasoned ideas. Your job as reader is to question such statements. Demand evidence and decide rationally, not emotionally, which opinions are valid, which are propaganda, and which are a mixture of both.

D *etecting Slanted Writing*

More difficult to detect than the bias of slogans is the subtle persuasion of *slanted writing*. Once you become aware of the emotional quality of many words, you'll not likely be taken in by slanted writing.

Be Cautious About Connotations

Words are symbols that can have both a *denotative* meaning (the actual meaning) and a *connotative* meaning (the emotional response to the word). The term *mother*, for instance, denotes a female who gives birth, but the word typically connotes warmth, love, comfort, and apple pie. Most words have connotations in varying degrees—some so strong as to be considered *loaded* or *slanted*. Whether you call the President a *statesman* or a *politician* may well reveal your political affiliation. Consider the connotations of these pairs of words with similar denotative meanings:

egghead	intellectual
pornographic	erotic
jock	athlete
penny-pinching	thrifty
mob	crowd
cur	doggie

Whether you choose from the negative words on the left or the favorable words on the right will reveal the writer's attitude to an alert reader.

Don't get the impression that connotative language is necessarily bad. It isn't. In fact, without the use of emotional words, writing would be fairly lifeless. But, you need to become alert to connotations.

The tone of righteous conviction achieved in the following passage is admirable. The argument is eloquent, emphatic, and persuasive. But it also is pure hogwash—blatant propaganda. See if you can pick out the emotionally charged words on which the appeal rests:

> If we stand idly by, if we seek merely swollen, slothful ease and ignoble peace, then bolder and stronger peoples will pass us by, and will win for themselves the domination of the world.

Note that the writer says not just "stand by" but "stand *idly* by." He fears we may seek "ease"—but not a good rest earned by hard work. No, it's a "*swollen, slothful* ease." Certainly the word "peace" alone would not serve his purpose: he makes it an "*ignoble* peace." Notice, too, that those who will "pass us by" are "*bolder* and *stronger* peoples," implying that only wimps would let them go unchallenged, for they are clearly standing in the way of our rightful, glorious conquest of the world.

That sentence, written by Theodore Roosevelt, deserves high marks as effective propaganda. But you as reader must be able to detect that the chinks in his logic are effectively plugged with rhetoric. It's this kind of misuse of the language that gives rhetoric a bad name.

You'll hear similar appeals every day, not just from politicians but from advertisers and special interest groups as well. Your best protection from slanted writing is your ability to think—to examine the language and the logic, to sort out the sound ideas from the sound effects.

Consider the Source

Anyone familiar with American history would know not to hope for an unbiased comment from Theodore Roosevelt concerning the causes of the Spanish-American War which he helped start. This doesn't mean, however, that you should ignore Roosevelt's statements if you're writing an appraisal of the reasons the United States began that war. Neither should you ignore the opinions of the opposing attorneys, William Jennings Bryan and Clarence Darrow, if you're analyzing the fairness of the Scopes trial concerning evolution in the 1920s. But you should be aware that the sources you're reading are not objective and let your readers know about these biases when you quote. Don't just report them at face value.

Some sources you would recognize as biased without even reading them. You would know to be suspicious of information on gun control published by the National Rifle Association, data about smoking from the Tobacco Institute, or views on racism from the Web page of the Ku Klux Klan. You would also know not to trust the *National Inquirer* if you're doing a paper on conspiracy theories surrounding the Kennedy assassination. But the bias in many other magazines is far more subtle. In a discussion of affirmative action you would want to balance the viewpoint of an article in *Ms.* magazine with that of a less liberal publication, like *U.S News and World Report*.

You could probably scare up most of the facts from reading one unbiased source, but the problem is discovering which one that is. The only way to make sure is to read widely. After you've read opinions on both sides of the issue, you should be able to recognize the center—if and when you find it.

Keep an Open Mind

Don't make the mistake of embracing what you consider a reliable source and then placing your trust in it till death do you part. Too many of us do just this: we plight our troth to the Bible, to *The Nation,* to *The Wall Street Journal,* or to *Newsweek* and assume we never have to think again. You will discover writers and publications whose viewpoint is similar to yours. These will naturally strike you as the most astute, cogent, perceptive, well-informed, reliable sources to consult. But be careful that you don't fall into the comfortable habit of reading these publications exclusively.

A *Quick Look at Logic*

Developing a logical mind is important for you, both as a reader and as a writer. Whenever you write—especially when you write to persuade—your aim is to convey your thoughts and ideas into the minds of your readers. To be convincing, these thoughts and ideas must be logical. You should know the important principles of logic so that you can apply them in your own thinking and writing—as well as in detecting slippery logic in the writing and arguments of others.

Cite Valid Authorities

You're probably going to cite authorities whenever you write on any controversial subject. But you need to be sure your authority is convincing to your audience. Some people think that once they've clinched a point with "The Bible says . . . ," they've precluded any rebuttal. If your reader happens to be one of the faithful, you'll be on solid ground. But not everyone would agree with the upright citizen who wrote a letter to the editor of our local paper offering this solution for helping the poor:

> The only remedy against poverty is to worship God as God, honor His word and obey His doctrines, call upon Him and humble ourselves. Then He will hear and heal the land.

Your more practical-minded readers are not likely to accept an argument requiring divine intervention to solve social problems. Cite authorities, by all means, but try for impartial authorities—noted scholars and researchers, who have published on your subject and are accepted as experts by most educated people.

TIP! Be especially questioning about sources from the Internet.

You'll find more extensive warnings about using electronic sources in Chapter 8.

Avoid Oversimplifying

Most of us have a tendency to like things reduced to orderly, easily grasped, *either/or* answers. The only problem is that things seldom are that simple. Be wary of arguments that offer no middle way—the "either we do away with affirmative action or else white males are going to go jobless" sort of reasoning.

Avoid Stereotyping

Stereotypes involve set notions about the way different types of people behave. Homosexuals, according to the stereotype, are neurotic, promiscuous, immoral people bent on sex and the seduction of innocents. Such stereotypes rarely give a truthful picture of anyone in the group and could never accurately describe all members.

Avoid Sweeping or Hasty Generalizations

You will do well to question easy solutions to complex problems. A faulty generalization (a general statement that is far too broad) can result from stating opinion as fact:

> Heavy metal music causes serious social problems by creating an attitude of irresponsibility in the listeners.

That statement needs evidence to prove its claim, and such proof would be nearly impossible to come by.

Since you can't avoid making generalizations, just be careful to avoid making them without sufficient evidence. At least, qualify your statements:

| (faulty) | All Siamese cats are noisy and nervous. |
| (better) | Many Siamese cats are noisy and nervous. |

Statements involving *all, none, everything, nobody,* and *always* are tough to prove. Instead try *some, many, sometimes,* or *often.*

Watch for Hidden Premises

Another sort of generalization that may prove deceptive involves a *hidden premise* (the basic idea underlying the main statement). The following observation, to those who accept information without questioning, may sound plausible:

> If those animal rights demonstrators had left when the police told them to, there would have been no trouble and no one would have been injured.

The hidden premise here assumes that all laws are just and fairly administered; that all actions of the government are honorable and in the best interest of all citizens. The statement presumes, in short, that the demonstrators had no right or reason to be there and hence were wrong not to leave when told to do so. Such a presumption overlooks the possibility that in a free country the demonstrators might legitimately protest the right of the police to make them move.

Use Analogy with Care

An *analogy* involves taking two similar situations and claiming that what holds true for one holds true for the other. For instance, psychologist Naomi Weisstein, in her article "Woman as Nigger," contends that women are conditioned with a slave mentality and exploited for the economic benefit of society just as African Americans were for centuries. As this example suggests, analogies can add interest and clarity to a persuasive paper, and they often illustrate points effectively. But conclusions derived from an analogy are not logical proof. Make certain your analogy is indeed convincing before giving it too much weight in your essay.

A *false analogy* occurs when the two situations are not comparable. For example, you often hear people say something like this:

> If we can put people on the moon, we should be able to find a cure for AIDS.

Although both of these situations involve solving a problem with scientific knowledge, the difficulties facing medical researchers are quite different from those solved by space engineers.

Do Not Dodge the Issue

People employ a number of sneaky logical fallacies in order to sidestep a problem while appearing to pursue the point.

1. *Appealing to Emotion*

   Perhaps the most common—and the most underhanded—involves playing on the emotional reactions, prejudices, fears, and ignorance of the audience instead of directly addressing the issue, like this:

   > If we allow condom distribution in the public schools, the moral fiber of the nation will be endangered.

   That sentence, which contains no evidence to prove that condom distribution is either good or bad, merely attempts to make it sound scary.

2. *Attacking the Person* (the *ad hominem* fallacy)

   Illogical thinkers and unprincipled people frequently attack the person they are arguing against, rather than addressing the issue being argued. They call their opponents "effete, effeminate snobs" and hope nobody notices that they haven't actually said anything convincing.

3. *Employing Circular Reasoning*

   People who use this dodge offer as evidence arguments that assume as true the very thing they are trying to prove, as a devout person might do by quoting the Bible to prove the divinity of Christ. Here's an example of circular reasoning:

   > If we want a society of people who devote their time to base and sensuous things, then pornography may be harmless. But if we want a society in which the noble side of humans is encouraged and mankind itself is elevated, then I submit that pornography is surely harmful.

   That writer says, in effect, that pornography is evil because pornography is evil. The statement might be true, but that doesn't make it logical or persuasive.

4. *Jumping to Conclusions*

   A common problem in reasoning is called the *post hoc* fallacy (from the Latin *post hoc, ergo propter hoc,* meaning "after this, therefore because of this"). This fallacy assumes—without any concrete evidence—that because one event follows another, the first is the cause of the second. Because we humans often employ cause-and-effect reasoning in attempting to make sense of our lives, *post hoc* reasoning is common.

   For example, suppose you've just read that the early symptoms of mercury poisoning are restlessness, instability, and irritability. Since ecologists have warned that our waters are polluted with mercury in dangerous amounts, and since everyone you know is restless, unstable, and irritable these days, you conclude that the population is succumbing to mercury poisoning. And we may well be, for that matter, but if you expect to convince anyone who wasn't already eager to make the same leap in logic, you'll need to gather more evidence—such as medical reports showing that human beings (as well as fish and cattle) are actually ingesting dangerous amounts of the poison.

T hink for Yourself

All of these techniques are frighteningly successful with untrained, unanalytical minds. Your best defense is critical thinking. Think while you're reading or listening, and think some more before you write. Be prepared to change your mind. Instead of hunting for facts to shore up your present opinions, let the facts you gather lead you to a conclusion.

And do not insist on a nice, tidy, clear-cut conclusion. Sometimes there isn't one. Your conclusion may well be that both sides for various reasons have a point. Simply work to discover what you honestly believe to be the truth of the matter, and set that down—as clearly and convincingly as you can.

D iscussion Exercise 7.1

Find, photocopy, and bring to class four copies of an example of the use of faulty logic. Good places to look include: TV or radio commercials (write a brief description and make copies), magazine ads, political speeches, letters to the editor, editorials, or opinion-page columnists. In a group with two or three fellow students, distribute and discuss everyone's examples. Identify the fallacies, and explain what makes the underlying thinking illogical.

R evising Exercise 7.2

Dig out the last paper you wrote that involved argument or persuasion. Jot down your main points and decide whether your logic was good or flawed. If you find flaws, figure out what went wrong and how to fix the problem.

$\boxed{\textbf{W}\textit{riting Exercise 7.3}}$

Think of a stereotype that you once believed in—for instance, the absent-minded professor, the dumb jock, the flighty blonde, the overbearing mother-in-law, the short-tempered redhead, the boring accountant, the greedy boss, the snobbish intellectual. Why did you believe this stereotype? How did you learn the stereotype was wrong? Write a paper in which you answer these questions.

II

How to Write a Research Paper

8

Conducting
Your Research

At some time you may be asked to write a paper that doesn't draw entirely on your own knowledge and experience. In fact, many kinds of writing involve the use of source materials. You may be required to do research: that is, to read fairly widely on a certain subject, to combine and organize this accumulated information, and then to present it in clear and coherent prose.

Traditionally, research papers involve *argument*. You may be expected to choose a topic which is somewhat controversial, investigate the issues on both sides, and take a stand. But you can, of course, engage in valuable and interesting research that simply involves finding and synthesizing information on any subject to increase your and your readers' knowledge.

In many ways, the writing process for a research paper is the same as for any other. You still need to narrow the subject to a topic that you can handle in the number of assigned pages, and you still have to come up with a thesis statement and outline or plan before you begin writing. But first you have to locate the material you're going to read; then you'll have to take notes as you read so that you can give credit to your sources as you write the paper.

S cheduling Your Research Paper

Writing a research paper is a time-consuming job. This is one paper that you simply cannot put off until the last minute. As usual, the writing will be better if you do it in stages. Dividing the project into units will allow you to keep the work under control.

Setting Deadlines for Yourself

If your completed paper is due in, say, six weeks, you could put yourself on a schedule something like this:

1st week:	Locate your possible sources, and record all the necessary bibliographical information about them.
	Try to narrow the topic to a workable thesis question to investigate.
2nd week:	Read and take notes.
	Settle on a preliminary thesis question.
	Try to come up with a preliminary outline.
3rd week:	Continue reading and taking notes.
4th week:	Complete your reading and note-taking.
	Turn your thesis question into a statement.
	Arrange your notes and organize your ideas.
	Develop a complete, detailed outline.
5th week:	Write the first draft and let it cool.
	Begin revising and editing.
	Get someone reliable to read your second draft and tell you whether the paragraphs are coherent, the sentences are clear, and the quotations are effectively integrated.
6th week:	Polish the second draft or write a third one.
	Type the final draft and let it rest at least overnight.
	Proofread and edit the final draft carefully.

This is a fairly leisurely schedule. You can, of course, do the work in a shorter time if required to. You will have to be more industrious about finding sources and taking notes. Some instructors deliberately ask students to complete the project within a month in order to prevent procrastination. Whatever your time limit, devise a schedule for yourself and stick to it.

Finding a General Topic

If allowed to select your own topic, you can begin by looking for information about any subject that interests you. Start by identifying a general subject that appeals to you, one that you can refine and narrow as you work through the process. This is an opportunity to learn about some aspect of your academic major, to investigate a career, to explore a personal interest or hobby, or to pursue some interesting topic that has come up in conversation or in a course you're taking.

One way to locate a fresh subject is to skim though the table of contents of a magazine that interests you. If you have access to the Internet, you can use its many resources to look for a topic. You might join a chat group or look through some online periodicals. Using a browser, you can check out listings and Web sites in a range of subject areas: arts and humanities, business and the economy, computers, education, entertainment, government, health, news and media, recreation and sports, science, society and culture. A quick look under entertainment, for instance, reveals a long list of topics—everything from "amusement and theme parks" to "comics and animation," "performing arts," and "television." If you want to write about television, you can look under that heading to lead you to more specific ideas, such as amateur television, ratings, TV violence, and the V-chip.

Narrowing Your Topic

If you have an area of interest but no ideas about any way to limit that topic, your first step might be to consult a good encyclopedia. Perhaps you have just taken up tennis, and you would like to know more about the sport. An encyclopedia article on tennis will give you information about the origin and history of the game, the court and the equipment, strategy and techniques, outstanding players, professional tournaments, and the state of the sport today. As you read, you will run across the comment that improved equipment and increased physical training have changed the nature of the game in the last twenty years. Precisely how has the game changed? In what ways has the equipment been improved and how have the improvements affected play? Have these changes been positive or negative? All it takes is a sentence, a subtopic, or an example in a general encyclopedia article on your subject to provide you with a focus for your research.

Topics for Researched Writing

If your mind remains a blank and your instructor will allow you to take one of our suggestions, here are some ideas that we think might be interesting to research.

For Informative Writing

1. Research the history of a familiar product or object, such as Coca-Cola, Mickey Mouse, the dictionary, disposable diapers, the nectarine, the title *Ms.*, frozen yogurt, the typewriter.
2. Research and analyze a fad, craze, custom, or holiday: fraternity hazing, body piercing, tattoos, quick weight-loss diets, Beanie Babies, St. Patrick's Day, Mother's Day, Kwanzaa, Cinco de Mayo, Victoria Day, Hanukkah, Juneteenth.
3. Research how a troubled group of people can be helped: autistic children, alcoholics, rape victims, anorexics, agoraphobics, battered women, people with HIV, nicotine addicts, steroid users.
4. Research the history of some feature of your hometown: a landmark, street names, architecture, an industry.
5. Research some hobby or job in order to inform someone unfamiliar with the activity.

For Persuasion or Argumentation

After doing the appropriate research, defend either side of one of the following issues:

1. The use of animals in research should (should not) be allowed.
2. It should (should not) be harder than it is now for married people to get a divorce.
3. Today's toys often contribute (do not contribute) to violent behavior in children.
4. Having a working mother does (does not) harm a child's welfare and development.
5. The fashion industry does (does not) exploit consumers. Or substitute another area of business: the cosmetics industry, the funeral business, car manufacturers, the oil industry.
6. Genetic screening of fetuses should (should not) be prohibited.
7. Sexual harassment is (is not) a serious problem in the workplace.
8. The government should (should not) cut welfare benefits for single parents.
9. News reporters should (should not) be required to reveal their sources in criminal cases.
10. English should (should not) be the only official language of the United States.
11. Affirmative action should (should not) be discontinued.
12. Homosexuals should (should not) be allowed to marry.

13. It is (is not) better for children if their incompatible parents get a divorce.
14. Teaching phonics would (would not) solve the literacy crisis in this country.
15. Laws restricting the use of pesticides should (should not) be repealed.
16. Free speech should (should not) be restricted on the Internet.

O *rganizing Your Search*

Once you have narrowed your topic, you need a plan for efficiently tracking down your source materials. Think about how much time you have and what kinds of sources you will probably be using. A good strategy is to begin with sources that give a broad overview of the subject and then move to ones that provide more detailed information. If you were to write about changes in tennis equipment, you might first look at a specialized reference work on the sport—something like *Bud Collins' Modern Encyclopedia of Tennis*, a book listed at the end of that encyclopedia article on tennis. Then you might search for articles of general interest and end with more technical articles in trade publications.

In order to locate all the relevant information in the library, you may need to think of headings under which your subject might be indexed. The encyclopedia and general reference works will supply you with some clues. The *Library of Congress Subject Headings (LCSH)* can be very useful in providing terms or key words to search with as well as additional terms that you might not have considered. Most of the entries in the *LCSH* give alternative terms listed as BT (broader topic), RT (related topic), and NT (narrower topic). For example, when we looked up "tennis," we found "racket games" and "ball games" as broader topics and "rackets (game)" and "rackets (sporting goods)" as narrower topics. You can use these alternative terms as you search for sources about the effects of improved equipment in tennis.

S *ome Suggestions for Using the Library*

One of the first things you need to do is get acquainted with your library. Most college libraries offer orientation courses to show students how to find materials. If the course in not required, take it anyway. An orientation course is the surest way of learning your way around the library. Libraries also have tours and guidebooks telling you where to find various materials. Taking one of these tours or studying the guidebook may save you many hours of aimless wandering.

TIP! **If you fail to find what you need, ask for help.**
Librarians are usually willing to answer questions and will often lead you to the material you want and give you valuable advice.

Searching for Sources

In the old days, the first things you were likely to see upon entering a library were imposing rows of polished wood cabinets with small drawers: the card catalog. In most libraries those cabinets have been replaced with row upon row of computers. It is almost certain that you will conduct your search for sources on a computer. Computer searches, online databases, and Internet search engines vary in the way you can use them; they are being expanded and improved all the time. Here are some general instructions to help you find your way around the modern library.

The Online Catalog

The computer version of the card catalog is called a public access catalog (PAC) or an online catalog (OC). The PAC or OC terminal itself will tell you how to use it. The opening screen on the OC at the library we use shows that we can search by subject, title, and author, as well as by call number, shelf position, and international standard book number (ISBN). We can search for books, titles of journals, and other items owned by our library or by other libraries in the state.

Using the online catalog, we are directed to enter the keywords of our topic on the subject line and press "enter." We're also reminded at this time that "You will achieve better results if you use a valid Library of Congress subject heading." Entering the topic "tennis" gets us a list of related subject headings with the number of titles for each heading indicated in parentheses; the general topic of "tennis" has 111 titles. We can view the detailed citations for these titles if we want to, or we can look down the list of more specific headings, such as "tennis coaching," "tennis courts," "tennis history," "tennis injuries," and so forth. We see there is only one title in our library for "tennis equipment and supplies"; when we call up the citation, we find details about a 1987 book entitled *Tennis Science for Tennis Players*. Although this source doesn't sound too promising, we jot down the call number and shelf location—and decide to search for articles in magazines and other periodicals.

Article Indexes and Databases

Most libraries now subscribe to one or more computerized bibliographic utilities such as *FirstSearch* (which indexes articles from academic journals, corporations, congressional publications, and medical journals) or EBSCO (which provides access to separate databases in the humanities, business, health, and the social and natural sciences) or Lexis-Nexis (an online commercial service that allows full-text access to a wide range of business, legal, medical, and political sources, including the *New York Times* from 1980 to the present). If your library subscribes to one or more of these services, you will find them on the OC terminal. You may also be able to access many of these databases from your computer at home or in your dorm room, if it has the necessary software and a modem (a device that connects your computer through the phone lines to other computer networks, like the ones in your school library).

The terminals in our library allow us to move from the online catalog to search more than eighty article indexes and specialized databases. These include general resources like CARL Uncover or WilsonSelectPlus, both of which provide citations, abstracts, and complete articles for most subject areas. But there are a number of indexes that allow us to search specific fields, such as African American Newspapers, AIDS/Cancer, Business Abstracts, Contemporary Women's Issues, Public Agenda Online, Health Reference Center Academic, PsycInfo, and Social Sciences Abstracts.

In our search for information about tennis rackets, we first choose SPORTDiscus, an index of articles and books on recreation, leisure studies, and sports. After typing in the search term "tennis equipment," we discover there are 597 references; so we narrow our search to "rackets," which yields 83 citations, most of them for periodical articles. Each citation includes the article title, the name of the magazine, the volume, date, and page number; it also supplies the call number of the magazine if our library owns it. We mark the items that appear relevant and print out this list of possible sources.

Because SPORTDiscus isn't a full-text database, we switch to *InfoTrac Expanded Academic Index ASAP,* which includes abstracts and many complete articles from scholarly and general interest publications. In our initial search of this database, we use the LCSH term "rackets (sporting goods)" and find 135 possible articles. Our search results also list a number of subdivisions that we can look

---

Booth Library, Eastern Illinois University

Expanded Academic ASAP

Time, August 24, 1998 v152 n8 p85(1)

   Tennis technology. (racquet designs)(Brief Article) *Joshua Quittner.*

Full Text: COPYRIGHT 1998 Time Inc. All rights reserved.

The physics of racquet design is changing the game. Are wider, longer and lighter better?

A few years ago, after my wife and I bought tennis racquets with heads the size of garbage-can lids, we became (arguably) the world's best Bad Doubles players. The oversize racquet head was only one of many weapons in our quiver. We are also the kind of Bad Doubles players who are not above yelling "Missssssss-it!" when someone on the far side of the net is serving. Plus we tend to do a little "chicken" victory dance after winning any point, to a loudly hummed rendition of Do the Hustle. Still, I'd have to say it was tech- nology--the oversize head--that catapulted us to the ranks of truly brilliant Bad Doubles players.

So it was more than simple competitive spirit that caused me to ridicule the new tennis racquets our friends wielded when they took to the court against us. "Hammer system?" I snickered, inspecting Goldberg's Wilson racquet as if it were poultry. "What is this '6.2' nonsense?" I said, mistaking the rac- quet's flexibility rating for a version number. "Do you get free software updates?" Needless to say, the Goldbergs proceeded to beat us like cheap rugs. New technology--combined with an unseemly willingness on their part to run for the ball--left us in the dust. Team Quittner needed an upgrade.

Ah, but so many racquets to choose from! Wilson sells not only Hammers but also SledgeHammers. And what of the Head and the Prince? In the years since we bought our racquets, tennis gear has evolved as human beings will over the millennium: heads are larger, necks longer and body weight is lighter. Mean- while high- tech jargon is used to justify racquet prices, which have zoomed to the $175-$300 range. I sought guidance from Howard Brody, a professor at the University of Pennsylvania and an expert in tennis physics.

Brody collects some laughable racquets, including one made from a tube filled with flowing fluid. Yet he endorses much of today's tennis tech. A larger rac- quet surface, he says, does help propel even off-center shots. And a thicker "beam" or frame produces more power and stability. "The extra length in the handle will give you something too," he notes, especially on the serve. (The higher up your serve starts, the better angle it has into the service box.) He's more dubious about the new ultralight titanium racquets. Although a lighter racquet is easier to maneuver, many players lose control when the thing collides with a heavy topspin shot.

Stiffer racquets offer more control, Brody notes, but flexible racquets are more comfortable. The professor pooh-poohs the digital precision of rating systems, at least for Bad Doubles players: "You cannot tell the difference between a 6.0 and a 6.2," he says. But even players like me should consider string tension: "The tighter the strings, the less power you get," he explains. Racquets strung less tightly launch the ball like a trampoline but with some loss of control.

FIGURE 8.1 *Sample Page from an Online Article*

under, so we choose "design and construction" (13 articles), "evaluation" (45 articles), and "innovations" (25 articles). We browse through these citations and find several to print out. Figure 8.1 shows the first page from one of these articles. We can also send the data from our searches to our home computers by way of e-mail.

Electronic Publications

These are just the first few steps in our search for possible sources. Our library computers also allow us to access books, journals, and reference works online. The electronic reference materials are extensive. They include directories, dictionaries, thesauruses, encyclopedias, and almanacs, as well as materials and resources on careers, grammar and writing, the arts, business, education and psychology, health and medicine, news and current events, political and social science, and science and technology. Some of these sources can be accessed directly on screen; many others are available through links to the World Wide Web (see page 127).

As you can see, the library's computers provide an overwhelming number of sources and service options. With so many possibilities, you can see why it's important, if not crucial, to take that orientation course we were talking about earlier. You will also have to spend some time with these data systems to find out how they work and how useful they are for your work. But it's time well spent. Once you get the hang of it, you will be able to research your topic or any other with astonishing ease and thoroughness.

TIP! **Remember that most libraries still hold almost all of this material in old-fashioned print.**
The *Readers' Guide to Periodical Literature,* for instance, still comes out in book form. If the computer terminals are crowded or not working—or if you simply want some peace and quiet while researching—your librarian can tell you where the references you seek are shelved.

U *sing the Internet*

The Internet links computers around the world; it's a vast storehouse of information that can be accessed in a number of ways. It's relatively easy to get on the Internet. All you need is a computer, a modem, and a browser (software that helps you find places on the Internet). If you don't have a computer at home, your college library probably has a bank of computers that are hooked up to the Net (as it's often called).

On the Net you can find government documents and archives, newsgroups, online publications, texts of published materials, and databases provided by commercial servers such as America Online, Prodigy, and Campus Networks. You can browse the noncommercial contents of the Internet through the World Wide Web.

It would take up too much space to give you detailed instructions for using the Internet, but we can briefly describe three of the basic tools that are available there: electronic mail, newsgroups, and the World Wide Web. If you are interested in finding out more, consult a book like *Casting Your Net: A Student's Guide to Research on the Internet*, 2nd ed. (Allyn & Bacon, 2001) by H. Eric Branscomb or *A Student's Guide to the Internet*, 2nd ed. (Prentice Hall, 1998) by Carol Clark Powell.

Electronic Mail

You're probably familiar with electronic mail (e-mail) as a way of communicating with friends and family. But e-mail can be a valuable research tool as well. Many people participate in special-interest discussion groups via e-mail; these groups are called *mailing lists,* and they use a *listserver* to automatically send mail to all the people on the list. Once you join a mailing list, the listserver will send you all messages on standard e-mail.

The easiest way to find a listserv is to check one of the directories on the World Wide Web (see page 127). One of the most popular is *Liszt,* which claims to list over 70,000 e-mail discussion groups. It's available at ⟨http://www.liszt.com⟩ and gives you simple instructions for searching and for subscribing to any list you might find useful.

TIP! Evaluate the reliability of an e-mail source in the same way you would judge any person you have interviewed. When referring to this source in your paper, provide background on the source and indicate why he or she is qualified to give information on your topic.

Newsgroups

A newsgroup is a kind of public bulletin board containing comments, questions, and responses on a particular topic. It's more extensive and more organized than an e-mail listserv. Asking a question of a mailing list or a newsgroup is a great way to get information about sources and to find people who can help you with your research. The newsgroup message board keeps track of several discussions at once and organizes the messages and replies in groups called *threads*. A thread begins with the original message, or *posting*, and includes all of the replies made by every participant in the discussion.

A program called a *newsreader* is used to read newsgroups and follow the threads. If your school subscribes to a news feed (a central computer that stores all messages and feeds them to other providers), you will have access to a newsreader and will be able to locate a newsgroup to follow. Another way to access newsgroups is through an Internet browser, although you may need to configure it to allow you to read the newsgroup. Once your system is appropriately configured, you might choose Netscape News, for example, from the browser menu to get a listing of the newsgroups to which your college subscribes.

TIP! Use material gathered from a newsgroup with caution. Try to confirm from other sources the reliability of any information from a newsgroup that you want to use in a research paper.

World Wide Web

The most popular tool for searching the Internet is the World Wide Web (also called the Web and WWW). The WWW is not the same thing as the Internet; the Web is a complex system for organizing and viewing information on the Internet. The primary attraction of this system is that its documents, called *Web pages*, are linked to other pages by a technique called *hypertext*. Hypertext links are usually underlined and in blue. By pointing and clicking at these links on a Web page, you can find paths to additional material, such as cross-references and explanations, on other pages and at other Web sites on the WWW. (A *Web site* is a collection of related Web pages.) To navigate the Web, you need a *browser* pro-

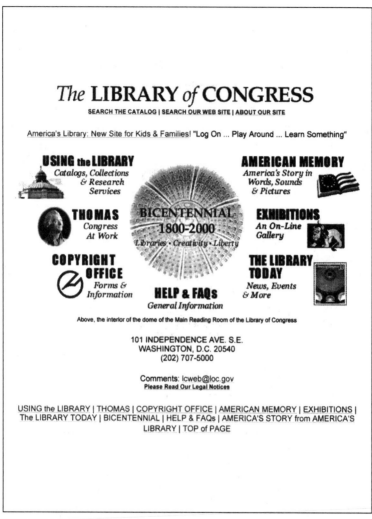

FIGURE 8.2   *Sample Web Page*

gram such as Netscape, Mosaic, or Microsoft Internet Explorer. Figure 8.2 shows the *home page* (the first page that appears when you access a Web site) for the Library of Congress, viewed through Microsoft Internet Explorer.

The WWW is also searchable. You can use one of several different *search engines*—such as Netscape, Lynx, or Microsoft Explorer— to search for key terms that you indicate. The search engine returns a list of sites that include the key terms. A subject-directory engine, such as Yahoo!, lets you look for specific information about a general topic (such as *finance*); a text-index engine, like AltaVista, Excite, Infoseek, HotBot, or Lycos, lets you look for specific words (such as *California deserts*) and gives links to documents containing these words. Figure 8.3 shows the first page of results from a search that was conducted on MSN Explorer using the key word "Kwanzaa."

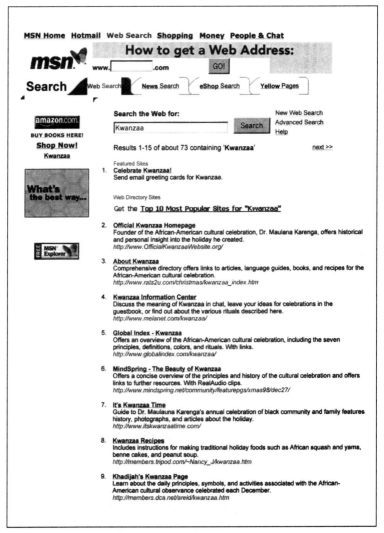

FIGURE 8.3 *Results from a Key Word Search*

When searching the Web, it's important to come up with a list of specific keywords as soon as possible. A single word like *cancer* will produce thousands of documents; using a phrase like *pancreatic cancer in teenagers* will limit the results. You can also narrow your search by using AND (for example, *Shakespeare AND sonnet*), which causes the engine to find only sites that include all the keywords you specify. (Some engines require a plus sign rather than AND.) When the search engine shows a list of "top" sites, survey the list to identify the most promising and click on these. When you find a useful site, print or download its pages for later examination. If you aren't satisfied with the first search results, try new search terms or a different search engine on your browser.

Some Advice About Using the Web

The Internet and the Web give you access to a great deal of information that is often more current than anything available in printed sources, and the Web's hyptertext feature allows you to explore a topic quickly and thoroughly. Nonetheless, there are a couple of serious pitfalls in using the Web that you need to consider:

1. It's difficult to know how to judge the vast array of material that's available. Some Web sites are filled with useful facts and helpful advice, but others are full of propaganda, unsupported opinion, inaccurate information, and tasteless junk. Anyone can publish on the Web; there is no editorial board to screen the material. So, you must apply sound judgment in evaluating each of your electronic sources, just as you would the print sources that you find in the library. Check the information against other sources, and consider carefully the credentials, and the biases, of the person or organization supplying the data. These sites give guidance on evaluating Internet sources:

    > Grassian, Esther. "Thinking Critically about World Wide Web Resources."
    > ⟨http://www.library.ucla.edu/libraries/college/help/critical/index.htm⟩
    > Kirk, Elizabeth E. "Evaluating Information Found on the Internet."
    > ⟨http://muse.mse.jhu.edu:8001/research/education/net.html⟩

2. Searching on the Internet, especially on the WWW, can eat up a lot of valuable time. Because it's so easy to move from site to site through numerous interlinked sources, you can spend hours browsing the Web. Your time might be better spent reading your source materials, taking notes, and writing your paper. To

avoid wasting your time, always go to the Web for specific purposes, skim the sites first, and note the size and downloading time of a document before printing it out. (The slow downloading time on some equipment can consume a lot of time.)

TIP! **Always record or store the address and references from an Internet source.**
You'll need them later.

S *weating Through the Research*

Once you've located the sources—the books and articles that you'll need to read and assimilate—you can begin reading, taking notes, and synthesizing the material.

Get It All Down

Every time you consult a new source, copy all the information necessary for indicating your source to the reader. If you fail to record all the pertinent data, you may find yourself tracking down a book or article weeks later in order to look up an essential publication date or volume number that you neglected to record initially. The book may by this time be checked out, lost, or stolen, so get it all down the first time.

We recommend that you use 3″ × 5″ note cards to keep track of this information. They are easy to carry with you to the library, and you can easily insert new entries in alphabetical order. Figures 8.4 through 8.7 give examples of what these cards should look like. If you work on a computer, you can create a separate file for your

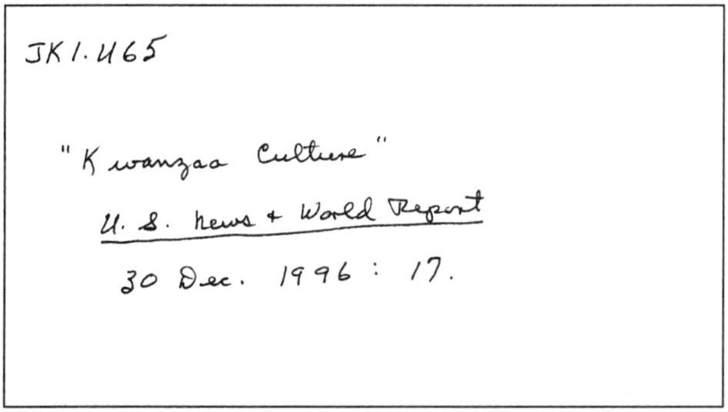

> JK 1. U 65
>
> " K wanzaa Culture "
>
> U. S. news + World Report
>
> 30 Dec. 1996 : 17.

FIGURE 8.4 *Article from a Magazine Without a Volume Number*

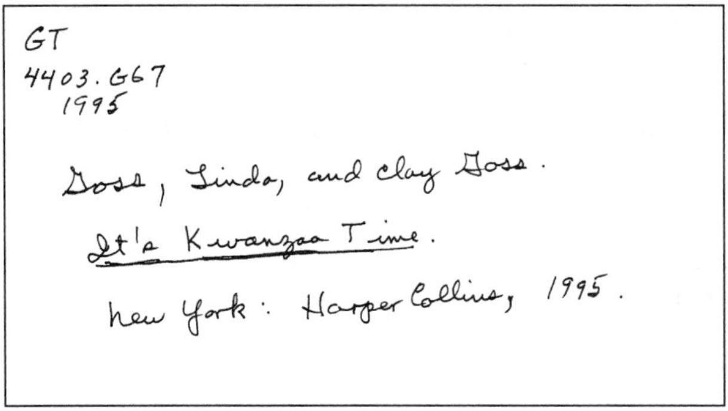

GT
4403.G67
 1995

Goss, Linda, and Clay Goss.
 It's Kwanzaa Time.
 New York: Harper Collins, 1995.

FIGURE 8.5 *Book*

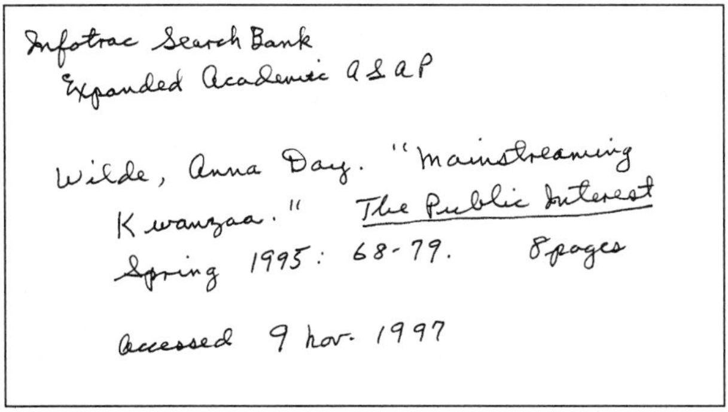

Infotrac Search Bank
 Expanded Academic ASAP

Wilde, Anna Day. "Mainstreaming
 Kwanzaa." The Public Interest
 Spring 1995: 68-79. 8 pages

Accessed 9 Nov. 1997

FIGURE 8.6 *Full-Text Article Available Through a Library Database*

list of sources and use a printout when you are not near your computer. Remember to keep the file up to date, and don't delete a citation until you're sure you will not be using that source.

TIP! Always remember to get *all* the pertinent data about your sources!

For whatever documentation system you are using, you will need to record the following information.

FOR BOOKS:
1. Title and author (or editor)
2. Publisher and place of publication
3. Date of publication (plus, date of edtion, if the book has more than one)
4. Library call number

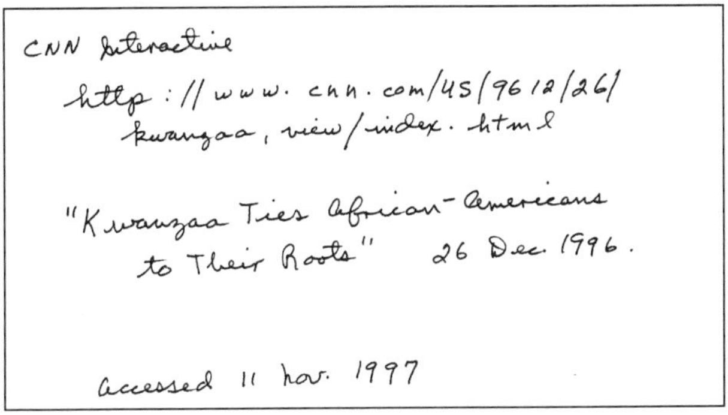

CNN Interactive

http://www.cnn.com/US/9612/26/kwanzaa,view/index.html

"Kwanzaa Ties African-Americans to Their Roots" 26 Dec. 1996.

Accessed 11 Nov. 1997

FIGURE 8.7 *Web Site Source*

FOR ARTICLES:
1. Author (or "no author")
2. Title
3. Name of magazine, newspaper, or journal
4. Volume number (if the journal uses them)
5. Date of the issue
6. Complete pages the article covers

FOR THE ELECTRONIC FORM OF EITHER BOOKS OR ARTICLES, YOU WILL ALSO NEED:
7. Title of database (if relevant)
8. Medium (like CD-ROM)
9. Name of the vendor or utility (like *FirstSearch* or *InfoTrac Expanded Academic ASAP*—if relevant)
10. Electronic publication date

On to the Reading

Using the list of sources you have developed so far, your next step is to locate all the materials that look promising and try to decide which ones will be genuinely useful. As you consider which articles and books to study thoroughly and which ones to eliminate at this stage, you need to give some thought to their reliability as well as their relevance to your thesis question.

TIP! **Just because a statement appears in print, it is not necessarily honest or accurate.**
You need to be wary as you read.

Evaluate Your Sources

You might expect an unbiased analysis of an event from journalists who were there, but again you must stay alert because not all publications present—or even try to present—objective reporting. The conservative *National Review* will give a substantially different assessment of an event than the ultraliberal *Mother Jones*. And the *Congressional Record*, which sounds like an impeccable source, is actually one of the least reliable, since any member of Congress can read any foolishness whatsoever into the *Record*. You must consult several sources and sample a variety of authorities to weigh the issues and discount the prejudices.

The date of publication often makes a difference in its value or reliability. If you are doing a paper about the treatment of AIDS, an article from 1980 will be of little use. If, on the other hand, you are writing a paper on the *history* of treating AIDS, then a 1980 article could be quite important. In general, we place the highest value on recent sources simply because the latest scholar or scientist has the advantage of building on all that has gone before.

TIP! Look for sources that address the topic from different perspectives. Avoid relying too heavily on a single source.

Tips on Note-Taking

Many researchers use note cards for keeping track of the information they find. If you decide to use note cards, work out some system for recording information. Here are some suggestions to guide you:

1. First record the essential information about the source on each and every card: the author's last name, an abbreviated title, and the page number or numbers. If you get in the habit of writing down these essentials before you start taking notes, there is less chance of forgetting an item.

2. Write only one idea or point of information on each card. This allows you to shuffle the cards as you figure out the precise organization of your paper. Taking notes consecutively on sheets of paper makes this handy sorting of ideas impossible.

3. Put subject headings on the cards: one or two words in the upper right-hand corner to tell you what each note is about. If all works well, these subject headings will probably correspond to sections of your outline.

4. Summarize the ideas in your own words. If you think you might want to quote directly from the source, copy the author's exact words and enclose them in quotation marks. If you forget the quotation marks and use those words in your paper, you will be guilty of *plagiarism* (claiming another person's work as your own), which is a serious academic offense.

Most computers now come with a note card program, or you can purchase software for a note card system. You can use the computer note cards just as you would use index cards: title each card by topic, and then type your notes onto the card provided by the computer. The only drawback is that computers are not as portable as note cards. Unless you have a laptop computer, you will have to type your notes at home or in your campus computer center.

The Printout/Photocopying Option

If the time you can spend in the library is limited, you might want to print out an online article or photocopy pertinent portions of books in order to have these materials available to study at your convenience. In fact, you might find it easier to take notes from a printout than from a computer screen. You can underline or highlight key ideas, even color coding these highlighted passages to fit different subtopics in your paper. You can also write comments or cross-references to other sources in the margins. It's a good idea to put the information from printouts and photocopies on note cards. This procedure forces you to summarize the material in your own words—and thus avoid plagiarism—and makes it much easier to sort the separate items into categories.

Constructing a Working Outline

At the time you're reading and taking notes, you should also be working on your outline. Chances are the best arrangement of points and ideas won't emerge until you're fairly well along with your research—possibly not until you've finished it. As you collect more and more cards, leaf through them occasionally to see if they can be arranged into three or four main categories to form the major headings of an outline. The sooner you can get one worked out, the more efficient your research becomes. You can see exactly what you're looking for and avoid taking notes that would prove irrelevant and have to be discarded.

If an idea sounds potentially useful, copy it down whether it fits exactly or not. If the idea recurs in your reading and gathers

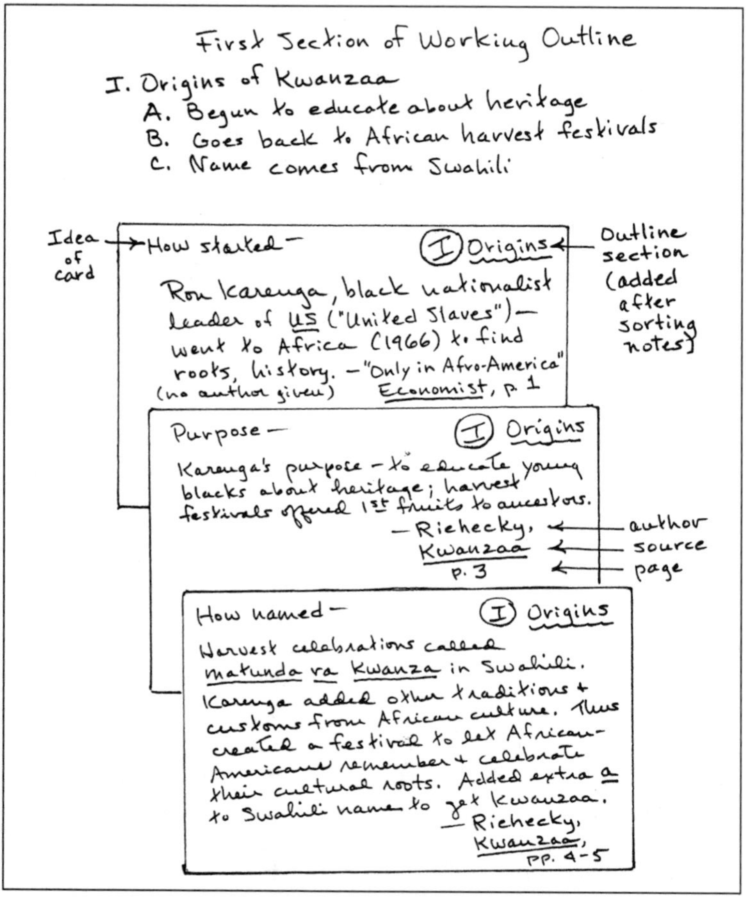

FIGURE 8.8 *Section of Working Outline with Note Cards*

significance, you may decide to add a section to your outline or to expand one of the present sections. Then later, at the organizing stage, if you have cards with points and ideas that just don't seem to fit in anywhere, let them go. Let them go cheerfully. Don't ruin the focus and unity of your paper by trying to wedge in every single note you've taken. Unless you're an uncommonly careful note-taker, you'll have a number of cards that you just can't use.

In Figure 8.8 you'll see the sample note cards for one section of a working outline. They may help you get the idea of how to label your cards. In the next chapter you will find advice on synthesizing all this diverse material into a unified, informative, well-documented research paper.

9

Using Your Sources

After you've read all the material you feel is necessary to cover your topic thoroughly, gather together your notes, your bibliography cards, your photocopied pages, your working outline, and anything else you need for writing your first draft. The actual drafting of the paper is a lot like writing any other paper, except that you'll incorporate the material from note cards into your text (either in your own words or through direct quotations) and give credit to the original authors for information, ideas, and quotations that you gathered from them. The following sections will give you advice on how to take all this raw material and craft it into a smooth, readable research paper.

F ocusing the Thesis

You first need to refine the thesis question or idea that you devised before you started reading on the subject. The refined thesis should convey the point you want to make after studying your sources. If, for instance, you began by investigating the question "Do breakfast cereal ads manipulate and exploit children?" you might, after doing your research, end up with a thesis statement something like this one written by our student Barb Taylor:

> Advertisers use jingles, slogans, cartoon characters, incentives, and promises of athletic prowess to lure and mislead young consumers into getting their parents to buy sugary, low-nutrient cereals.

TIP! Your thesis may change as you work with your source material, but get a fairly clear idea of where you're going before you start your draft.

Imagine Your Readers

If your teacher doesn't specify an audience for you, you'll find it helpful to think of your readers as people who want to learn about your topic but don't know a lot about it. Your focus will be clearer if you have in mind a specific group of readers and perhaps a specific publication your writing could appear in. For example, Barb Taylor's research essay could be directed at parents of small children and might appear in *Parents, Good Housekeeping,* or *Mother Jones,* magazines that often criticize shoddy television fare and falsity in advertising.

O *rganizing Your Notes*

Once you have a clearly focused thesis and a strong sense of your target audience, go back and read through your note cards. Use the headings that you put on the cards while taking notes, and group the cards with similar ideas together in stacks. (If you photocopied most or all of your sources, write headings on the first page of the photocopy and sort the articles that way.) Then consult your working outline, and arrange the stacks in the order that the headings appear there. As you write, following this plan, you will have the information you need in front of you, ready to be incorporated into the first draft of your paper.

If your stacks of cards don't match the outline but lie there in a confused, overlapping, mind-boggling mess, all is not lost. You can still bring order out of chaos. Here are a few methods:

1. *Tinker with your outline.* It may seem like a step backward, but now that you have new information from your research, the whole topic may look different. Look at the main headings and change any that don't seem to fit; add others that you have good material for but overlooked when you made the working outline.

2. *Cluster your note cards again.* This process may suggest an organizing strategy that you wouldn't think of any other way.

3. *Put your notes aside and begin writing*—even if you begin in the middle of a thought. Force yourself, as in freewriting, to keep going, even if your paper seems repetitive, disorganized, and sketchy. Eventually, the writing will begin to take shape, giving you an idea about where to start your first draft.

4. *Find a key article on the topic, and examine its structure.* You may be able to find an organizational scheme that will work for your paper.

I ntegrating Sources

One important difference between writing a paper using your own ideas and writing a paper incorporating research involves acknowledging your sources. Whether you are quoting directly or simply paraphrasing someone else's ideas and observations, you should always give credit in the text of your paper to the person from whom you are borrowing. Both the MLA and APA documentation styles require you to cite all sources *within* the paper. Many people who do researched writing make no attempt to work in direct quotations or provide complete citations in the first draft because pausing to do so interrupts the flow of their ideas. They just jot down the name of the person who has provided the information or idea; they go back later to fill in page numbers and integrate exact quotations.

Use the "Hamburger" Model

Think of each use of a source as a hamburger, with its two buns and a burger. The top bun is your introduction of the source, telling your reader that material from some authority is coming up, who or what the source is, and what the person's credentials are, if you know them. The burger is the information from the source, quoted or paraphrased. The bottom bun is the *parenthetical documentation*, which tells your reader that your use of the source is over and gives the page number for the source of that particular material.

The hamburger model is crucial because your reader needs to know where your own ideas stop and others' begin—and end. The following example from student Bob Harmon illustrates the hamburger approach to documentation:

> Behavior research has clearly shown that different types of music have different effects on different people. Music can increase or decrease anxiety, but its use in business to improve morale is questionable. In the *Journal of Marketing*, researcher John Milliman points out that past decisions to use music in the marketplace have been based on folklore or intuition rather than on empirical results (88). His study focused primarily on the experimental manipulations of no music,

slow music, and fast music. The results indicate music does control the speed with which subjects move through a store. Slow music results in subjects spending more time, and fast music means less time spent (Milliman 86–91). If music does affect the speed with which people move through a store, does it affect their perceptions of time? If fast music is used for music-on-hold, it may decrease people's sense of how long they are on hold; and slow music may expand the perceived length of time. Here again, proper selection is critical.

In this example, you see Harmon's transition from a preceding paragraph, his use of a paraphrase of the thesis of Milliman's article, then his summary of Milliman's research, and then his own application of the research. And you never confuse which is which, because the hamburger system of source citation makes clear where all the ideas come from.

TIP! Attribute sources ("According to Professor White, . . .") in the text of your paper, not just in parenthetical citations.

T o Cite or Not to Cite

The main purpose of documentation—of citing sources used in a research paper—is to give credit for ideas, information, and actual phrasing that you borrow from other writers. You cite sources in order to be honest and to lend authority to your own writing. You also include citations to enable your readers to find more extensive information than your paper furnishes, in case they become engrossed in your subject and want to read some of your sources in full.

We are all unsure occasionally about when a citation is necessary. We can say with authority that you must include a citation for:

1. All direct quotations
2. All indirect quotations
3. All major ideas that are not your own
4. All essential facts, information, and statistics that are not general knowledge—especially anything controversial

The last category is the one that causes confusion. In general, the sort of information available in an encyclopedia does not need a citation. But statements interpreting, analyzing, or speculating on such information should be documented. If you write that President Warren G. Harding died in office, you do not need a citation because that is a widely known and undisputed fact. If you write that Harding's administration was one of the most corrupt in our history, most people would not feel the need for a citation because authorities agree that the Harding scandals were flagrant and abundant. But if you write that Harding was sexually intimate with a young woman in the White House cloakroom, you should cite your source. Because such information is not widely known and is also debatable, you need to identify your source so that your readers can judge the reliability of the claim. Then, too, they might want further enlightenment on the matter, and your citation will lead them to a more complete discussion.

TIP! It's better to bother your readers with too many citations than to have them question your integrity by having too few.

Accuracy Is the Aim

Get the form of your citations correct every time, right down to the last comma, colon, and parenthesis. After years of being told to be original and to think for yourself, you are now being told—on this one matter, at least—to fall into line and slavishly follow the prescribed format. What you might consider a blessed bit of variety will not be appreciated in citing your source information. That information (date, publisher, place of publication) is located on the title page and on the back of the title page of each book. For magazines you usually can find it all on the cover.

When in Doubt, Use Common Sense

Keep in mind that the purpose of documentation is two-fold:

1. To give credit to your sources
2. To allow your readers to find your sources in case they want further information on the subject

If you are ever in doubt about documentation form (if you are citing something so unusual that you can't find a similar entry in the samples here), use your common sense and give credit the way you think it logically should be done. Be as consistent as possible with other citations.

To Quote or Not to Quote

Never quote directly unless (1) the material is authoritative and convincing evidence in support of your thesis, or (2) the statement is extremely well phrased, or (3) the idea is controversial and you want to assure your readers that you are not slanting or misinterpreting the source. You would probably quote an observation as well-put as this one:

> Charles Darwin concluded that language ability is "an instinctive tendency to acquire an art."

There is no need, however, for the direct quotation in the following sentence:

> The ICC, in an effort to aid the rail industry, has asked for a "federal study of the need and means for preserving a national passenger service."

You could phrase that just as well yourself. But remember, even after you put the statement into your own words, you still have to indicate (in a parenthetical citation) where you got the point.

Quoting Quotations

Sometimes in your reading you will come across a quotation that says precisely what you've been looking for and says it well. If the quotation is complete enough to serve your purpose, and if you honestly don't think you would benefit from tracking down the original, then don't bother. Instead, include that quotation in the usual way. But notice that your parenthetical citation will include "qtd. in" before the source and page number:

> Oscar Wilde once said about education, "It is well to remember from time to time that nothing that is worth knowing can be taught" (qtd. in Pinker 19).

TIP! **Too much quotation can suggest that you have too few ideas of your own.**
Use quotations to support your points, not to make them for you.

W *orking Quotations in Smoothly*

If you want your research paper to read smoothly, you must take care when incorporating quotations into your writing. You'll need to have a ready supply of introductory phrases to slide the quotations in gracefully—phrases like "As Le Seure discovered," "Professor Weber notes," and "According to Dr. Carter." These attributions help your readers to evaluate the source material as they read it and distinguish source material from your remarks about it. If you run through the examples in this section on quoting, you will find a generous assortment of these phrases. Borrow them with our blessing.

Notice, please, that the more famous the person, the less likely we are to use Mr., Miss, Mrs., or Ms. in front of the name. "Mr. Shakespeare" sounds quite droll. If the person has a title, you can use it or not, as you think appropriate: Dr. Pauling or Pauling, Senator Feinstein or Feinstein, President Wilson or Wilson.

Lead into Your Quotations

Don't drop quotations in without preparing your readers. Provide clear lead-ins, usually including the author's name, to connect the quotation to your text:

> Many fluent native speakers of English will claim they don't understand grammar. As Professor David Crystal points out, "Millions of people believe they are failures at grammar, say that they have forgotten it, or deny they know any grammar at all—in each case using their grammar convincingly to make their point" (191).

For variety, you may want to place the connecting phrase in the middle every so often, this way:

> The fundamental purpose of language is to communicate intelligibly. "But if thought corrupts language," warns George Orwell, "language can also corrupt thought" (38).

You don't always have to quote full sentences from your sources. You can quote only the telling phrases or key ideas of your authority, like this:

> Barbara Strang remarks that worrying about split infinitives is "one of the most tiresome pastimes" invented by 19th-century grammarians (95).

Or like this:

> The play's effectiveness lies, as E. M. W. Tillyard points out, in "the utter artlessness of the language" (34).
>
> The self-portraits of Frida Kahlo are bold and personal. Art critic Hayden Herrera describes them as "autobiography in paint" (xii).

But do introduce your quotations, please. Identifying the source before presenting the borrowed material helps your readers to know which ideas are yours and which come from sources.

TIP! If you have difficulty finding new ways to introduce your authorities in the text of your paper, perhaps you are using too many direct quotations.

Make the Grammar Match

When you integrate a quotation into your own sentence, you are responsible for making sure that the entire sentence makes sense. You must adjust the way your sentence is worded so that the grammar comes out right. Read your quotations over carefully to be sure they don't end up like this one:

> When children are born, their first reactions are "those stimuli which constitute their environment."

"Reactions" are not "stimuli." The sentence should read this way:

> When children are born, their first reactions are to "those stimuli which constitute their environment."

What a difference a word makes—the difference here between sense and nonsense. Take particular care when you are adding someone else's words to your own; you get the blame if the words in the quotation do not make sense, because they *did* make sense before you lifted them out of context.

Use Special Punctuation: Ellipsis Dots and Brackets

When you write a documented paper, you may need to use *ellipsis dots* and *brackets* to condense quotations and blend them in smoothly with your text.

To shorten a quoted passage, use *ellipsis dots* (three periods with spaces between) to show your readers that you've omitted some words. To distinguish between your ellipsis points and the spaced periods that sometimes appear in written works, put square brackets around any ellipsis dots that you add:

"The time has come [. . .] for us to examine ourselves," declares James Baldwin, "but we can only do this if we are willing to free ourselves from the myth of America and try to find out what is really happening here" (18).

Ellipsis dots are not needed if the omission occurs at the beginning or end of the sentence you are quoting. But if *your* sentence ends with quoted words that are not the end of the original quoted sentence, then use ellipsis dots:

> Thoreau insisted that he received only one or two letters in his life "that were worth the postage" and commented summarily that "to a philosopher all news, as it is called, is gossip [. . .]."

That fourth dot is the period. If you include documentation, such as a page number, add the period after the parentheses:

> "is gossip [. . .]" (27).

Use *brackets* to add words of your own to clarify the meaning or make the grammar match:

> In her memoir, Jessica Mitford confirms that "In those days [the early 1940s] until postwar repression set in, the [Communist] Party was a strange mixture of openness and secrecy" (67).

Handling Long Quotations

If you quote more than four typed lines of prose or more than three lines of poetry, you set the quotation off by indenting it one inch or ten spaces. Introduce the quotation, usually with a complete sentence followed by a colon; begin the indented quotation on the next line; double-space the quotation and do not use quotation marks (since the indention signals that the material is quoted).

> In 1892 George Bernard Shaw wrote to the editor of the London *Chronicle,* denouncing a columnist who had complained about split infinitives:
>
> > If you do not immediately suppress the person who takes it upon himself to lay down the law almost every day in your columns on the subject of literary composition, I will give up the *Chronicle* [. . .]. I ask you, Sir, to put this man out [. . .] without interfering with his perfect freedom of choice between "to suddenly go," "to go suddenly" and "suddenly to go." Set him adrift and try an intelligent Newfoundland dog in his place. (qtd. in Crystal, 195)

Notice that in an indented quotation, the page number is cited in parentheses *after* the period. The quotation marks within the indented material indicate that Shaw punctuated those phrases in that way.

A voiding Plagiarism

Plagiarism means using somebody else's writing without giving proper credit. You can avoid this dishonesty by using a moderate amount of care in taking notes. Put quotation marks around any material—however brief—that you copy verbatim. As you're leafing through your note cards trying to group them into categories, circle the quotation marks in red so you can't miss them, or else highlight the quoted material as a reminder.

You must also avoid the author's phrasing if you decide not to quote directly but to paraphrase. You naturally tend to write an idea down using the same language as your source, perhaps changing or omitting a few words. This close paraphrasing is still plagiarism. To avoid it, read the passage first, then look away from the original as you put the idea down in your own words. You will scarcely be able to fall into the original phrasing that way.

TIP! When you summarize, try to condense several pages of reading on a single note card.

Writing an Acceptable Paraphrase

Sometimes, of course, you must do fairly close paraphrasing of important ideas. Because plagiarism can often be accidental, we will give you a couple of examples to show you exactly what unintentional plagiarism looks like. Here is a passage from *The Language Instinct* by Steven Pinker. Assume that you want to use this idea to make a point in your paper.

> Language is not a cultural artifact that we learn the way we learn to tell time or how the federal government works. Instead, it is a distinct piece of the biological makeup of our brains. Language is a complex, specialized skill, which develops in the child spontaneously, without conscious effort or formal instruction.

If you incorporate this material into your paper in the following way, you have plagiarized:

(wrong)   Humans do not learn language the way we learn to tell time or how the federal government works. Language is a part of the biological makeup of our brains, a complex skill that a child develops spontaneously, without conscious effort or formal instruction (Pinker 18).

The fact that the source is cited suggests that this plagiarism perhaps resulted from ignorance rather than deception, but it is plagiarism nonetheless. Changing a few words or rearranging the phrases is not enough. Here is another version, somewhat less blatant but still plagiarism:

(wrong) Humans do not learn language in the way we learn to count or understand how a steam engine works. Language is part of our physical makeup, a complex, specialized skill that develops automatically, without conscious effort or formal instruction (Pinker 18).

There are still two phrases that are distinctly Pinker's: "a complex, specialized skill" and "without conscious effort or formal instruction." It is quite all right to use those phrases but *only if you put them in quotation marks.* You should also acknowledge your source in the text of your paper whenever possible, like this:

(right) According to linguist Steven Pinker, humans do not learn language in the way we learn to count or understand how a steam engine works. Language is part of our physical makeup, "a complex, specialized skill" that develops automatically, "without conscious effort or formal instruction" (18).

Notice, by the way, that the phrase "in the way we learn" and the words "makeup" and "develops" do not have quotation marks around them, even though they appear in the original. These words are so common, so frequently used that quotation marks are unnecessary. Here is another acceptable paraphrase in which none of the original phrasing is used:

(right) Linguist Steven Pinker claims that human beings do not learn language in the way that we learn to count or understand how a steam engine works. Language is a part of our physical makeup; it's a sophisticated skill that children acquire automatically and effortlessly without explicit training (18).

Writing Exercise 9.1

Write paraphrases of two of these paragraphs from Chapter 4: Floyd Skoot's paragraph on neurological tests (p. 56), Stephen Jay Gould's paragraph on dinosaurs (p. 59), Steven Brill's paragraph on handguns (p. 66), and Anthony Wilson-Smith's paragraphs on crime in Canada (pp. 66–67, 69–70). If you have the chance, compare your paraphrases with your classmates' to see how well you did at capturing the original meaning and avoiding plagiarism.

R *evising the Draft*

Because a research paper requires the incorporation of other people's ideas and the acknowledgment of these sources, you need to take special care in revising. Consult the Revising Checklist for Researched Writing in Figure 9.1.

Preparing the Final Copy

Before you work on your final draft, give your entire attention to the following instructions on form.

1. Provide margins of at least one inch at the top, bottom, and sides.

Check the Usual Things
1. Be sure the introduction states your thesis.
2. Be sure each paragraph is unified, coherent, and directly related to your thesis.
3. Be sure that the transitions between paragraphs are clear and effective.
4. Be sure your conclusion evaluates the results of your research. If the paper is argumentative, be sure the last sentence is emphatic.

Check the Special Things
1. Be sure that you have introduced direct quotations gracefully, using the name and, if appropriate, the title or occupation of the person quoted.
2. Be sure each citation is accurate.
3. Be sure that paraphrases are in your own words and that sources are clearly acknowledged.
4. Be sure that you have not relied too heavily on a single source.
5. Be sure that you have written most of the paper yourself; you need to examine, analyze, or explain the material, not just splice together a bunch of quotations and paraphrases.
6. Be sure always to separate quotations with some comment of your own.
7. Be sure to use ellipsis dots if you omit any words from a quotation; never leave out anything that alters the meaning of a sentence.
8. Be sure to use square brackets, not parentheses, if you add words in a quotation.
9. Be sure to underline the titles of books and magazines; put quotation marks around titles of articles and chapters in books.
10. Be sure to indent long quotations ten spaces—without quotation marks.

FIGURE 9.1 *Revising Checklist for Researched Writing*

2. Double-space throughout.

3. Do not put the title of your own paper in quotation marks.

4. Put page numbers in the upper right-hand corner. But do not number the title page or the first page of the paper. After the title page (and the outline, if you include one), count all pages in the total as you number. Note correct page numbering on the sample student paper, which follows.

5. Proofread. You may well be close to exhaustion by the time you finish typing the final copy, and the last thing you will feel like doing is rereading the blasted thing. But force yourself. Or entice somebody else to do it. But do not skip the proofreading.

6. Edit. If you find mistakes, insert the corrections neatly in ink *above the line* (if allowed by your instructor) or re-type the page (which is easy to do on a word processor).

Discussion Exercise 9.2

Interview someone who has written a successful research paper and find out what the person did to make the process work. Report back to your class on this interview, and discuss what advice and warnings you picked up.

S *ample Student Research Paper*

The following documented essay was written by Amelia Doggett, a student at Eastern Illinois University. Amelia chose to follow the MLA (Modern Language Association) style commonly used in the humanities. She included a title page and an outline, which are not always required of research papers. We have annotated Amelia's paper to call your attention to certain features of this style. Complete instructions for using the MLA style of documentation follow in Chapter 10.

If you want to use the APA (American Psychological Association) style of documentation, which is used in the social sciences, you will find directions for its use on pages 173–79. You should, of course, use the format and documentation style that your teacher requests.

Center your title
about one-third
down the page. ————— Kwanzaa: An American Creation

Center your
name near the ————————— Amelia Doggett
middle of the
page.

Course name, ————— English 1091C, Section 095
section number,
professor's   Professor Robert Funk
name, and date
are centered near   5 December 1997
the bottom of
the page.

Doggett i

– Number outline pages with small roman numerals.

Outline

Thesis: Now that Kwanzaa has become ———— Outline begins with thesis.
mainstream, its legitimacy is
being questioned.

Introduction: Brief overview of
acceptance and current
questioning

I. Origins
   A. Started to educate about African
      heritage
   B. Rooted in African harvest
      festivals
   C. Uses Swahili word for harvest
      festival
II. Description of festival
   A. Seven letters in name, seven days
      in celebration
   B. Seven candles stand for seven
      principles (list)
   C. Symbolic elements of celebration
   D. Gift-giving each night or just at
      family feast
   E. Tributes to ancestors or famous
      African Americans
III. Controversy and Divisiveness
   A. Grew out of black power
      movement
   B. Rhetoric of Kwanzaa changing

Your last name
and page num-
ber are typed ½
inch from top of
each page.

        C. Dissenting opinions about Kwanzaa

  IV. Entering the mainstream

        A. Fosters cohesiveness in black
           community

        B. Evidence of widespread acceptance

        C. Questions about commercialism

Conclusion: No longer a tool for racial
              separatism, Kwanzaa is now a
              force for cooperation.

Doggett 1

Kwanzaa: An American Creation

Many people have heard of the African American celebration called Kwanzaa, but few outside the African American community know exactly what it is about. In fact, many African Americans do not know all the details about the origins and purposes of this festival. Although an estimated 18 million people celebrate Kwanzaa worldwide ("Kwanzaa Culture" 17), there are those who question the holiday's legitimacy and others who claim its goals and values are already being compromised and commercialized.

Origins

Kwanzaa is a recent invention. In 1966 Ron Karenga, a leader of a black nationalist group called US ("United Slaves"), traveled to Africa to learn more about the history of his people ("Only" 1). According to author Janet Riehecky, Karenga wanted to educate African Americans, especially young people, about their rich heritage (3). While in Africa he observed the celebrations of many tribes when the first crops of the year were harvested. In Swahili these celebrations were called <u>matunda ya kwanza</u>, meaning first fruits; according to Karenga the Africans offered the first

Give your paper a title that suggests not only the topic but also your point of view or main idea.

— This article had no author byline. Use the article title, in its entirety or shortened, within quotation marks. Alphabetize in the Works Cited by the first main word of the title.

Here the title of the article is shortened from "Only in Afro-America."

— The 3 is the exact page number that the information in the sentence came from.

Doggett 2

fruits of their harvest to their ancestors. Karenga decided to combine these
commemorative celebrations with other
African traditions and with customs borrowed from other holidays to create a
festival in which African Americans could
rejoice and remember their culture and
their ancestors. He took the word <u>kwanza</u>
from the Swahili phrase, added an extra
<u>a</u>, and called the new holiday <u>Kwanzaa</u>
(Riehecky 4-5).

This citation shows that the information in the last 3 sentences came from pages 4-5 of the Riehecky book. Provide just the pages you use, not the whole page span of the article.

The Seven-Day Festival

The extra <u>a</u> was added to give the
word seven letters. Karenga wanted the
seven-letter name to go along with the
seven days of the celebration, the seven
candles lit for each day, the seven symbols, and the seven principles he created
for the holiday. The basic doctrines of
Kwanzaa, the <u>Nguzo Saba</u> (seven principles), come from the values that Karenga
saw in the harvest festivals. These are
<u>umoja</u> (unity), <u>kujichagulia</u> (self-deter-
mination), <u>ujima</u> (collective work and
responsibility), <u>ujamaa</u> (cooperative economics), <u>nia</u> (purpose), <u>kuumba</u> (creativity), and <u>imani</u> (faith). These values are
celebrated over seven days and nights,
from December 26 through January 1, with
each day focused on one of the seven

Doggett 3

principles (Goldsmith 8-10). Most fami-
lies light a candle each night in honor
of the principle of the day. The candles
(called <u>mishumaa saba</u>) are black (repre-
senting the African people), red (symbol-
izing their struggles), and green (denot-
ing both Africa itself and the hope of
deliverance from the struggles) and are
placed in a simple seven-candle holder
called a <u>kindra</u>, reminiscent of a
Hanukkah menorah (Goss 2). ─────── Notice that there
is no punctua-
      The rituals, as described by Karenga,   tion between the
                                              author's name
also involve fruits and vegetables, each   and the page
identified by its Swahili name and sym-   number—just a
                                              space. The same
bolizing "the rewards of collective pro-   goes for an arti-
                                              cle title in your
ductive labor" (<u>mazao</u>); a straw mat sym-   parenthetical ci-
bolizing tradition or history (<u>mkeka</u>);   tations: only a
                                              space before the
ears of corn for each child in the family   page number.
(<u>vibunzi</u>); and simple, homemade gifts
that emphasize education and African culture (<u>zawadi</u>) (Wilde 3). The <u>kindra</u> is
placed on the straw mat among the fruits
and vegetables. The gifts are distributed
each night or just on the final night,
December 31, when family members gather
for the communal feast (<u>karamu</u>). This
closing feast often includes some kind of
tribute or salute to ancestors or famous
African Americans, usually in the form of
a song or poem or even a speech by a
guest (Goss 2-3).

Doggett 4

Use subheadings to help your reader grasp your organization.

Controversy and Divisiveness

Kwanzaa is the product of the American civil rights and black power movements of the 1960s. Its creator, Ron Karenga, is now a professor black studies at California State University in Long Beach, and he has changed his first name to Maulana ("master teacher"). In the '60s, however, Karenga was the leader of a Los Angeles-based organization called US (as opposed to "them") and became an important figure in the rebuilding of Watts after the riots there (Early 2). Kwanzaa was born in the aftermath of Watts and was an attempt "to reaffirm African culture," says Karenga; "it was at the same time a political act of self-determination. . . . We were talking about

The *qtd. in* means that the person's words were quoted in the cited article.

re-Africanization" (qtd. in "Kwanzaa Culture" 1). And, indeed, one of the common features in some larger Kwanzaa ceremonies has been a name-changing ceremony, in which the participants convert their "slave names" into African ones (Wilde 3).

If you use more than four typed lines of direct quotation from a source, indent all the lines 10 spaces (or 1 inch) from the left margin. Don't use quotation marks around the indented material.

In the beginning, Karenga's Afrocentric and anti-white rhetoric was often polemical and confrontational:

> The more you learn, the
> more resentful you are of this
> white man. Then you see how

Doggett 5

he's tricking your people,

emasculating your men, raping

your women and using his power

to keep you down. (qtd. in

Wilde 3)

But since that time, Karenga has mel-

lowed, and Kwanzaa has lost much of its

polemical style and content. The inventor

of the holiday now describes its goals in

more general and tranquil terms, saying

that it promotes "The good life. The good

of existence. The good of family, commu-

nity and culture. The good of the awesome

and the ordinary. The good of the divine,

the natural and the social" (qtd. in

"Kwanzaa Ties" 1).

   While Kwanzaa has been transformed

in the thirty years since its original

conception, it still retains some traces

of divisiveness and anti-white senti-

ment. Professor Gerald Early, director

of the African and Afro-American Studies

Program at Washington University in

St. Louis, points out that "Kwanzaa's

success depends on exacerbating, con-

sciously or un-consciously, black

people's sense of alienation from

Christmas" (4). In this respect, then,

Kwanzaa becomes, as the Afrocentrist

writer Haki Madhubuti claims, an

"Afro-American celebration [that] is

When you give the name of the person or author you're using and you place a parenthetical citation at the end of the same sentence as the name, put only the page number in the parentheses.

truly progressive and revolutionary"
(qtd. in Early 4).

The divided opinion about Kwanzaa ex-
tends into the black community. Although
many African Americans embrace the holiday, others think that it presents a
false history (Wilde 4). They question
the need to celebrate an idealized
African past, especially when there is so
much to celebrate in the real history of
blacks in America. "It's not an authentic
black American holiday, not a part of our
tradition," says Clarence Walker, a black
professor at the University of California
at Davis (qtd. in "Only" 2).

Professor Early feels that the seven
principles of Kwanzaa are "less ideas
than a set of slogans." He describes the
philosophical foundation of the holiday
as a "pastiche" drawn from a range of political and cultural sources:

> There's a good deal of the
> African political philosopher
> Julius Nyerere, some of the
> former Senegalese president
> Leopold Senghor's "Negritude,"
> a bit of Mao, a dash of Marx, a
> serving of Garveyite Pan-
> Africanism, and a pinch of na-
> ture religion. (2)

Because it's in an indented quotation without quotation marks, the word "Negritude" has double quotations marks around it, just as it appeared in the source.

Doggett 7

But this concoction of ideas is entirely
fitting for an American creation: Americans have been inventing their culture
from scratch since the country began.
Early concedes that the principles of
Kwanzaa "combine the beatitude of
willpower, an old American preoccupation,
with the righteousness of racial uplift,
an old African-American preoccupation"
(2-3).

Entering the Mainstream
    Kwanzaa was originally intended as a
way to unite African Americans against
those (whites) who are trying to hold
their race back, but its positive goal of
increasing community cohesiveness has di-
minished the racial resentment. Yes, there
is still some anti-white feeling, but as
Anna Day Wilde observes, "Most African
Americans view Kwanzaa not as an opportunity to bash whites but as a force for
oneness among blacks" (7). This constructive concern has made it a holiday that
many people feel comfortable embracing.
    And there are many signs that African
Americans have enthusiastically embraced
Kwanzaa. Bookshops carry Kwanzaa cook-
books and audiotapes; schools and museums
include Kwanzaa in their holiday cel-

Doggett　8

ebrations; communities hold parades and
public celebrations; Kwanzaa expositions
draw thousands of merchants and cus-
tomers; and Hallmark since 1992 has been
selling Kwanzaa cards, featuring designs
by African-American artists, as part of
its Mahogany line (Wilde 3-4). As journalists Kenneth Woodward and Patrice
Johnson point out, "All this activity
means that Kwanzaa has made it into the
mainstream. If it's featured in shop windows and McDonald's ads, then it has arrived" (2).

Some people do not approve of the increased popularity of the holiday. They
fear that commercial exploitation will
take away from the positive communal
goals of Kwanzaa (Horne 2) and contribute
to its decline. After all, many people
say the main reason they started cele-
brating this new holiday was to escape
the over-commercialism of Christmas
(Wilde 4). "I'm wondering when they're
going to announce a big Kwanzaa clearance
sale," says Dawad Phillip, an editor at
the Daily Challenge, a black newspaper in
Brooklyn (qtd. in Woodward and Johnson
2). But others feel that the holiday is
safe because most people who really celebrate Kwanzaa realize what it stands for
(Horne 3). Gerald Early thinks that the

Notice that the
quotation
marks close the
sentence. Then
the parenthetical
citation appears,
followed by the
period to close
the whole thing. —

Whenever possi-
ble, give the cre-
dentials and ti-
tles of the people
you quote.

Doggett 9

commercialization of Kwanzaa is not a
sign of the corruption of the holiday but
an indication of the increasing economic
power of blacks (6).

Conclusion

There are those who feel that no matter how commercialized the holiday becomes it will not endure. These cynics
scoff at this relatively new holiday and
dismiss it as "a marginal, slightly ludi-
crous idea that is unlikely to last long,
let alone 2,000 years"--like Hanukkah and
Christmas ("Only" 2). But behind all the
commercialism and controversy, there is a
holiday moving steadily toward its potential. Kwanzaa is no longer a tool for
racial separatism, as it was when it
started. It has become, instead, a strong
force for cooperation and unification in
the African American community and in
American society in general.

Doggett 10

Works Cited

The Early article appeared in print in *Harper's* magazine but was accessed online through InfoTrac.

Early, Gerald. "Dreaming of a Black Christmas." <u>Harper's</u> Jan. 1997: 55-61. <u>InfoTrac Expanded Academic Index ASAP</u>. Eastern Ill. U Lib. 9 Nov. 1997.

Goldsmith, Diane Hoyt. <u>Celebrating Kwan-zaa</u>. New York: Holiday House, 1993.

With multiple authors, reverse the order of only the first author's name.

Goss, Linda, and Clay Goss. <u>It's Kwanzaa Time</u>. New York: HarperCollins, 1995.

Horne, Malaika. "The Seeds of Kwanzaa Have Spawned a Cultural Revival."

In the Works Cited listing for a printed article, give the number for the whole span of the article, even if you used material from only one or a few pages. This article spanned pages 2 and 3.

<u>Crisis</u> Nov. 1994: 2-3.

"Kwanzaa Culture." <u>U. S. News & World Report</u> 30 Dec. 1996: 17.

"Kwanzaa Ties African-Americans to Their Roots." CNN Interactive. 26 Dec. 1996. ⟨http://www.cnn.com/US/9612/26/kwanzaa.view/index.html.⟩ 11 Nov. 1997.

"Only in Afro-America." <u>The Economist</u> 17 Dec. 1994: A32. <u>InfoTrac Expanded Academic Index ASAP</u>. Eastern Ill. U Lib. 11 Nov. 1997.

Riehecky, Janet. <u>Kwanzaa</u>. Chicago: Chil-

The Works Cited form for a book gives the city of publication, the publisher's name, and the copyright date—but no page numbers.

dren's Press, 1993.

Wilde, Anna Day. "Mainstreaming Kwanzaa." <u>The Public Interest</u> Spring 1995: 68-79. <u>InfoTrac Expanded Academic Index ASAP</u>. Eastern Ill. U Lib. 9 Nov. 1997

Woodward, Kenneth L., and Patrice Johnson. "The Advent of Kwanzaa." <u>Newsweek</u> 11 Dec. 1995: 88. <u>InfoTrac Expanded Academic Index ASAP</u>. Eastern Ill. U Lib. 9 Nov. 1997.

10

Documenting Your Sources

In this chapter you will find complete instruction for documenting papers according to the two most widely used academic styles:

1. MLA (Modern Language Association) for the humanities
2. APA (American Psychological Association) for the social sciences

If you are writing a paper using library sources for any of the remaining academic disciplines, you should identify a leading journal in that field and follow the style used there.

T *he MLA Documentation Style for the Humanities*

The Modern Language Association (MLA) recommends that source citations be given in the text of the paper, rather than in footnotes or endnotes. This in-text style of documentation involves parenthetical references. Throughout this chapter, titles of books and periodicals are underlined (a printer's mark to indicate words to be set in italic type). When you have italic lettering on a computer, you can use italics instead of underlining, as long as your instructor approves.

A. Normally you will introduce the cited material by mentioning the name of the author in your lead-in and giving the page number (or numbers) at the end in parentheses, like this:

```
Edmund Wilson tells us that the author of Uncle Tom's
Cabin felt "the book had been written by God" (5).
```

B. Your readers can identify this source by consulting your Works Cited at the end of your paper (see items H through K). The entry for the source cited above would appear like this:

```
Wilson, Edmund. Patriotic Gore: Studies in the Litera-
     ture of the American Civil War. New York: Oxford
     UP, 1966.
```

C. If you do not mention the author in your lead-in, then include his/her last name in parentheses along with the page number, like this:

```
One of the great all-time best-sellers, Uncle Tom's
Cabin sold over 300,000 copies in America and more
than 2 million copies world wide (Wilson 3).
```

D. If you have to quote indirectly—something from another source not available to you—use "qtd. in" (for "quoted in") in your parenthetical reference. The following example refers to a book written by Donald Johanson and Maitland Edey.

```
Richard Leakey's wife, Maeve, told the paleoanthropolo-
gist David Johanson, "We heard all about your bones on
the radio last night" (qtd. in Johanson and Edey 162).
```

E. If you are using a source written or edited by more than three people, use only the name of the first person listed, followed by "et al." (meaning "and others") in your lead-in:

```
Blair et al. observe that the fine arts were almost
ignored by colonial writers (21).
```

F. If you refer to more than one work by the same author, include a shortened title in the parenthetical reference:

```
(Gould, Mismeasure 138).
```

G. If the author's name is not given, then use a shortened title instead. Be sure to use at least the first word of the full title to send the reader to the proper alphabetized entry on your Works Cited page. The following is a reference to a newspaper article entitled "Environmental Group Calls DuPont's Ads Deceptive":

```
The Friends of the Earth claimed that, despite
DuPont's television ads about caring for the environ-
ment, the company is the "single largest corporate
polluter in the United States" ("Environmental
Group" F3).
```

H. On a separate page at the end of the paper, alphabetize your Works Cited list for all sources mentioned in your paper. Use *hanging indention;* that is, after the first line of each entry, indent the other lines five spaces.

I. Omit any mention of *page* or *pages* or *line* or *lines.* Do not even include abbreviations for these terms. Use numbers alone:

```
Kinsley, Michael. "Continental Divide" Time 7 Jul.
     1997: 89-91.
```

J. Shorten publishers' names: for example, use Allyn instead of Allyn and Bacon, Inc. or Norton instead of W. W. Norton and Co. or Oxford UP instead of Oxford University Press or U of Illinois P instead of University of Illinois Press. See sample entries 1 through 13.

K. Use regular (not roman) numerals throughout, even to indicate act and scene in plays: "In Othello 2.1, the scene shifts to Cyprus." Exceptions: Use *lowercase* roman numerals (ii, xiv) for citing page numbers from a preface, introduction, or table of contents; use roman numerals in names of monarchs (Elizabeth II).

L. Use raised note numbers for *informational notes* only (that is, notes containing material pertinent to your discussion but not precisely to the point). Include these content notes at the end of your paper just before your Works Cited page, and use the heading Notes.

M. Abbreviate months and titles of magazines as shown in the sample entries.

S *ample Entries for a Works Cited List*

The following models will help you write Works Cited entries for most of the sources you will use. If you use a source not illustrated in these examples, consult the more extensive list of sample entries found in the *MLA Handbook for Writers of Research Papers,* 5th ed., or ask your instructor for guidance.

Books

1. Book by one author

> Chused, Richard H. <u>Private Acts in Public Places: A</u>
> <u>Social History of Divorce</u>. Philadelphia: U of
> Pennsylvania P, 1994.

2. Two more books by the same author

> Gould, Stephen Jay. <u>The Mismeasure of Man</u>. New York:
> Norton, 1981.

> ---. <u>The Panda's Thumb: More Reflections in Natural</u>
> <u>History</u>. New York: Norton, 1980.

3. Book by two or three authors

> Anderson, Terry, and Donald Leal. <u>Free Market Environ-</u>
> <u>mentalism</u>. Boulder: Westview, 1991.

> McCrum, William, William Cran, and Robert MacNeil. <u>The</u>
> <u>Story of English</u>. New York: Viking, 1986.

4. Books by more than three authors

> Medhurst, Martin J., et al. <u>Cold War Rhetoric: Strat-</u>
> <u>egy, Metaphor, and Ideology</u>. New York: Greenwood,
> 1990.

[The phrase *et al.* is an abbreviation for *et alii,* meaning "and others."]

5. Book by an unknown author

> <u>Literacy of Older Adults in America: Results from the
> National Adult Literacy Survey</u>. Washington: Center
> for Educ. Statistics, 1987.

6. Book with an editor

> Gallegos, Bee, ed. <u>English: Our Official Language?</u> New
> York: Wilson, 1994.

[For a book with two or more editors, use "eds."]

7. Book with an editor and author

> Whorf, Benjamin. <u>Language, Thought, and Reality: Se-
> lected Writings of Benjamin Lee Whorf</u>. Ed. J. B.
> Carroll. Cambridge: MIT P, 1956.

8. Book by a group or corporate author

> National Research Council. <u>The Social Impact of AIDS
> in the United States</u>. New York: National Academy
> P, 1993.

[When a corporation, organization, or group is listed as the author on the title page, cite it as you would a person.]

9. Work in a collection or anthology

> Gordon, Mary. "The Parable of the Cave." <u>The Writer on
> Her Work</u>. Ed. Janet Sternburg. New York: Norton,
> 1980. 27-32.

10. Work reprinted in a collection or anthology

> Sage, George H. "Sport in American Society: Its Per-
> vasiveness and Its Study." <u>Sport and American
> Society</u>. 3rd ed. Reading: Addison-Wesley, 1980.
> 4-15. Rpt. in <u>Physical Activity and the Social</u>

```
Sciences. Ed. W. N. Widmeyer. 5th ed. Ithaca:
     Movement, 1983. 42-52.
```

[First give complete data for the earlier publication; then add "Rpt. in " and give the reprinted source.]

11. Multivolume work

```
Blom, Eric, ed. Grove's Dictionary of Music and Musi-
     cians. 5th ed. 10 vols. New York: St. Martin's,
     1961.
```

12. Reprinted (republished) book

```
Jespersen, Otto. Growth and Structure of the English
     Language. 1938. Chicago: U of Chicago P, 1980.
```

13. Later (second or subsequent) edition

```
Gibaldi, Joseph. MLA Handbook for Writers of Research
     Papers. 5th ed. New York: MLA, 1999.
```

14. Book in translation

```
Grmek, Mirko D. History of AIDS: Emergence and Origin
     of a Modern Pandemic. Trans. Russell C. Maulitz
     and Jacalyn Duffin. Princeton: Princeton UP, 1990.
```

Newspapers

15. Signed newspaper article

```
Krebs, Emilie. "Sewer Backups Called No Problem." Pan-
     tagraph [Bloomington] 20 Nov. 1985: A3.
```

[If the city is not part of the name of a local newspaper, give the city in brackets, not underlined, after the newspaper's name.]

```
Weiner, Jon. "Vendetta: The Government's Secret War
     Against John Lennon." Chicago Tribune 5 Aug. 1984,
     sec 3:1.
```

[Note the difference between "A3" in the first example and "sec. 3:1" in the second. Both refer to section and page, but each newspaper indicates the section in a different way. Give the section designation and page number exactly as they appear in the publication.]

16. Unsigned newspaper article

    "No Power Line-Cancer Link Found." <u>Chicago Tribune</u> 3
    July 1997, final ed., sec. 1: 5.

    [If an edition is specified on the paper's masthead, name the edition (late ed., natl ed., final ed.) after the date and before the page reference. Different editions of the same issue of a newspaper contain different material.]

17. Letter to the editor

    Kessler, Ralph. "Orwell Defended." Letter. <u>New York</u>
    <u>Times Book Review</u> 15 Dec. 1985: 26.

18. Editorial *written by staff member*

    "From Good News to Bad." Editorial. <u>Washington Post</u> 16
    July 1984: 10.

Magazines and Journals

19. Article from a monthly or bimonthly magazine

    Lawren, Bill. "1990's Designer Beasts." <u>Omni</u> Nov.-Dec.
    1985: 56-61.

    Rosenbaum, Dan, and David Sparrow. "Speed Demons:
    Widebody Rackets." <u>World Tennis</u> Aug. 1989: 48-9.

20. Article from a weekly or biweekly magazine (signed and unsigned)

    Coghlan, Andy. "Warring Parents Harm Children as Much
    as Divorce." <u>New Scientist</u> 15 Jun. 1991: 24.

    "Warning: 'Love' for Sale." <u>Newsweek</u> 11 Nov. 1985: 39.

21. Article from a journal with continuous pagination throughout the whole volume

    ```
    Potvin, Raymond, and Che-Fu Lee. "Multistage Path Mod-
        els of Adolescent Alcohol and Drug Use." Journal
        of Studies on Alcohol 41 (1980): 531-42.
    ```

22. Article from a journal that paginates each issue separately or that uses only issue numbers

    ```
    Holtug, Nils. "Altering Humans: The Case For and
        Against Human Gene Therapy." Cambridge Quarterly
        of Healthcare Ethics 6.2 (Spring 1997): 157-60.
    ```

    [That is volume 6, issue 2.]

Other Sources

23. Book review

    ```
    Emery, Robert. Rev. of The Divorce Revolution: The Un-
        expected Social and Economic Consequences for
        Women and Children in America by Lenore Weitzman.
        American Scientist 74 (1986): 662-63.
    ```

24. Personal interview or letter

    ```
    Ehrenreich, Barbara. Personal interview. 12 Feb. 1995.

    Vidal, Gore. Letter to the author. 2 June 1984.
    ```

    [Treat published interviews and letters like articles, with the person being interviewed as the author.]

25. Anonymous pamphlet

    ```
    How to Help a Friend with a Drinking Problem. American
        College Health Assn., 1984.
    ```

26. Article from a reference work (signed and unsigned)

    ```
    "Psychopharmacology." The Columbia Encyclopedia. 5th
        ed. 1993.
    ```

```
Van Doren, Carl. "Samuel Langhorne Clemens." The Dic-
     tionary of American Biography. 1958 ed.
```

[Treat a dictionary entry or an encyclopedia article like an entry from an anthology, but do not cite the editor of the reference work.]

27. Government publication

```
United States Dept. of Labor, Bureau of Statistics.
     Dictionary of Occupational Titles. 4th ed. Wash-
     ington: GPO, 1977.
```

[GPO stands for Government Printing Office.]

28. Film or videotape

```
Citizen Kane. Dir. Orson Welles. Perf. Orson Welles,
     Joseph Cotton, Dorothy Comingore, and Agnes Moore-
     head. RKO, 1941. 50th Anniversary Special Edition
     videorecording: Turner Home Entertainment, 1991.
```

29. Lecture

```
Albee, Edward. "A Dream Or a Nightmare?" Illinois
     State University Fine Arts Lecture. Normal, IL. 18
     Mar. 1979.
```

For any other sources (such as televised shows, performances, advertisements, recordings, works of art), include enough information to permit an interested reader to locate your original source. Be sure to arrange this information in a logical fashion, duplicating so far as possible the order and punctuation of the entries above. To be on safe ground, consult your instructor for suggestions about documenting unusual material.

Electronic Sources

If you use material from a computer database or online source, you need to indicate that you read it in electronic form. In general, follow the style for citing print sources, modifying them as appropriate to the electronic source. Include both the date of

electronic publication (if available) and the date you accessed the
source. In addition, include the Uniform Resource Locator (URL)
in angle brackets. If a URL must be divided between two lines,
MLA style requires that you break it only after a slash and not introduce a hyphen at the break.

30. Article in an online reference book or encyclopedia

```
Daniel, Ralph Thomas. "The History of Western Music."
     Britannica Online: Macropaedia. 1995. Online Ency-
     clopedia Britannica. 14 June 1995. ⟨http//
     www.eb. com:180/cgi-bin/g:DocF=macro/5004/45/
     0.html⟩.
```

31. Article in an online magazine

```
Yeoman, Barry. "Into the Closet: Can Therapy Make Gay
     People Straight?" Salon.com 22 May 2000. 23 May
     2000. ⟨http://www.salon.com/health/feature/2000/
     05/22/exgay/html⟩.
```

32. Article from an online full-text database
    To cite online material without a URL that you get from a ser-
    vice to which your library subscribes, complete the citation
    by giving the name of the database (underlined), the library,
    and the date of access.

```
Viviano, Frank. "The New Mafia Order." Mother Jones
     May–June 1995: 44–56. InfoTrac Expanded Academic
     Index ASAP. Eastern Ill. U Lib. 17 July 1995.
```

33. Article from a commercial online service

```
Howell, Vicki, and Bob Carlton. "Growing up Tough: New
     Generation Fights for Its Life: Inner-city Youths
     Live by Rule of Vengeance." Birmingham News. 29
     Aug. 1993: 1A+. Lexis-Nexis. Eastern Ill. U Lib.
     26 Apr. 1997.
```

[Lexis-Nexis is both the database and the name of the online
service.]

34. Material accessed on a CD-ROM

Shakespeare. <u>Editions and Adaptations of Shakespeare</u>.
Interactive multimedia. Cambridge, UK: Chadwick-
Healey, 1995. CD-ROM. Alexandria: Electronic Book
Technologies, 1995.

"Silly." <u>The Oxford English Dictionary</u>. 2nd ed. CD-
ROM. Oxford: Oxford UP, 1992.

35. Web site

Cummings, Shelly. "Genetic Testing and the Insurance *published*
Industry." <u>Electronic Genetics Newsletter</u> 18 Mar
1996 17:442. 23 Dec. 1997. ⟨http:// Date took
www.westpub.com/Educate/mathsci/insure.htm⟩.

For more detailed information about citing electronic sources, consult *The MLA Handbook for Writers of Research Papers,* 5th ed. (1999); the MLA's World Wide Web site ⟨http://www.mla.org⟩; or Janice Walker's Web site, "MLA-Style Citations of Electronic Sources" at ⟨http://www.columbia.edu/cu/cup/cgos/idx_basic.html⟩.

The APA Documentation Style for the Social Sciences

The APA style puts more focus on the date of the source than the MLA style does; it's also called the author-date system. The year appears in the parenthetical documentation in the text, instead of only in the References list. It works this way:

A. Always mention your source and its date within the text of your paper in parentheses, like this:

The study reveals that children pass through identifi-
able cognitive stages (Piaget, 1954).

B. Your readers can identify this source by consulting your References list at the end of your paper. The entry for the information above would appear like this:

> Piaget, J. (1954). *The construction of reality in the child*. New York: Basic Books.

[Note the use of sentence capitalization for titles in the References section. Note, too, that APA style requires you to italicize the punctuation that follows underlined titles.]

C. If you are quoting directly or if you want to stress the authority of the source you are paraphrasing, you may mention the name of the source in your sentence. Then include just the date in parentheses, like this:

> In *Words and Women*, Miller and Swift (1976) remind us that using the plural is a good way to avoid "the built-in male-as-norm quality English has acquired . . ." (p. 163).

D. If the author's name is not given, then use a shortened title instead. Be sure to use at least the first word of the full title to send the reader to the proper alphabetized entry on your References page. The following is a reference to a newspaper article entitled "Environmental Group Calls DuPont's Ads Deceptive":

> The Friends of the Earth claimed that, despite DuPont's television ads about caring for the environment, the company is the "single largest corporate polluter in the United States" ("Environmental Group," 1991).

E. If you are using a source written or edited by more than two people and fewer than six, cite all authors the first time you refer to the source. For all subsequent references use only the surname of the first person listed, followed by *et al.* (meaning "and others") in your lead-in:

> Blair et al. (1980) observe that the fine arts were almost ignored by colonial writers.

When there are only two authors, join their names with the word *and* in the text:

Hale and Sponjer (1972) originated the Do-Look-Learn theory.

In parenthetical materials, tables, and reference lists, join the names with an ampersand (&):

The Do-Look-Learn theory (Hale & Sponjer, 1972) was taken seriously by educators across the country.

F. If you are quoting more than *forty* words, begin the quotation on a new line and indent the entire quotation five spaces, but run each line to the usual right margin. Omit the quotation marks. Do not single-space the quotation.

In *Language and Woman's Place* (1975) Lakoff has concluded that

men tend to relegate to women things that are not of concern to them, or do not involve their egos. . . . We might rephrase this point by saying that since women are not expected to make decisions on important matters, such as what kind of job to hold, they are relegated the noncrucial decisions as a sop. (p. 9)

G. If there are two or more works by the same author in your References list, put the earliest one first. When more than one work has been published by the same author during the same year, list them alphabetically, according to the name of the book or article, and identify them with "a," "b," "c," etc., following the date. (Include the "a," "b," "c," etc. in your in-text citations, too.)

Graves, D. (1975). An examination of the writing processes of seven-year-old children. *Research in the Teaching of English*, 9, 227-241.

Graves, D. (1981a). *Writers: Teachers and children at work.* Exeter, NH: Heinemann Educational Books.

Graves, D. (1981b). Writing research for the eighties: What is needed. *Language Arts, 58,* 197-206.

S *ample Entries for a References List*

The following models will help you write entries for most of the sources you will include in your References list. If you use a source not illustrated in these samples, consult the more extensive *Publications Manual of the American Psychological Association,* 5th ed. (Washington: APA, 2001), or ask your instructor.

Alphabetize your list by the author's last name. If there is no author given, alphabetize the entry by the title. Use hanging indention; use author's initials for given names; put the dates after the authors' names; and use sentence capitalization for article and book titles, but capitalize the first word in the subtitle after a colon.

Books

1. Book by one author

Abernathy, C. F. (1980). *Civil rights: Cases and materials.* St. Paul: West Publishing.

2. Book by two or more authors

Cook, M., & McHenry, R. (1978). *Sexual attraction.* New York: Pergamon Press.

Brusaw, C., Alfred, G., & Oliu, W. (1976). *The business writer's handbook.* New York: St. Martin's.

[Note: in the list of references, use the ampersand sign instead of writing the word *and*.]

3. Book by a group or corporate author

National Research Council. (1993). *The social impact of AIDS in the United States.* New York: National Academy Press.

4. Book with an editor

```
Gallegos, Bee (Ed.). (1994). English: Our official
    language? New York: Wilson.
```

5. Article in a collection or anthology

```
Emig, J. (1978). Hand, eye, brain: Some basics in the
    writing process. In C. Cooper & L. Odell (Eds.),
    Research in composing: Points of departure (pp.
    59-72). Urbana, IL: National Council of Teachers of
    English.
```

6. Multivolume work

```
Asimov, I. (1960). The intelligent man's guide to sci-
    ence. (Vols. 1-2). New York: Basic Books.
```

7. Later (second or subsequent) edition

```
Gibaldi, J. (1999). MLA handbook for writers of re-
    search papers (5th ed.). New York: MLA.
```

Periodicals

8. Article from a journal paginated by volume

```
Messner, M. (1990). When bodies are weapons: Masculin-
    ity and violence in sport. International Review for
    the Sociology of Sport, 25, 203-220.
```

[Do not put quotation marks around article titles. Capitalize all important words in journal or magazine titles.]

9. Article from a journal paginated by issue

```
Holtug, Nils. (1997). Altering humans: The case for
    and against human gene therapy. Cambridge Quarterly
    of Healthcare Ethics, 6(2), 157-160.
```

10. Article from a magazine

> Neimark, J. (1991, May). Out of bounds: The truth
>   about athletes and rape. *Mademoiselle,* 196-199.

11. Article from a newspaper

> Eskenazi, G. (1990, June 3). The male athlete and sex-
>   ual assault. *The New York Times,* Section 8, 1.

Other Sources

12. Personal or telephone interview
    Not cited in References list, only within your paper.

13. Article from a specialized dictionary or encyclopedia
    Treat as an article in a collection (item 5 above).

Electronic Sources

14. Article retrieved from a database.

> Viviano, F. (1995, May/June). The new mafia order.
>   *Mother Jones 38,* 44-56. Retrieved 17 July 1996 from
>   InfoTrac Expanded Academic Index ASAP.

15. Article from an online magazine

> Yeoman, B. (2000, May 22). Into the closet: Can ther-
>   apy make gay people straight? *Salon.com.* Retrieved
>   23 May 2000 from http://www.salon.com/health/
>   feature/2000/05/22/exgay/html

16. Article from an online newspaper

> Hopper, D. (2001, December 4). 'Goner' virus infects
>   PCs worldwide. *Chicage Tribune Internet Edition.*
>   Retrieved December 4, 2001, from
>   http://www.chicagotribune.com/technology/
>   sns-virus?coll=ch%2Dtechnology%2Dhed

17. Article from an online encyclopedia

> Pisani, E. (2001). Africa's struggle against AIDS. *En-*
> *cyclopedia Britannica Online.* Retrieved November
> 17, 2001, from http://members.eb.com/bol/
> topic?tmap_id=4028008map_typ=by

Divide a URL only after a slash or before a period. There is no period after a URL at the end of a citation so that readers will not think the period is part of the URL. For more information, consult the APA Web site at http://www.apastyle.com/elecref.html

III

How to Make Your Writing Clear and Correct

11

Reviewing
the Basics
of Grammar

You do not need an extensive knowledge of grammar in order to write well. What you do need is a basic vocabulary, shared by you and your teachers and other writers, in which you can talk about sentences. Learning grammatical terms and concepts can help you identify and correct sentence fragments, comma splices, and run-on sentences; it can also help you decide where to put commas and semicolons and how to untangle sentences that are marred by dangling modifiers or piled-up prepositional phrases.

A *Quick Look at the Parts of Speech*

The sentence is the basic unit of communication in English. But sentences are, of course, made up of words, each of which can be classified as a *part of speech*. Learning these parts of speech and how they work will help you to understand how sentences operate.

NOUNS are names. A noun may name a person, place, thing, or idea: *Maria, brother, Chicago, beach, shoe, cat, daffodil, iron, courage.*
Most nouns can be made plural (*dog, dogs*) and possessive (my *dog's* name; the *dogs'* fleas). Subjects of sentences are usually nouns.

PRONOUNS replace or refer to nouns. The noun that a pronoun replaces or refers to is called the *antecedent* of that pronoun:

antecedent   pronoun

<u>Paula</u> took three suitcases with <u>her</u> to Vancouver.

English has several different kinds of pronouns; the most frequently used are the *personal pronouns:* I, me, you, she, her, him, it, we, us, they, and them. Other types include *relative pronouns* (that, who, whose, whom, which), *indefinite pronouns* (each, some, many, one, few, everything, and so forth), *demonstrative pronouns* (this, that, these, those), and *interrogative pronouns* (what, who, which, whose).

VERBS say something about the subject of a sentence. They express actions, describe occurrences, or establish states of being.

Action: The umpire <u>called</u> the runner out.

Occurrence: A hush <u>settled</u> over the stadium.

State of being: The umpire <u>was</u> wrong.

A complete sentence always has a main verb. Many verbs combine with *auxiliary* (or *helping*) verbs; the most common auxiliaries are forms of *be, have,* and *do:*

Silvio <u>is taking</u> a course in ballroom dancing. He <u>has taken</u> three lessons already. The instructor <u>did tell</u> him not to give up too soon.

ADJECTIVES describe or limit the meaning of nouns (and sometimes pronouns).

Descriptive adjectives answer the question "what kind?":

red hair, *heavy* load, *expensive* car, *unbelievable* story

Many descriptive adjectives change form to show a comparative and superlative degree:

heavy, heavier, heaviest; expensive, more expensive, most expensive

Limiting adjectives tell "which one" or "how many":

this problem, *any* car, *few* questions, *his* hair

Limiting adjectives do not have comparative or superlative forms.

ADVERBS usually modify verbs, describing *how, when, where,* and *how much* the action of the verb is performed:

Garfield <u>ran</u> *upstairs quickly.* Robert <u>will arrive</u> *soon.*

Some adverbs can modify an adjective or another adverb:

Ian <u>is</u> a *very* cautious driver. He <u>drives</u> *quite* carefully.

Although many adverbs in English are formed by adding -*ly* to an adjective (*happily, expensively*), many others are not: *already, always, seldom, never, now, often, here, there, up, down, inside,* and so forth. Like adjectives, many adverbs change form to indicate the comparative and superlative degree: *carefully, more carefully, most carefully.*

PREPOSITIONS are connecting words. Each of the following prepositions shows a different relation between the noun *stump* and the actions expressed by the verbs:

> The rabbit jumped *over* the stump, ran *around* the stump, sat *on* the stump, hid *behind* the stump, crouched *near* the stump.

The group of words beginning with a preposition and ending with a noun or pronoun (its *object*) is called a *prepositional phrase.* For a list of common prepositions, see Figure 11.1.

CONJUNCTIONS join words or groups of words.

A *coordinating conjunction* (and, but, or, nor, for, yet, so) joins words or word groups of the same kind and same importance:

> Clovis forgot the extra nails *and* sealing tape. He also stepped on the drywall *and* ruined it. We wanted to fire him, *but* his dad owns the business.

about	below	in	since
above	between	into	through
across	by	like	till
after	down	of	to
against	during	off	until
at	except	on	up
before	for	outside	upon
behind	from	over	with

Prepositions made up of more than one word are called *compound prepositions:*

according to	in addition to	in spite of
because of	in back of	instead of
contrary to	in case of	on account of
except for	in front of	out of

FIGURE 11.1 *Common Prepositions*

after	only	till
although	since	unless
as, as if	so as	until
because	so far as	when, whenever
before	so that	whereas
if	though	while

FIGURE 11.2 *Common Subordinating Conjunctions*

A *subordinating conjunction* (if, because, although, when, etc.) joins a dependent (subordinate) group of words to an independent sentence:

If you love me, you will buy me a new car.

I love you *because you are so generous.*

Figure 11.2 gives a list of common subordinating conjunctions.

Conjunctive adverbs are adverbs used as conjunctions or transitional words. The most common are *however, thus, therefore, consequently, indeed, furthermore,* and *nevertheless.*

He used the wrong nails to put up the drywall; **thus,** they popped right out when spring came. His daughter told him to use special nails; **however,** he hated to follow her advice.

P utting the Words Together

Knowing a word's part of speech tells only part of the story. You must understand how the word operates in the pattern or structure of a particular sentence to get the full message.

Basic Sentence Patterns

There are five basic patterns for sentences in English. Each pattern contains a subject and a verb. Depending on the nature of the verb, the pattern may also contain *objects* or *complements* that complete the meaning of the verb.

subject / intransitive verb
        S   V
    Her tires squealed.

subject / transitive verb / direct object
        S   V   DO
    Flying gravel hit the sidewalk.

subject / transitive verb / indirect object / direct object

          S   V   IO   DO

Shana's driving almost gives her father a heart attack.

subject / transitive verb / direct object / object complement

          S   V   D   OC

Shana's driving makes her father nervous.

  S   V   DO   OC

Shana calls her father a big worrywart.

subject / linking verb / subject complement

       S   V   SC

Her father was her driving teacher.

  S   V SC

He usually seems calm, though.

Phrases

A phrase is a string of related words that does *not* include a subject and verb combination. There are several common types of phrases:

1. *Noun phrase.* A noun plus its modifier: *a delicious six-foot submarine sandwich*

   Noun phrases serve as subjects, objects, and complements:

   We ate <u>a delicious six-foot submarine sandwich</u> for lunch. (direct object)

   <u>The delicious six-foot submarine sandwich</u> was too big for three people. (subject)

2. *Prepositional phrase.* A preposition, its object, and the object's modifiers: *with dill pickles.*

   Prepositional phrases can modify nouns or verbs:

   Give me a hamburger <u>with dill pickles</u>. (adjectival phrase, describes "hamburger")

   I'll eat it <u>in the car</u>. (adverbial phrase, tells "where")

3. *Infinitive phrase.* The base form of a verb preceded by *to*, plus any modifiers and complements: *to eat the delicious sandwich.*

   Infinitive phrases can function as nouns, adjectives, or adverbs:

   He wants <u>to eat the F sandwich</u>. (noun, direct object)
   The best thing <u>to have for lunch</u> is a salad. (adjective, identifies "thing")

   I am lucky <u>to have two hours for lunch</u>. (adverb, tells "why")

4. *Gerund phrase.* An *-ing* verb form plus its modifiers and complements: *eating the six-foot sandwich.*

> Gerund phrases are used as nouns:

> <u>Eating the six-foot sandwich</u> took us two hours. (subject)

> We enjoyed <u>eating the six-foot sandwich.</u> (direct object)

5. *Participle phrase.* An *-ing*, *-ed*, or *-en* verb form plus its modifiers and complements: *putting lettuce and mayonnaise on her hamburger, topped with pickles and onions.*

> Participle phrases are used as adjectives:

> The woman <u>putting lettuce and mayonnaise on her hamburger</u> is my mother. (tells "which woman")

> She also likes her hamburgers <u>topped with pickles and onions.</u> (describes "hamburgers")

Clauses

Clauses contain both subjects and verbs plus all their related modifiers and complements. The two kinds of clauses are *independent* (sometimes called *main*) and *dependent* (sometimes called *subordinate*).

Independent Clauses. An independent clause is a complete sentence. It contains a subject and verb plus any objects, complements, and modifiers of that verb. We have already described the typical patterns for independent clauses: see the Basic Sentence Patterns, pages 186–87.

Dependent Clauses. A dependent clause does not sound like a complete sentence when it is spoken or written by itself. It *depends* on an independent clause to complete its meaning. The word that makes all the difference is the subordinating conjunction or relative pronoun that introduces the clause. For instance, suppose a stranger walked up to you and said, "I eat blue bananas." You would understand those words as a complete, though odd, utterance. In contrast, suppose the stranger said, "Since I eat blue bananas" or "That I eat blue bananas" or "After I eat blue bananas." You would think this even more unusual: you would want the stranger to finish the sentence. The words *since, that,* and *after* make the clauses dependent.

Dependent clauses can be used as nouns, adjectives, and adverbs:

> I know <u>who ate that banana</u>. (noun, direct object)
>
> <u>Why he ate it</u> does not concern me. (noun, subject)
>
> The lawyer <u>whose donut you ate</u> is famous. (adjective, identifies "which lawyer")
>
> The things <u>we try most to forget</u> are the things <u>we always remember</u>. (adjective clauses, identify "which things")
>
> <u>After Clothilde ate the blue banana</u>, her stomach felt funny. (adverb, tells "when")
>
> The banana was blue <u>because it was a mutation</u>. (adverb, tells "why")

Exercise 11.1

In the following sentences, label parts of speech, phrases, and independent and dependent clauses.

1. Many cures for insomnia exist.
2. Drinking warm milk is a common home remedy for sleeplessness.
3. Milk contains calcium, which is a natural tranquilizer.
4. When you heat the milk, you make the calcium in it easier for your body to absorb.
5. The warm milk cure does not work for everyone.
6. Some people believe in counting sheep.
7. This boring activity quickly makes them drowsy.
8. Others claim that long 19th-century novels will produce sleep efficiently.
9. Alarmed at such barbarism, 19th-century fiction scholars are frantically trying to find alternative sedatives.
10. Their most recent work, which is now in experimental stages, involves Wordsworth's *Prelude*.

12

Punctuating for Clarity and Effectiveness

When we speak, we nod, gesture, change facial expression, and raise and lower the tone and volume of our voice to help communicate the meanings of our words. When we write, the only aids we have are word choice, word order, and punctuation. The conventions for punctuating our written sentences are not numerous, but they are complicated and flexible enough to give some writers more trouble than help.

S *eparating and Connecting*

Punctuation marks have one main function: to signal the separation between ideas. For example, if you want to show that two ideas are completely separate, you put a period or question mark after one and start a new sentence. On the other hand, if you want to show that two parts of a sentence (like the subject and verb) are closely connected, you don't put in any punctuation at all. The following list of punctuation marks describes the amount of separation (from most to least) that you can signal within and between sentences:

- period, question mark, exclamation mark: maximum separation
- semicolon: medium separation
- colon: medium separation (anticipatory)
- dash: medium separation (emphatic)
- comma: minimum separation
- no mark: no separation

As the list suggests, the colon and the dash signal more than just the amount of separation. Their precise uses will be explained later.

Another way of understanding the differences among these punctuation marks is to look at the grammatical units they separate. These units can be divided into two kinds: independent clauses and non-independent elements. You'll remember that an independent clause is a group of words that contains a subject and a verb and can stand alone as a sentence. Non-independent elements include words, phrases, and dependent clauses that do not stand alone as sentences. Figure 12.1 presents the list of punctuation marks arranged according to the grammatical units they separate.

To separate independent clauses   Use **periods, question marks,** or **semicolons**

American novelist Willa Cather was born in Virginia. When she was ten her family moved to Nebraska.

Have you read any of Cather's novels? Many of them deal with the immigrant settlers of the western prairies.

The Cather family settled near the Kansas border; they later moved from the prairie to Red Cloud.

To separate independent clauses   Use **dashes** or **colons**
or to separate non-independent
elements from independent clauses

Cather came to know various immigrant groups who settled on the Divide—a high area of grassy, windblown plains.

The plains area was often affected by harsh conditions: blizzard, droughts, and invasions of insects.

To separate non-independent   Use **commas**
elements from independent clauses

Six years after her family moved to Red Cloud, Cather enrolled in the University of Nebraska.

Planning to study science, Cather, however, turned to writing.

Several of Cather's early novels, such as *My Antonia* and *O Pioneers!*, deal with the people of the prairies.

In 1912 Cather visited the Southwest, an area that influenced her later novels.

FIGURE 12.1 *Using Punctuation to Separate Sentence Elements*

With these differences in mind, we can now look at the specific conventions for using punctuation marks both within and between independent clauses. And we'll begin with the most frequently used mark of punctuation, the comma.

P *unctuation Within Sentences: Using Commas*

Commas are used to set off non-independent elements within sentences. Learn to look at a basic English sentence—with a subject, verb, and completer—as a single structure (an independent clause):

subject	verb	completer
Liz	loves	cleaning the house.

You don't want to separate the three parts of an independent clause with commas. But when you attach non-independent elements (words, phrases, dependent clauses) to this structure, you need to put in commas.

You can add non-independent attachments in three places: before the independent clause, after the independent clause, and in the middle of the independent clause.

(before)   Though it seems odd to most of us, Liz loves cleaning the house.

(after)   Liz loves cleaning the house, a preference we find hard to believe.

(middle)   Liz, who hates to do laundry, loves cleaning the house.

These non-independent additions are usually separated from the independent clause by commas. If you leave the commas out, the reader may be confused or disconcerted, because your punctuation has not marked off where the main (independent) clause begins and ends.

Using Commas to Set Off Beginning Elements

Put a comma after an introductory word or phrase, a dependent clause, or a long phrase that precedes an independent clause. Dependent clauses, you will remember, contain a subject and a verb but do not make complete sense by themselves. (See pages 188 and 207 for more information about dependent clauses.)

After a heavy downpour with lightning and high winds, the yard was littered with branches.

Surprisingly, the roof was still intact.

Before going outside, my roommate checked the basement.

Indeed, he found an inch and a half of water down there.

Because the electricity had gone out, the sump pump quit working.

Sighing heavily, we got out the wet-vac and went to work.

Using Commas to Set Off Ending Elements

Put a comma before a word, phrase, or dependent clause tacked on the end of an independent clause.

The counselor intended to help you, obviously.

Her advice wasn't all that bad, considering the hopelessness of the situation.

Do not be angry with her, whatever you decide to do.

She was completely honest, which suggests she had your best interests at heart.

Dependent clauses that begin with *after, as soon as, before, because, if, since, unless, until,* and *when* are not set off with a comma when they follow an independent clause:

You will feel better after you get a good night's sleep.

But dependent clauses that begin with *although, even though, though,* and *whereas* convey a contrast and are usually set off when they come after an independent clause:

The play seemed to go on for hours, although my watch said it lasted only forty minutes.

Using Commas to Set Off Elements in the Middle

Put commas before and after a word, phrase, or dependent clause that interrupts the flow of thought in an independent clause.

Honesty, in my opinion, should always be tempered with kindness.

Being totally honest is, after all, sometimes an excuse for being cruel.

Winifred, my friend from school, has taught me a lot about etiquette.

A noncommittal remark may be, it seems, the proper response to questions about personal appearance.

George, taking into account my frame of mind, told me that my swimsuit had beautiful colors.

My swimsuit, which is bright red and flaming orange, does fit a bit tightly.

In those last two sentences, the interrupters (the parts between commas) could be dropped out of the sentence without changing the overall meaning, like this:

George told me that my swimsuit had beautiful colors.

My swimsuit does fit a bit tightly.

TIP! You can use this dropout rule to decide whether to enclose an interrupter in commas.

Using Dashes and Parentheses to Set Off Elements

You can also use dashes or parentheses instead of commas to set off non-independent elements.

A *dash* is a comma with clout. Dashes are used for emphasis or variety—to highlight whatever they set off.

In the twentieth century it has become almost impossible to moralize about epidemics—except those which are transmitted sexually.

—Susan Sontag

The real interest rate—the difference between the nominal rate and the rate of inflation—has averaged about 3 to 4 percent over long periods.

—Milton Friedman

If the interrupting material contains commas, dashes will help to make the sentence easier to read:

But when TV is forced upon us, all the things that give it power—intimacy, insularity, intensity—are deadened.

—Jennifer Cowan

TIP! Remember the difference between a hyphen and a dash: Hyphens connect, dashes separate.
On your keyboard, strike two hyphens to make a dash.

Parentheses function just the opposite of dashes. (Parentheses downplay whatever they enclose.) Use parentheses to separate material that is indirectly related or less crucial to the main idea in a sentence.

John Stuart Mill (1806–1873) promoted the idea of women's equality.

Although Ernest has lapses of memory (often forgetting what he went to the store to buy), he is the best auditor in the company.

Using Commas to Separate Items in a Series

Put commas between elements in a series—words, phrases, or short parallel clauses. The comma before the final item (usually before the *and*) is now optional, but we recommend using it.

The restaurant in the elegant shopping mall specialized in fresh fish, lobster, shrimp, clams, and crabs.

We strolled through the mall, looked at expensive clothes, and admired the fountains.

Jeanne lusted for a diamond pin, she panted for a crystal vase, she pined for a chiffon gown, but she bought a pair of pre-torn blue jeans.

TIP! **For variety you can sometimes omit the *and*:**
Some values never go out of style: love, pity, compassion, honesty.

For emphasis, you can replace the commas with *ands*:
We could all be more loving and compassionate and honest and caring.

When writing descriptive modifiers in series, put in a comma only if you could insert the word *and* between the modifiers:

Jeanne loves fresh, creamy lobster thermidor.

You could easily say "fresh *and* creamy." You could not sensibly say "creamy *and* lobster," though. Neither would you say "lobster *and* thermidor." Consider this one:

Jeanne bought pre-torn, stonewashed blue jeans.

You could say "pre-torn *and* stonewashed," so the comma is all right. But you can't reasonably say "stonewashed *and* blue jeans," nor would you say "blue *and* jeans."

Using Semicolons with Items in a Series

If one or more of the items in a series already includes commas or if the individual items are lengthy, *semicolons* will increase the amount of separation and help the reader to sort out the boundaries between items:

> Rich asked me to bring wine, preferably a chablis; baby Swiss cheese; and freshly baked whole wheat rolls.

Using Commas with Dates, Addresses, and Titles

In dates, the year is set off from the rest of the sentence with a pair of commas:

> On May 5, 1993, I'll be moving to Ontario.

If you give only the month and year, you don't need to separate them with a comma:

> July 1997 was an extremely hot month.

The elements in an address or place name are separated by commas, although a zip code is not preceded by a comma:

> My new address will be 4378 Oak Street, Englewood, Colorado 81118.

> Our aunt in Pine Bluff, Arkansas, sent us some gold-plated candlesticks.

If a title follows a name, separate it from the rest of the sentence with a pair of commas:

> The committee chose Delores Sanchez, attorney-at-law, to represent them.

Using Commas to Prevent Confusion

Occasionally you may need to put in a comma simply to make the sentence easier to read:

> The main thing to remember is, do not light a match.

> Everything that we thought could happen, happened.

> Before kicking, a player may want to visualize her target.

TIP! Don't write an unclear sentence and depend on a comma to make it intelligible. If in doubt, rewrite the sentence.

Exercise 12.1

Try your hand at putting commas in the following sentences to separate non-independent elements from the independent clause and to separate elements in series.

1. My father who leads a sheltered life took a dim view of my being arrested.
2. My mother however saw the injustice involved.
3. All students who can't swim must wear life jackets on the canoeing trip.
4. Melvin's cousin who can't swim has decided to stay home.
5. Date rape after all occurs in a culture that still expects men to be assertive and women to be resistant.
6. Before you complete your plans for vacationing at Lake Louise you should make plane reservations.
7. Reservations which may be submitted either by mail or by phone will be promptly acknowledged.
8. Reservations that are not secured by credit card or check will be returned.
9. If you go out please get me some cheese crackers pickles and a case of cola.
10. Anyone who wants the most from a college education must study hard.
11. Maureen who was born November 15 1950 in Santa Fe New Mexico moved to Dallas Texas before she was old enough to ski.
12. Before getting all excited let's find out if the money is real.
13. Irving can't seem to pass math although he studies for hours and hours.
14. My cousin Clarice is the tall willowy red-haired girl with the short bow-legged long-haired dog.
15. Robert Frost tells of a minister who turned his daughter his poetry-writing daughter out on the street to earn a living saying there should be no more books written.

When Not to Use Commas

Remember that commas separate or set off non-independent elements from the rest of the sentence. If you toss in commas whenever you feel the need, you may confuse or mislead your readers. Here are some situations that seem particularly tempting to comma abusers.

1. *When main sentence parts are long.*
   Some writers mistakenly separate the subject from the verb or the verb from the complement. These are required parts of the independent clause and should not be separated from each other.

(misleading)   A lively lecture followed by a good discussion, is entertaining, and instructive.

(clear)   A lively lecture followed by a good discussion is entertaining and instructive.

(misleading)   I was told by several people, that this speaker would be boring.

(clear)   I was told by several people that this speaker would be boring.

In that second example, the dependent clause serves as the completer of the verb *told* and thus should not be set off with a comma.

2. *When a restrictive clause occurs in the sentence.*
   The term *restrictive* means that the modifier is necessary to the meaning of the sentence or is needed to identify the word it modifies.

(restrictive)   People who compose on word processors can use spell checkers to catch their misspellings.

In this example, the modifier "who compose on word processors" identifies the subject of the sentence, "people"; it tells us which people are being talked about.

(nonrestrictive)   Sid, who composes on a word processor, is too lazy to use the spell checker.

In this example with the subject identified as *Sid*, the modifier adds some information but does so without changing the basic meaning of the sentence. Since you could drop the modifier out, you set it off with commas—one before and one after.

3. *When the word* and *appears in the sentence.*
   Some people always put a comma before the word *and*, and they are probably right more than half the time. It's correct to put a comma before *and* when it joins the last item in a series or when it joins independent clauses. But when *and* does not

do either of these things, a comma before it is usually inappropriate.

(nonstandard) His problems with spelling, and his reluctance to proofread make Ned's writing seem illiterate.

(standard) His problems with spelling and his reluctance to proofread make Ned's writing seem illiterate.

P *unctuation Between Sentences*

Most of your writing will consist of multiple independent clauses. To guide your readers through your sentences and paragraphs, you need to mark the places where the independent clauses begin and end. If you don't, your writing will be confusing and difficult to follow.

There are two devices for marking the boundaries of independent clauses: conjunctions and punctuation marks. The rules for using these devices effectively are not complicated, but they offer you several choices that require thought and understanding.

Using Periods and Other End Marks

A period, question mark, or exclamation mark provides the greatest amount of separation between independent clauses. Each of these marks tells the reader to come to a full stop.

Use a *period* to end sentences that make statements or give mild commands:

Professional tennis players keep their eye on the ball until the point of impact with the racket.

Keep your head down, and swing through the ball.

Also use a period to close an indirect question, one which reports a question instead of asking it directly:

The players wondered whether the tournament will start on time.

Many parents ask if their children need individual tutoring.

Use a *question mark* to end a direct question. Direct questions often begin with an interrogative word (like *who, when, what, how, why,* and so forth) and usually have an inverted word order, with the verb in front of the subject.

When will the tournament start?

Does my child need individual tutoring?

Use *exclamations points* to end sentences that express very strong feelings or deserve special emphasis.

> O kind missionary, O compassionate missionary, leave China! Come home and convert these Christians!
>
> —Mark Twain, "The United States of Lyncherdom"

> I'm mad as hell, and I'm not going to take it anymore!
>
> —Paddy Chayefsky, *Network*

But don't use an exclamation point just to punch up an ordinary sentence; instead, write a good emphatic sentence.

(ineffective)   LeRoy was in a terrible accident!

(improved)   LeRoy, whose motorcycle collided with a semi on US 51, lies near death from head injuries.

Using Coordinating Conjunctions and Commas

To mark the boundary between two independent clauses, you can use a coordinating conjunction (*and, but, or, nor, for, yet,* and *so*) with a comma before it.

> Children's reactions to grief vary, *yet* educators have found a well-defined set of common responses.

> Children intuitively know something is wrong, *and* they fill in the gaps with their fantasy thinking.

> Educators must pay attention to the warning signs, *for* the key to successful grief counseling is early intervention.

> Children at this age are interested in tangible things and want to know the facts about death, *but* they are also interested in causality and want to know why someone has died.

Notice, there are three coordinating conjunctions in that last example, but a comma precedes only one of them. The *ands* connect compound verb phrases ("are interested in *and* want to know"), not independent clauses the way the *but* does. Thus, a comma before a coordinating conjunction signals your readers that another complete sentence is coming up.

If the independent clauses are short and parallel, you can use the coordinating conjunction without the comma:

> Adults seek emotional help but children do not.

TIP! If the independent clauses are short and parallel in structure, separate with commas for stylistic effect.

> We shall fight on the beaches, we shall fight on the landing grounds, we shall fight in the fields and in the streets, we shall fight in the hills; we shall never surrender.
>
> —Winston Churchill

Using Semicolons

A *semicolon* functions very much like a period but doesn't provide as much separation. Thus, you can use a semicolon between two independent clauses that are closely related in thought.

> Sebastian Lareau must rethink his strategy; he is losing more games than he's winning.

> Perhaps he needs better equipment; a wider racquet and some lightweight tennis shoes might help him.

You should also use a semicolon to separate two independent clauses, even though they appear to be connected with a conjunctive adverb *(therefore, nevertheless, consequently, then, thus, however, indeed, furthermore, besides, otherwise, moreover, hence, meanwhile, instead)*.

> Practicing more might help Sebastian; however, he already practices four hours a day.

> He should skip the next tournament; then he and his coach can decide how to improve his game.

For more on conjunctive adverbs, see page 203.

Notice that when independent clauses are connected with a coordinating conjunction *(and, but, or, for, nor, yet, so)*, you do not need a semicolon. A comma is enough.

> Practicing more might help Sebastian, but he already practices four hours a day.

> He should skip the next tournament, and he and his coach can then decide how to improve his game.

TIP! Memorize the seven coordinating conjunctions—*and, but, or, for, nor, yet, so*—so that you won't be fooled into mistaking a conjunctive adverb for a coordinating conjunction.

Both clauses connected by a semicolon should be independent clauses.

(nonstandard)	I thought surely Lareau would win the tournament; although I didn't bet any money on him.
(standard)	I thought surely Lareau would win the tournament, although I didn't bet any money on him.
(standard)	I thought surely Lareau would win the tournament; I didn't bet any money on him, though.

Using Colons

You can use a *colon* to separate independent clauses, but the colon marks more than a separation. It also signals that an explanation or summary is coming. So use a colon between independent clauses only when the second clause summarizes or explains the first, as these examples demonstrate:

John Merrick, the Elephant Man, was not a pretty sight: his forehead and the right side of his face were so hideously deformed that he always wore a large bag over his head.

The students had an inspired idea: they would publish a course guide for next year's class.

If the second clause poses a question, begin with a capital letter:

Our policy makers should ask themselves this question: Are we doing everything we can to reduce poverty?

You can also use a colon after a single independent clause to call attention to a list or a quotation.

You will need the following supplies for this course: three camel's hair brushes, one 15-by-30-inch watercolor pad, and ten tubes of paints.

Oscar Wilde's epigrams are often thought-provoking: "The truth is rarely pure," he said, "and never simple."

M *arking Sentence Boundaries Clearly*

If you run independent clauses together without any punctuation or with only a comma, you may confuse some readers and annoy others. Sentences that are run together with no conjunction or no punctuation are called *fused* or *run-on sentences*. Here is an example:

(run-on)   Oubykh is a highly complex language it has eighty-two consonants but only three vowels.

Sentences that are separated by just a comma are called *comma splices*. A comma alone is not enough to divide independent clauses.

(comma splice)   Almost all languages change in one way or another, the written form of Icelandic is a rare exception.

Using Conjunctive Adverbs and Semicolons

Only coordinating conjunctions—*and, but, or, nor, for, yet, so*—can link two independent clauses with just a comma. If you use another connective word with a comma, you will write a comma splice:

(comma splice)   We read our papers aloud first, then we discussed them.

Other connective words—also known as *conjunctive adverbs*—may seem like coordinating conjunctions, but they are not. Figure 12.2 provides a list of the most commonly used conjunctive adverbs.

One way to tell a conjunctive adverb from a coordinating conjunction is to see if you can reasonably move the word

also	however	nevertheless	still
besides	indeed	next	then
consequently	instead	nonetheless	therefore
finally	likewise	otherwise	thus
furthermore	meanwhile	similarly	hence

FIGURE 12.2   *Commonly Used Conjunctive Adverbs*

around in the sentence. If you can move it, it's a conjunctive adverb:

> We read the poem first; *then* we analyzed it.
>
> We read the poem first; we *then* analyzed it.
>
> We read the poem first; we analyzed it *then*.

If you use a conjunctive adverb between independent clauses, you must put a semicolon in front of it:

> Learning a language is a challenging experience; therefore, a learner must be persistent and hardworking.
>
> Children pick up languages easily; however, the older we get, the harder it becomes to learn a new language.

Many common transitional expressions also act like conjunctive adverbs:

as a result	in addition	of course
for example	in fact	on the other hand

You should put a semicolon in front of these expressions when you use them between two independent clauses:

> Language acquisition is natural; in fact, every normal human child learns to speak at least one native language.

Revising Run-Ons and Comma Splices

You can revise these two sentence boundary problems—*run-ons* and *comma splices*—in a number of ways. You have to decide which method fits your writing situation.

1. *Use a semicolon:*
   Oubykh is a highly complex language; it has eighty-two consonants but only three vowels.
2. *Use a period and a capital:*
   Almost all languages change in one way or another. The written form of Icelandic is a rare exception.
3. *Use a comma plus a coordinating conjunction:*
   Oubykh is a highly complex language, for it has eighty-two consonants but only three vowels.
4. *Use a semicolon plus a conjunctive adverb:*
   Almost all languages change in one way or another; however, the written form of Icelandic is a rare exception.

5. *Use subordination to eliminate one independent clause:*
   Although almost all languages change in one way or another, the written form of Icelandic is a rare exception.

Exercise 12.2

Revise any run-ons or comma splices in the following sentences. You may be able to revise them in more than one way.

1. Many people are left-handed, some of them belong to an organization called Lefthanders International.

2. Lefthanders International fights discrimination against the left-handed, it informs the public about the special problems of left-handed people.

3. More men than women are left-handed hand preference doesn't become established until about the age of six.

4. The right side of the brain controls the sense of space, in addition it governs the left side of the body.

5. Left-handed people can drive or sew or paint as well as any right-hander, still it is not easy for them to use many ordinary tools and mechanical gadgets.

6. Stores now sell objects designed especially for left-handed people these include watches, scissors, cameras, and pencil sharpeners.

7. Creativity is not the same thing as intellect, in fact there is no relation between intelligence and originality.

8. Intelligence tests measure knowledge and skill, however they do not accommodate inventiveness.

9. Creative people ask questions intelligent people want to know the answers.

10. Creative scientists have a lot in common with creative artists, they both prefer things to be complex instead of simple.

Revising Exercise 12.3

Rewrite the following paragraph; revise the six run-on sentences and comma splices by using the methods described in this chapter.

WATER SUPPLY

Years ago river water and rain water provided all the water people needed. The farmer working in the fields used river water, the people in the towns used rain water. There was no shortage in the water supply, however, population growth and town development have changed the situation. Nowadays geologists are looking for new underground reserves, engineers are trying to find cheap ways to get drinking water from the salty sea. Newspaper advertisements ask people to save water towns have passed ordinances against watering lawns in the summer, farmers who have no irrigation system fear a dry winter. Townsfolk once disliked the winter rains, they now wait for the clouds that will bring the needed water.

R ecognizing and Revising Sentence Fragments

A *sentence fragment,* as the term suggests, is only part of a sentence but punctuated as if it were a complete sentence. Many accomplished writers use fragments for emphasis, or simply for convenience, as in the portions we have italicized in the following examples:

Man is the only animal that blushes. *Or needs to.*

—Mark Twain

As a rule, more thought goes into the purchase of a stereo than a tattoo. *With predictable results.*

—John Gray

If there is to be a new etiquette, it ought to be based on honesty, mutual respect and responsiveness to each other's real needs. *Regardless of sex.*

—Lois Gould

Although professional writers sometimes use grammatically incomplete sentences for emphasis and variety, the writing that you do in school and in business should be in complete sentences. To make sure that you are not writing sentence fragments, you first need to be able to recognize a complete sentence. Then, you need to know how to revise the fragments.

Recognizing a Complete Sentence

A group of words must meet three grammatical tests to be a complete sentence:

1. It must contain a subject
2. It must contain a verb

3. It must contain at least one clause that does not begin with a subordinating word

Groups of words that do not pass all three tests are fragments and need to be revised.

TIP! A clause is a group of words that has a subject and a verb. Subordinating words—such as *if, when, although, who, which, that*—turn independent clauses into dependent fragments

---

Subjects and Verbs

Look at the following examples, and notice the difference between the ones that contain a subject and a verb (the sentences) and the ones that don't (the fragments). Subjects are underlined once and verbs are double underlined.

(sentence)	My <u>uncle</u> in New Jersey <u>has worked</u> in a zinc mine most of his life.
(fragment)	My uncle in New Jersey.
(sentence)	This <u>mine</u> in New Jersey <u>produces</u> the richest zinc ore in the world.
(fragment)	Produces the richest zinc ore in the world.

Dependent Clauses

Some groups of words may contain a subject and a verb but do not pass the third test for grammatical completeness: they need at least one clause that does not begin with a subordinating word. Look at the following examples to see the difference:

(fragment)	When I was twelve years old.
(sentence)	I started mining when I was twelve years old.
(fragment)	Who worked here forty years ago or more.
(sentence)	On the walls I can read the names of miners who worked here forty years ago or more.
(fragment)	Although mining may not be the easiest job in the world.
(sentence)	Although mining may not be the easiest job in the world, I don't think it's dangerous.
(fragment)	Because the mine is never too hot or too cold.
(sentence)	I like working underground because the mine is never too hot or too cold.

after	in order that	when, whenever
although	once	where, wherever
as	since	whereas
as if	so that	whether
because	thanA	which
before	that	while
even though	though	who, whom, whose
ever since	unless	whoever
how	until	why
if, even if	what, whatever	

FIGURE 12.3 *Subordinating Words*

Word groups that begin with a subordinating word are fragments because they *depend* on another statement to complete the thought. *When I was twelve years old* leaves the reader hanging, expecting to find out what happened when the writer was twelve years old. These word groups are called *dependent clauses*. Unlike independent clauses, which can stand alone as sentences, dependent clauses don't make complete sense by themselves. Figure 12.3 gives you a list of words that begin dependent clauses. Whenever you begin a sentence with one of these words, be sure to attach it to another clause so that the whole thought sounds complete.

Verbal Phrase Fragments

Some groups of words that appear to be grammatically complete may be verbal phrases. These fragments usually begin with a word that looks and sounds like a verb but isn't. Some words ending in *-ing* (working, repairing, using) or with *to* in front of them (to love, to produce) name actions but are not complete verbs. Notice the differences in the following examples (subjects are underlined once and verbs are double underlined):

(verbal phrase)	Working underground for eighteen months.
(sentence)	<u>Daniel Flores</u> from Argentina <u>has been</u> working underground for eighteen months.
(verbal phrase)	To love his job in the mine.
(sentence)	<u>He</u> <u>seems</u> to love his job in the mine.
(verbal phrase)	Repairing machinery in the mine.
(sentence)	<u>Richard Vreeland</u> <u>has worked</u> for five years repairing machinery in the mine.

(verbal phrase)	Using modern machinery.
(verbal phrase)	To produce the richest zinc ore in the world.
(sentence)	The <u>miners</u> <u>work</u> nearly 2,000 feet under the ground, using modern machinery to produce the richest zinc ore in the world.

Revising Sentence Fragments

In general, you can revise a fragment by combining it with an independent clause or by turning it into an independent clause. The following examples will show you how to eliminate sentence fragments from your writing:

1. A group of words that lacks a subject or verb can often be joined to the independent clause that comes before or after it, like this:

(fragment)	A steeplejack paints and fixes church roofs, clocks, and steeples. *The highest parts of tall church buildings.*
(revised)	A steeplejack paints and fixes church roofs, clocks, and steeples—the highest parts of tall church buildings.
(fragment)	*The entire O'Neil family, Jerry O'Neil, his wife Beverly and their two sons and the sons' wives.* They all work as steeplejacks.
(revised)	The entire O'Neil family, Jerry O'Neil and his wife Beverly and their two sons and the sons' wives, all work as steeplejacks.

2. Dependent clauses can be attached to an nearby independent clause or rewritten as complete sentences:

(fragment)	*Because many old church buildings became damaged by wind and water.* Their roofs began to leak, the paint peeled, and the decorations wore off.
(revised)	Because many old church buildings became damaged by wind and water, their roofs began to leak, the paint peeled, and the decorations wore off.
(fragment)	The church members then decided to hire someone to make repairs. *Which can be very expensive.*
(revised)	The church members then decided to hire someone to make repairs, which can be very expensive.
(revised)	The church members then decided to hire someone to make repairs. Such work can be very expensive.

3. Verbal phrases can be combined with an independent clause or turned into separate sentences:

(fragment)   The O'Neils enjoy working together. *Traveling around the country. Finding jobs as they go.*

(revised)   The O'Neils enjoy working together, traveling around the country and finding jobs as they go.

(revised)   The O'Neils enjoy working together. They travel around the country, finding jobs as they go.

TIP!   **It's OK to use fragments in asking and answering questions, even in formal writing.**
When should the reform begin? At once.
How? By removing self-serving politicians from office.

Revising Exercise 12.4

Rewrite the following paragraphs, correcting any fragments that you find. The first one has three fragments in it.

1.   Next year I am going to cooking school. I got the idea from a friend of my brother's. A business manager for a cruise line. He said that cruise ships build their reputations on the meals they serve. Which must be superbly prepared and elegantly presented. Consequently, cruise lines are always looking for chefs. Trying to find people who are well trained as expert cooks.

2.   There are many ways to exercise and have fun at the same time, Such as, swimming, hiking, or playing tennis. But Some people are exercise puritans, Insisting that exercise must be serious and painful. My next door neighbor, for example, makes fun of me because I prefer walking to jogging. But I walk several miles every day. While he jogs only once or twice a week. I figure that exercise isn't going to help if a person doesn't do it regularly. So why not find something enjoyable to do?

3.   To do their work, steeplejacks have to sit on seats that hang down from ropes. Attached to the very tops of the church steeples. If you watch them at work, you can see them. Swinging gently in midair. While they repair a roof. Or replace the old numbers on a church clock. With newly painted ones. Would you have the nerve to do that kind of work? Probably not. Most people wouldn't.

C *oping with Apostrophes*

Apostrophes probably cause more problems than any other mark of punctuation. Many experienced writers feel shaky about using them. If you study carefully the various uses of the apostrophe, you should be able to straighten them out.

1. Use an apostrophe plus *s* with singular nouns to show possession.

the length of the rope	the rope's length
the star of the show	the show's star
a lease of one year	a year's lease

As you can see from the above examples, the *'s* ending is a substitute for a phrase beginning with *of* that shows possession.

2. Do not use an apostrophe to form the plural of a noun.
You may have problems with the apostrophe plus *s* ending because the letter *s* gets pressed into service in a number of ways. Its most common use is to show that a noun is plural (more than one of whatever the noun names). No apostrophe is needed:

three professors

two encyclopedias

two athletes

3. Use an apostrophe with plurals that are possessive.

three professors' letters of recommendation

two encyclopedias' different interpretations

two athletes' difficulties with drugs

You do not need another *s* after the apostrophe in the above examples because it can't be pronounced aloud.
In deciding where to place an apostrophe to show possession with plural nouns, first write down the plural form. Then add just an apostrophe to those plurals ending in *s*.

Singular	*Plural*	*Plural Possessive*
lady	ladies	ladies' lunch
society	societies	societies' problems
bartender	bartenders	bartenders' tips

212 Chapter 12 *Punctuating for Clarity and Effectiveness*

But if the plural does *not* end in *s*, then you have to add an apostrophe plus *s:*

child	children	children's clothes
man	men	men's fashions

4. Use an apostrophe plus *s* with singular nouns ending in *s.*

the boss's daughter	Janis's singing
Keats's poetry	the albatross's curse

If pronouncing the added 's would be awkward, some writers use only the apostrophe. Either use is acceptable.

Jesus' teachings	Jesus's teachings
Socrates' death	Socrates's death

5. Do not use an apostrophe with any of the possessive pronouns. You won't even be tempted to use an apostrophe with most of the possessive pronouns—*his, hers, theirs, ours, yours.* But one of these pronouns—*its*—causes considerable grief because it gets confused with the contraction *it's.* Notice the difference:

That dog just bit *its* kindly owner.

It's an ungrateful beast.

TIP! If you simply can't keep track of the difference between *it's* and *its*, the only safe thing to do is to quit using the contraction entirely. Then all you have to remember is that *its* never takes an apostrophe.

---

6. Use an apostrophe to show omissions in contractions and numbers.
   The apostrophe goes where the letters are left out, not where the two words are joined.

   does not = doesn't (not *does'nt*)

   will not = won't (not *wo'nt*)

   would not = wouldn't (not *would'nt*)

   class of '75 = class of 1975

7. If you wish, use an apostrophe in forming the plural of numerals, letters, words used as words, and abbreviations.

   Your 5's look like 8's to me.

   This paragraph has three *very*'s in it.

Her last name contains three m's.

The 1960's were years of great social change.

He claims to have three Ph.D.'s.

You may also correctly add the s with no apostrophe.

Your 5s look like 8s to me.

The 1960s were years of great social change.

Exercise 12.5

Copy the following sentences, inserting an apostrophe or an apostrophe plus s as needed.

1. Many adults distrust of computers stems from lack of understanding the way that the machines function.
2. Childrens love of computers may indicate that they are not concerned with the machines internal workings.
3. Grade school teachers are often surprised by their students achievements on computers.
4. One students accomplishments were the main topic of talk in the teachers lounge.
5. Students attendance improves when they are allowed to do assignments in class on computers.
6. When he was given a computer, James attitude changed completely, greatly to his mothers surprise.
7. "For goodness sake," his mother exclaimed. "I used to question James intelligence."
8. Many of societys problems have been eased by computer use.
9. But the computers usefulness is offset by problems caused by programmers mistakes.
10. A computers mistake can ruin a persons credit, for instance.

Exercise 12.6

Using *its* or *it's*, fill in the blanks in the following sentences with the correct form.

1. The army forces _____ recruits to do aerobic exercise.
2. Undoubtedly _____ it's _____ a good idea to keep the soldiers fit.
3. The military needs _____ its _____ forces in fighting shape.

4. To gain ___its___ full benefits, exercise must be strenuous.
5. In order to exercise regularly, ___it's___ helpful to have a drill sergeant to force you.

P unctuating Quotations

If you want to report the actual words that someone has spoken or written, you need to enclose those words in *quotation marks*. It is customary to use a *reporting tag* to identify the person being quoted: "she said" or "he replied" or "Darwin observed" or some such phrase. For variety, these reporting tags can appear at the beginning, in the middle, or at the end of the quoted material.

Identifying Quotations at the Beginning

Put a comma after the reporting tag and before the opening quotation marks:

> Samuel Johnson observed, "Marriage has many pains, but celibacy has no pleasures."

If you quote a full sentence, capitalize the first word in that sentence, unless it blends into the sentence that introduces it:

> In his essay on punctuation Lewis Thomas writes, "The commas are the most useful and usable of all the stops."

> It is Thomas's opinion that "exclamation points are the most irritating of all."

Punctuating the Ends of Quotations

If the quotation ends the sentence, put a period, a question mark, an exclamation mark, or a dash before the final quotation marks:

> The mayor announced, "Our landfills are completely full."

> The city manager asked, "What are we going to do?"

> A concerned citizen shouted, "We *must* begin recycling!"

> One board member smugly observed, "I'm recycling already, but you folks—"

The dash in this last example indicates that the speaker stopped in mid-sentence—or was interrupted.

If a question mark or an exclamation mark belongs to the whole sentence, not just to the quoted material, put this mark after the closing quotation marks:

> Did the mayor actually say, "Let's postpone this issue"?
>
> I could not believe that the mayor said to the council, "Let's table this recycling business tonight"!

If you are not reporting the exact words that were spoken, you don't need quotation marks:

> Did the mayor actually want to postpone recycling?
>
> He told the city council he wanted to table the recycling proposal.

Identifying Quotations in the Middle

If your reporting tag interrupts a sentence, set it off with commas:

> "I hope," sniffed the mayor, "that we can remain civil about this matter."

If a complete sentence comes before the reporting tag, put a period after the reporting tag and capitalize the first word of the rest of the quoted material:

> "You cretin!" shouted the concerned citizen. "Can't you see that this is a pressing issue?"
>
> "What do you mean?" asked the mayor. "I don't feel any great need for haste."

If the reporting tag is placed between two independent clauses that are separated by a semicolon, the semicolon follows the tag:

> "Everyone needs to calm down," pleaded the city manager; "we must try to discuss this issue rationally."

Identifying Quotations at the End

If the quoted sentence would ordinarily end in a period, put a comma before the quotation marks:

> "We must come to some decision tonight," said the city manager.

But use a question mark or an exclamation mark when it is appropriate:

> "Why do we have to decide tonight?" the mayor asked.
>
> "Because time is running out!" yelled the manager.

In these cases, do not add a comma as well.

Punctuating Dialogue

When you are writing dialogue or reporting a conversation, you should start a new paragraph when there is a change in speaker, no matter how brief the quoted remarks may be:

> "I saw you listening to those two little creeps," she hissed. "Were they talking about me?"
>
> "I don't know," I said.
>
> "You don't know! Why not?"
>
> "They were speaking Spanish."

Quoting Within Quotations

When you need to put quotation marks around material that is *already* inside quotation marks, use single quotation marks around the material inside.

> Jim whispered, "I think I heard one of them say, 'We launch the attack as soon as it gets dark.'"

Notice that both single and double quotation marks go outside the period.

Using Quotation Marks to Punctuate Titles

Put quotation marks around the titles of short works—such as the titles of short stories and poems that are usually part of a longer work like a book or magazine:

> "A Cap for Steve"—a short story by Morley Callaghan
>
> "We Real Cool"—a poem by Gwendolyn Brooks
>
> "Not Poor, Just Broke"—an essay by Dick Gregory
>
> "Your Reflex Systems"—a chapter in a book by Jonathan Miller

Exercise 12.7

Copy the following paragraphs, inserting quotation marks in the appropriate places.

Motherhood is not for every woman, moaned Michelle, as she wiped up the milk. Why doesn't anyone ever tell you that having children can be hazardous to your health?

Do you mean your mental health? inquired her friend Laverne, who was holding the dripping Billy at arm's length.

" That too! snapped Michelle, stripping off the milk-soaked T-shirt. This makes the third time today I've changed Billy's clothes. And it's not even afternoon yet!"

" But he's so cute, observed Maureen, glancing at the grinning Billy who was already planning more mischief. Isn't he your pride and joy? "

" Maybe, if I live through his childhood, sighed Billy's mother, I may be able to see some profit in this venture. But right now I agree with Roseanne, When my husband comes home at night, if those kids are still alive—I've done my job. " '

U *sing Italics (Underlining)*

Italic type slants upward to the right. We use *italics* to set off words and phrases for emphasis or special consideration. Some word processors and printers can produce italic type. In handwritten or typed papers, you underline material that would be italicized if set in type.

Italicizing Titles and Names

We generally italicize (or underline) the titles of long or complete works. Figure 12.4 gives you a list of examples of titles to italicize.

The titles of sacred books, such as the Bible or the Koran, and of public documents, like the Bill of Rights or the Constitution,

Books	**Long Poems**
The Dance of the Happy Shades	*The Odyssey*
The Internet for Dummies	*In Memoriam*
Plays	**Films**
The Glass Menagerie	*The Sweet Hereafter*
A Midsummer Night's Dream	*Citizen Kane*
Long Musical Works	**Paintings and Sculptures**
Gershwin's *Rhapsody in Blue*	Rodin's *The Thinker*
the Beatles' *Abbey Road*	the *Mona Lisa*
Television and Radio Programs	**Magazines and Newspapers**
The West Wing	the *St. Louis Post Dispatch*
As It Happens	*Entertainment Weekly*

FIGURE 12.4 *Titles to Italicize*

are not italicized or underlined. The titles of shorter works—such as poems, short stories, songs, and essays—are enclosed in quotation marks: "My Last Duchess," "Girls and Boys," "Dancing in the Dark," "On Keeping a Notebook." The same is true for sections of works, such as chapter titles ("The Rise of the Middle Class") or titles of magazine articles ("An Interview with Adrienne Clarkson").

Italicizing Words and Phrases

We underline (italicize) foreign words and phrases that have not yet been adopted into English:

> Standing *en pointe* is useful only if the candy bars are on the top shelf.

Words and phrases used so frequently that they have become part of the English language—for example, "pasta," "bon voyage," "habeas corpus" and "karate"—do not need to be underlined or italicized. Most dictionaries will tell you whether the words you want to use should be underlined or marked for italics.

We also underline (or italicize) words, letters, or numbers referred to as words:

> In current usage, the pronouns *he*, *him*, and *his* outnumber *she*, *her*, and *hers* by a ratio of almost 4 to 1.

> Some people have trouble pronouncing the letter *r*, especially when it follows an *i* or an *a*.

Using Italics for Emphasis

Underlining (or italics) can add emphasis to written language:

> We want our freedom *today*, not tomorrow.

But this means of adding emphasis is obvious and easy to overdo. It is usually more effective to create emphasis through sentence structure and word choice.

U *sing Hyphens*

1. Use a *hyphen* to connect two or more words that go together to modify a noun.

hard-hearted lover	up-to-date sources
lighter-than-air balloon	world-renowned pianist

Do not hyphenate the modifiers when they come after the noun.

lover with a hard heart	sources that are up to date
balloon lighter than air	pianist who is world renowned

Do not use a hyphen between an *-ly* adverb and the word it modifies:

a hopelessly dull person	a happily divorced couple

2. Use a hyphen to connect *all-, self-, ex-,* and *-elect* to other words.

self-esteem	ex-wife	all-important	governor-elect

Never use a hyphen with the following words:

yourself	himself	itself
themselves	herself	oneself
ourselves	myself	selfless

3. Use a hyphen when spelling out fractions and compound numbers from twenty-one to ninety-nine.

People over fifty-five make up almost two-fifths of the population.

4. Use a hyphen to avoid ambiguous or awkward combinations of letters. For instance, *re-creation* means "create anew"; the hyphen distinguishes it from *recreation,* which means "a refreshing or diverting activity." Words like *anti-inflammatory, cross-stitch,* and *bell-like* are easier to read with the hyphens.

5. Consult a dictionary about compound words: some are two words, some are hyphenated, some are written as a single word. Usage changes rapidly and is unpredictable. Even compounds that begin with the same word are treated differently: blue cheese, blue-collar, blueprint.

6. Use a hyphen to divide a word at the end of a line of type. Words can be divided only between syllables. Consult your dictionary when in doubt. The tendency today is to *avoid* dividing words if at all possible.

13

Working with Verbs

You probably remember from somewhere back in junior high school that in English subjects have to agree with their verbs in *number,* meaning a singular subject takes a singular verb and a plural subject takes a plural verb. And then lots of people need to watch their irregular verbs. Most of the time getting your verbs right is easy, but complications can occur.

G *etting Subjects and Verbs to Agree*

When the Bible declares that "The wages of sin is death," we're not supposed to question—either grammatically or theologically. But if you write, "The wages at McDonald's is lousy," you'll likely get corrected by someone saying your subject–verb agreement is off. There's no point in protesting the inequity of this double standard. Just grant poetic license to the Bible and concentrate on making your own subjects and verbs agree.

Singular Verb Forms

In English the only singular verb form occurs in the present tense. We add an *-s* or *-es* ending to a present-tense verb when its subject is a singular noun or the pronoun *he, she,* or *it.*

Our biology <u>instructor</u> <u>wants</u> us to write three lab reports a week. <u>She</u> <u>expects</u> them to be handed in on Friday.

My <u>roommate</u> <u>washes</u> his hair twice a day. <u>He</u> <u>flosses</u> his teeth after every meal.

That <u>color</u> <u>looks</u> good on you; <u>it</u> <u>matches</u> your eyes.

Two verbs—*have* and *be*—are exceptions to this rule. *Have* changes to *has*, and *be* changes to *is*.

> My <u>uncle</u> <u>has</u> false teeth.

> <u>He</u> <u>is</u> only thirty-five years old.

Be is the only verb that has a singular form in the past tense. Use *was* with *I*, with singular nouns, or with *he, she,* or *it*.

> <u>I</u> <u>was</u> late for class yesterday.

> My <u>teacher</u> <u>was</u> not happy with me.

Otherwise, use *were*.

> The other <u>students</u> <u>were</u> all on time.

Most of the time subject–verb agreement poses no problem. With a plural subject *(wages)*, supply a plural verb *(are)*, and everybody's happy:

> The <u>wages</u> at McDonald's <u>are</u> lousy.

Only it's not always that simple because we don't always use the normal *subject-followed-by-verb* sentence pattern. In this chapter, we'll explain a few of the less-than-simple situations. For variety, we shuffle the order around so that sometimes the verb gets ahead of the subject—or sometimes modifiers crop up between the subject and verb, causing confusion. Another construction you need to watch out for involves *expletives*, words which often pose alluringly like subjects, even though they're not. You also have to be alert for collective nouns and indefinite pronouns, which can sometimes lead to agreement problems.

Subject–Verb Reversals in Questions

You naturally expect one of the first words in a sentence to be the *subject*—what the sentence is about. Usually the *verb* follows, telling what's going on with the subject or what the situation is, like this:

> These <u>papayas</u> <u>taste</u> delicious.

But questions often reverse this normal order:

> Where <u>are</u> the <u>papayas</u>?

TIP! **To find the subject, turn the question into a statement.**
If you'll make a statement out of a question, you'll usually end up with the subject at the beginning of the sentence:

The papayas are where.

As you can see, the reversal won't necessarily make sense. But the real subject becomes clear—*papayas* (plural)—so the verb should be *are* (plural). No problem.

The going sometimes gets tricky when the questions get longer, like this:

(wrong)   Which version of the ending has the show's producers decided to use?

If you turn that into a statement, you can see that the agreement is off:

(wrong)   The show's producers has decided to use which version of the ending.

Since the subject—*producers*—clearly is plural, you need a plural verb:

The show's producers have decided to use which version of the ending.

(right)   Which version of the ending have the show's producers decided to use?

If you have difficulty with agreement in questions, get into the habit of quickly changing them into statements as part of your editing process. Once you get the subject and verb in the normal order, you're not likely to go wrong.

Subject–Verb Reversals for Style

Sometimes you may deliberately put a verb ahead of its subject as a stylistic device. If not overdone, this technique is a dandy. The variation from the expected sentence pattern automatically produces emphasis:

(wrong)   In poverty, injustice, and discrimination lie the cause of many social problems.

But just glance at that sentence again. What is the subject? Not *poverty, injustice, and discrimination*: those words are the object of the preposition *in*. Since a noun can't serve as the subject *and* as an object in the same sentence, you need to look elsewhere. The subject actually is *cause*—and *the cause lie* doesn't sound right. It should be *the cause lies* or *the causes lie*. You could change either word, but both words have to be singular or both plural to make subjects and verbs agree.

(right)   In poverty, injustice, and discrimination lies the cause of many social problems.

(right)   In poverty, injustice, and discrimination lie the causes of many social problems.

Of course, we know that most people who aren't composition teachers probably wouldn't be much bothered by the lack of agreement in that sentence. But see if you pick up the problem in this less complex construction:

(wrong)   Here comes the defending champions.

Of course it should be,

(right)   Here <u>come</u> the defending <u>champions</u>.

TIP! *Here* and *There* can never be subjects.
    If a sentence begins with either of those words, turn it around, find the true subject, and make the verb agree.

          (right)   There <u>are</u> a few <u>flaws</u> in your plan.
          (right)   Here <u>is</u> a small <u>case</u> of larceny.

Agreement with Intervening Modifiers

Sometimes even when the subject–verb order is normal, a modifier gets sandwiched between them and confuses things, like this:

(wrong)   The seriousness of these injustices have been revealed to the public.

Injustices have been revealed sounds fine, but the subject of that sentence happens to be *seriousness*, with *injustices* serving as the object of the preposition *of* (which means that it can't also be the subject). So, how does *The seriousness have been revealed* sound? Not good, since *seriousness* is clearly singular. The sentence should read,

(right)   The <u>seriousness</u> of these injustices <u>has been revealed</u> to the public.

Because this problem won't be revealed by simply turning the sentence around, let's look at a few more examples. You have to recognize the intervening modifiers and take them out in order to get the subject and verb next to each other. Try this sentence:

(wrong)   The boredom of dusting furniture, folding laundry, cleaning floors, cooking meals, and washing dishes have driven many women to drink.

Doesn't sound bad, does it? But actually all those plural-sounding tasks are objects of the preposition *of*. The true subject is quite singular—*boredom*. The sentence should read,

(right)   The <u>boredom</u> of dusting furniture, folding laundry, cleaning floors, cooking meals, and washing dishes <u>has driven</u> many women to drink.

Here's one more:

(wrong)   Ling's reasons for developing his gymnastics style was essentially the same as Jahn's—to promote nationalism.

Style was sounds fine. But *style* is not the subject. It's the object of the gerund *developing;* the subject is *reasons*. So, *reasons was* can't be right. The verb needs to be plural:

(right)   Ling's <u>reasons</u> for developing his gymnastics style <u>were</u> essentially the same as Jahn's—to promote nationalism.

Agreement with Compound Subjects

Sentences having *compound subjects* (meaning more than one subject) usually cause no bother. With singular compound subjects connected by *and*, you can apply simple arithmetic:

The <u>pitcher</u> and the<u> catcher</u> <u>are</u> both fine players.

Pitcher + *catcher* = 2 people = plural subject requiring plural verb. But matters can get a tad more complicated:

1. *When you have more than one singular subject connected with "but," "or," or "nor."*
   These subjects take singular verbs, even though the idea expressed may be quite plural:

   Not only the pitcher <u>but</u> the catcher also <u>is</u> tired.

Both are tired, but the verb arbitrarily should be singular. Go figure. If you use *nor*, the agreement is at least a bit more logical:

   Neither the pitcher <u>nor</u> the catcher <u>is playing</u> well.

Both are still tired but neither one is playing well.

2. *When you have one singular and one plural subject.*
The verb agrees with the one that's closest:

> Champagne or sad <u>movies</u> <u>remind</u> me of you
> Sad movies or <u>champagne</u> <u>reminds</u> me of you.

3. *When you have subjects that sound plural but really are not.*
Singular subjects followed by any of these terms remain singular:

with	like	along with
besides	including	together with
as well as	namely	no less than

The meaning of the sentence may be distinctly plural but the subject is still grammatically singular:

> The Attorney General, as well as the President, is responsible for the decision.

Obviously, two people are responsible, but the verb remains faithful to the singular subject. This next example is more logical:

> Seymour, together with his St. Bernard, his pet alligator, and his seventeen goldfish, is planning to move in with us.

Although the group moving in is incontestably plural, only Seymour is doing the plan. As you can see, commas often set off these constructions, giving you a good clue that the subject remains separate.

The Expletive *There*

Although an indispensable little word, the expletive *there* causes more than its share of bother. An *expletive* is a filler word that stands enticingly at the beginning of a sentence, looking for all the world like the subject, when actually it's nothing of the kind. It's just taking up space until the real subject comes along. The word *there* is either an expletive or an adverb. You need to find out what the subject really is before sliding in a verb.

(wrong)   There is among all the weeds in my garden several exquisite begonias.

The actual subject is *begonias*:

(right)   There <u>are</u> among all the weeds in my garden several exquisite <u>begonias</u>.

Expletives in Questions. Don't forget that *there* can complicate questions as well as statements (and *there* won't necessarily be the very first word, either):

(wrong)   Is there in this line of work many opportunities for advancement?

Ask yourself, *what* is? Answer: *opportunities is.* But *opportunities* always *are*, so the verb needs changing. Or you can make those *opportunities* singular and write the sentence that way.

(right)   <u>Are</u> there in this line of work many <u>opportunities</u> for advancement?

(right)   <u>Is</u> there in this line of work any <u>opportunity</u> for advancement?

Collective Nouns and Indefinite Pronouns

Collective nouns, which name a group or a collection of people, usually are considered singular:

Theodore's <u>family</u> <u>is</u> quite small.

Our school <u>orchestra</u> <u>plays</u> extremely well.

The <u>audience</u> <u>was clapping</u> wildly.

Sometimes, if the members of the group are acting as individuals, a plural verb is used to indicate that the group is not considered a single unit:

The curriculum <u>committee</u> <u>disagree</u> on every issue.

Our old <u>gang</u> <u>have gone</u> their separate ways.

Even when a plural verb is used correctly with a collective noun, it may not sound correct. Some writers add a clearly plural noun, like *members,* to underscore the notion of individuality that the sentence is supposed to convey.

Some <u>members</u> of the curriculum committee <u>disagree</u> on every issue.

All the <u>members</u> of our old gang <u>have gone</u> their separate ways.

Several collective nouns (like *rest, remainder,* and *number*) and some *indefinite pronouns* (*some, all, enough, neither,* and *none*) can be either singular or plural, depending upon how they are used:

(singular)   The <u>rest</u> of the movie <u>is</u> sloppy and sentimental.

(plural)   The <u>rest</u> of us <u>are</u> leaving.

(singular)   <u>Some</u> of the pizza <u>has</u> anchovies on it.

(plural)   <u>Some</u> of players <u>are</u> already on the bus.

(singular)	<u>All</u> of the pizza <u>is</u> stone cold by now.
(plural)	<u>All</u> of the seats <u>are</u> taken.

TIP! When referring to *a number,* use a plural verb; when referring to *the number,* use a singular verb.

<u>A</u> <u>number</u> of students <u>are</u> ill; <u>the</u> <u>number</u> <u>is</u> getting larger every day.

When the indefinite pronouns *none* and *neither* are used alone, they take a singular verb:

(singular)	<u>None</u> <u>is</u> immune to this disease.
(singular)	<u>Neither</u> <u>has</u> arrived.

But when followed by phrases with a plural meaning, usage varies:

(plural)	<u>None</u> of us <u>are</u> ever going to eat there again.
(singular)	<u>None</u> of us <u>is</u> sick today, at least.

TIP! Be warned that some writers and editors insist that *none* and *neither* should always be singular.

The rest of the indefinite pronouns are singular and cause little trouble with verbs: *anyone, something, any, anybody, each, either, everybody, everyone, everything, nobody, no one, somebody, someone.*

<u>Anyone</u> <u>is allowed</u> to attend.

<u>Everything</u> <u>seems</u> in order.

<u>Somebody</u> <u>is pounding</u> on the door.

Exercise 13.1

Revise any of these sentences whose subjects and verbs do not agree. Some may be correct.

1. A child's personality and behavior is influenced to a great extent by environment.
2. In this new stage of our relationship comes new adjustments.
3. There has never been any concerted attempts to solve the mystery.
4. Financial support, like volunteer workers and effective speakers, are hard to get.
5. Movies packed with violence is still a favorite with the public.
6. There by the bank of that stream is a mass of lovely flowers.

7. Melba Starstruck, along with her agent, her latest husband, and her Bengal tiger, are staying at the Plaza.

8. In the center of the superstore lies various departments ranging from electronics to kitchenware.

9. Where has my toothbrush and the toothpaste gone?

10. The prime audience for advertising, mainly young people, are an easy target.

Exercise 13.2

If you still feel shaky about subject/verb agreement, see how you do choosing the correct word in the following sentences.

1. There (is/are) Yolanda and Chris, talking furiously.

2. Bananas and peanut butter (make/makes) a tasty snack.

3. Peanut butter and bananas (make/makes) a tasty snack.

4. The major impact of these statistics (has/have) not yet been analyzed.

5. Ingesting tar, as well as nicotine, (cause/causes) cigarette smoking to be hazardous to your health.

W atching Out for Irregular Verbs

Although sometimes the language seems irritatingly irregular, English is actually a well-patterned language. Only because we are accustomed to its regularity do we get thrown off track by its quirks—like irregular verbs.

Verbs in English regularly form their past tense and their past participle by adding -d or -ed or -t. The past participle is the form used with the helping verbs *has, have,* or *had* and with forms of *be* in passive verbs *(are used, was seen, will be changed)*.

I hope today, I hoped yesterday, I have hoped always.

I laugh today, I laughed yesterday, I had laughed before.

I spend today, I spent yesterday, I have spent too much.

As you can see, the past tense and past participle are the same for regular verbs.

But with the irregular verbs, you just have to memorize the principal parts. Here are the most common irregular verbs:

Present	Past	Past Participle
bring	brought	brought
begin	began	begun
break	broke	broken
burst	burst	burst
choose	chose	chosen
come	came	come
do	did	done
drag	dragged	dragged (not drug)
drink	drank	drunk
forget	forgot	forgotten (or forgot)
get	got	gotten
go	went	gone
lay	laid	laid (meaning placed)
lead	led	led
lie	lay	lain (meaning reclined)
ride	rode	ridden
rise	rose	risen
run	ran	run
see	saw	seen
swim	swam	swum
take	took	taken
wake	waked (or woke)	waked (or woke)

You can also look up the principal parts of verbs in your dictionary. If you don't find any listed, that means the verb is regular, adding -d, -ed, or -t.

Dictionary Exercise 13.3

Look up in a dictionary the principal parts of these verbs

climb	dive
freeze	awake
say	go
drown	shine
eat	drag

Were any alternate forms presented? Did any of the answers surprise you? If so, why?

Exercise 13.4

In the following sentences insert the form of the verb given in parentheses beforehand. Check the verbs against the list on p. 229. The first one is done for you as an example.

1. (*break*: past participle) You have <u>broken</u> your promise.
2. (*lay*: past) Yesterday I _____ my watch on the sink.
3. (*lie*: past) She was so tired that she _____ down.
4. (*set*: past) I _____ my watch ten minutes fast.
5. (*lie*: past participle) We had just _____ down when the telephone rang.
6. (*lay*: past participle) The goalie _____ down his face mask and chin protector.
7. (*drown*: past) His son almost _____ in the pool.
8. (*cost*: past participle) It has _____ me a lot to move.
9. (*go*: past participle) She has _____ to Montreal.
10. (*begin*: past participle) I have just _____ to fight.
11. (*see*: past) The director _____ to it that I knew my part.
12. (*bring*: past participle) What have you _____ to the picnic?
13. (*be*: past participle) They had _____ soundly defeated.
14. (*do*: past participle) You have _____ it again.
15. (*swim*: past) We _____ to the other side of the lake.

S taying in the Same Tense

Sometimes your prose gets rolling along and you shift into the wrong gear while moving, which causes an unpleasant grinding noise in your readers' heads. You should choose either present or past tense and stay with it. *Tense* in verbs has nothing to do with being uptight; it just indicates time. Here's an example of present tense:

Savio <u>is swimming</u> in his running shorts.

Past tense would be

Savio <u>was swimming</u> yesterday, too.

or

Savio <u>has been swimming</u> every day this week.

English has three simple tenses and three perfect tenses. There is a progressive form of each of these six tenses:

	Basic Form	Progressive Form
SIMPLE PRESENT	walk(s)	is (are) walking
SIMPLE PAST	walked	was (were) walking
SIMPLE FUTURE	will walk	will be walking
PRESENT PERFECT	has (have) walked	has (have) been walking
PAST PERFECT	had walked	had been walking
FUTURE PERFECT	will have walked	will have been walking

Simple present describes habitual actions (*Jamal walks to work*) and events that are happening now (*I see a blue heron by the dock*). Simple past describes actions completed entirely in the past (*Yesterday Jamal walked to work*). Simple future describes actions that have not yet happened (*Jamal will walk to work tomorrow*).

Present perfect describes actions that began in the past and might still be going on (*Jamal has walked to work for years*) or actions that occurred at some unspecified time in the past (*The leaves have turned yellow already*). Past perfect describes a past action that ended before another past action began (*Jamal hailed a cab after he had walked several blocks in the rain*). Future perfect tense describes actions that will be completed before or by a certain future time (*Jamal will have left by the time you get there*).

Progressive forms describe actions in progress: *Jamal is walking to work this morning. He was working on our tax accounts last night; he has been working on them for three days and will be working on them again this weekend.*

FIGURE 13.1   *Survey of Tenses*

There's a good bit of variety within the tenses. These variations are summarized for you in Figure 13.1. The main point to remember is to choose one tense and stay in it—unless you have some reason to change, like this:

> Savio is swimming today, but yesterday he played tennis.

Here's an example of a faulty tense shift, the kind that happens by accident and needs to be changed when you revise:

(inconsistent)   Savio was swimming across the pool, when suddenly he sinks under the water and failed to come up. I yell and jumped in to rescue him, when he shoots to the surface and laughed at me.

The passage sounds much better this way:

(consistent)   Savio was swimming across the pool, when suddenly he sank under the water and failed to come up. I yelled and jumped in to rescue him, when he shot to the surface and laughed at me.

TIP!   Remember to be consistent: choose present tense or past tense and stick with it.

Using the Literary Present Tense

If you are writing about literature, you will probably want to use the present tense even though you may be referring to works written decades ago, authors long dead, and characters never alive. The use of the present tense makes sense if you consider that the works, the authors, and the characters still live in our imaginations.

Adventures of Huckleberry Finn by Mark Twain <u>is</u> one of our greatest American novels.

Despite his deep and abiding cynicism, Mark Twain <u>remains</u> our most famous American humorist.

Huck Finn <u>tells</u> fibs to get himself and Jim out of scrapes, yet honesty <u>is</u> one of his great virtues.

W*riting Exercise 13.5*

Think about some person, some friend or relative, whom you have known for years. How has this person changed? How does he or she act toward you now that you are older? Write a paragraph that describes how your friend or relative has changed. Use present tense verbs to describe how the person is now and past tense verbs to describe how the person used to be.

R*evising Exercise 13.6*

The following paragraph contains uncalled for tense shifts. First, revise it to make all the verbs present tense; then go through it again and make all the verbs past tense.

(1) Bowser, the huge sheep dog who lives next door, had a shaggy coat and a loud, resounding bark. (2) He was friendly and loves to be petted, but his size frightened children. (3) He got so excited when kids came around that he knocks them down like bowling pins. (4) So, he spent his time barking at squirrels, or else he gallops along the fence and terrorized our tiny fox terrier. (5) Bowser really needed to live on a farm and have animals his own size to play with.

14

Managing
Pronouns
and Modifiers

Pronouns, for the most part, don't cause any more bother than do nouns, the words they replace. But you remember that pronouns must agree with their antecedents in number (singular or plural) and gender (male or female). Gender never causes agreement problems, but agreement in number can get tricky.

And modifiers usually know their place, but an occasional one will stray off and nudge up next to the wrong word, leaving your readers either puzzled or amused. But more on that later. We'll take up pronouns first.

S orting Out Agreement with Indefinite Pronouns

The indefinite pronouns that have been decreed singular (like *everyone, everybody, anyone, anybody, everything*) can cause confusion with pronouns referring to them. Consider these grammatically correct sentences:

Everyone applauded, and I was glad *he* did.

After *everybody* finished writing, the instructor passed among *him* and collected the papers.

The lack of logic in such constructions has always made the rule difficult to follow. So, standard usage is changing to allow these once singular indefinites to be followed by plural pronouns:

Everyone should wear *their* seat belts.

None of those arrested would admit *they* were involved.

That takes care of what used to be a truly troublesome problem with pronoun agreement.

TIP! **Be warned: some people do not like this usage.**
Some may declare you in error if you write *everyone* followed by *their*. To avoid ruffling such readers, you can use both singular pronouns, this way:

> *Everyone* should wear *his or her* seatbelt.
>
> *None* of those arrested would admit *he or she* was involved.

Or rewrite to avoid the issue:

> Everyone should wear *a* seatbelt.
>
> None of those arrested would admit being involved.

Srategies for Avoiding Sexist Pronouns

If your indefinite pronoun is singular in meaning, standard English once required you to write,

> *Each* student must show *his* permit to register.

Writers now take care to avoid sexist language that makes all people appear to be male. You can totally eliminate the difficulty by writing in the plural:

> *Students* must show *their* permits to register.

Or, you can do it this way:

> *Each* student must show *a* permit to register.

Occasionally, you may need to write a sentence in which you emphasize the singular:

> *Each* individual must speak *his* own mind.

But the sentence will be just as emphatic this way:

> *Each one of us* must speak *our* own mind.

TIP! **If you write in the plural, the problem disappears.**

Exercise 14.1

In the following sentences, select one or more pronouns to fill in the blanks. If you can't think of suitable words, rewrite the sentences in the plural.

1. Anyone living outside of town should leave _his / her_ job early to avoid getting _his / her_ car stuck in a snow drift.
2. A good student does _his or her_ own homework.
3. Someone has left _the_ carlights on.
4. Anyone wishing to improve _their_ tennis game should work on _their_ backhand.
5. Each must cast _our_ own vote.

C *onfusion with the Pronouns* **This** *and* **Which**

Most of the time when you use the pronoun *this*, your meaning is clear. You say, "This is my new tennis racquet," and because you're standing there holding it, your meaning is quite clear. But at other times, when you use *this* to refer to ideas or events, your meaning becomes hazy, especially if the pronoun gets too far away from its antecedent (the noun that names the idea or event you're talking about).

TIP! Whenever you use the word "this," try to follow it with a noun telling what "this" refers to.

If you're going to write,

> The importance of this becomes clear when we understand the alternatives.

at least give your readers a clue: this *plan,* this *principle,* this *problem,* this *stipulation,* this *qualification,* this *dichotomy,* this *stalemate,* this *whatever.* And if you have trouble supplying a noun to follow *this,* that's nature's way of telling you that the whole idea is vague, and you need to go back and clarify what *this* means in your own mind before you totally befuddle your readers.

The word *which* causes similar problems. Often this handy pronoun refers to an entire clause preceding it. Sometimes the meaning is clear, sometimes not. Suppose you write,

(unclear)   Germaine has received only one job offer, which depresses her.

That sentence can be interpreted two ways:

Germaine is depressed about receiving only one job offer, even though it's a fairly good one.

or

Germaine has received only one job offer—a depressing one at that.

Whenever you use the word *which*, make sure that your readers will be able to tell exactly what it means.

R*evising Exercise 14.2*

Revise the following sentences to eliminate any unclear pronoun reference.

1. Al asked if Jose allowed a speck of egg yolk or a particle of grease to get into the egg whites. This might keep the whites from fluffing up the way they should.

2. Meg ate Chinese food and went out jogging, which caused her to feel unwell.

3. Eating a simple meal in an outdoor setting, which I prefer, relaxes me after a hard day.

4. This makes all my symptoms of stress disappear.

5. I was late and skipped dinner, which got me in trouble.

C*hoosing Pronoun Case*—I *or* Me? He *or* Him?

Nouns do not change form when they move from being subjects to objects in a sentence. For instance, you can write,

Kesha resembles my sister.

My sister resembles Kesha.

But alas, as a holdover from Old English, pronouns still show *case* (subjective, objective, or possessive). So, with pronouns, we write,

She resembles my sister.

My sister resembles *her*.

The case forms are easy.

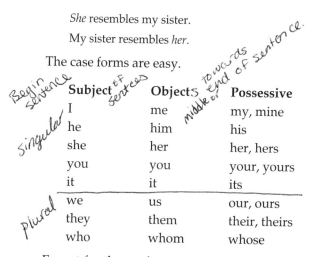

Subject	Objects	Possessive
I	me	my, mine
he	him	his
she	her	her, hers
you	you	your, yours
it	it	its
we	us	our, ours
they	them	their, theirs
who	whom	whose

Except for the confusion of *its* with the contraction *it's* and *whose* with *who's*, the possessives cause no concern. But you must make choices among the other forms in constructions like these:

1. *When you have more than one subject or object.*

(wrong)	Adrian and *me* went to a lecture.
(right)	Adrian and *I* went to a lecture.
(wrong)	LaWanda sat with Seymour and *I*.
(right)	LaWanda sat with Seymour and *me*.

Drop the word before (or after) the "and" to see how the pronoun sounds alone.

Me went to a lecture or *I* went to a lecture?

LaWanda sat with *I* or LaWanda sat with *me*?

You choice is now a no-brainer.

TIP! **Although prepositions are usually short words (***in, on, at, by, for,* **and the like), a few are deceptively long—** *through, beside, among, underneath, between.*

Long or short, prepositions always take object pronouns:

between Clyde and *me*

among Clyde, Clarence, and *him*

beside Clyde and *me*

---

2. *When pronouns are used as appositives.*

You remember what appositives are. They go like this:

we football fans	us football fans
we pizza lovers	us pizza lovers
we students	us students
we teachers	us teachers

Whether you choose *we* or *us* depends on whether the construction is the subject or the object.

(wrong)	*Us* fitness freaks are slaves to exercise.
(right)	*We* fitness freaks are slaves to exercise.
(wrong)	Weather can be bad news for *we* joggers.
(right)	Weather can be bad news for *us* joggers.

TIP! **If you're in doubt, just drop the appositive.**
Would you say "*Us* are slaves" or "*We* are slaves"? Your ear should tell you that *we* is the correct choice. And would it be "bad weather for *we*" or "bad weather for *us*"? Of course, it's "bad weather for *us*."

---

3. *When pronouns are used in comparisons.*

(wrong)	My sister is smarter than *me*.
(right)	My sister is smarter than *I*.

Just finish the incomplete comparison in your mind. Would you say, "My sister is smarter than *me* am"? If so, you're right about your sister but wrong about the pronoun. Most of us would say, "smarter than *I* am."

4. *When choosing between "who" and "whom."*
In speaking, you don't have to worry about this choice anymore; you can just use *who* in any construction. But if you're writing, you're expected to figure out whether to use the subject *who* or the object *whom*.

> Kate Chopin was a superb writer (who/whom) literary critics have neglected until recently.

Substitute the subject *he* (or *she*) or the object *him* (or *her*). Then ask yourself, "Critics have neglected *she*"? or "Critics have neglected *her*"? We would all choose *her*, of course. Because *her* is an object, the sentence needs the object *whom*:

> Kate Chopin was a superb writer *whom* literary critics have neglected until recently.

TIP! You can avoid the choice by using "that":

> Kate Chopin was a superb writer *that* literary critics have neglected until recently.

---

5. *Do not substitute* which *for* who *or* whom.

Standard usage still does not allow *which* to refer to people.

(unacceptable)	the candidate *which* I admire
(acceptable)	the candidate *whom* I admire
(acceptable)	the candidate *that* I admire

E*xercise 14.3*

Choose the correct pronoun in each sentence.

1. You can't win if you run against Malcolm and (she/her).
2. At the prom next Saturday Ashley and (I/me) are going to wear blue jeans.
3. For too long (we/us) taxpayers have been at the mercy of Congress.
4. (Who/Whom) is going to deliver the keynote address?
5. Stanley went to visit his mother (who/whom) he called "Muma."
6. Renato and (I/me) are planning to become vegetarians as soon as we finish our Big Macs.
7. Did both (she/her) and Cecil promise to come early to help?
8. The Senator is the person on (who/whom) I base all hope of the future.
9. We should be spared commercials (who/whom/that/which) are an insult to our intelligence.
10. We arranged to study for the big exam with Selina and (she/her).

R *evising Dangling and Misplaced Modifiers*

The word *modify* means to change. Thus a modifier in a sentence changes in some way the meaning of whatever it modifies. Here's a sentence with no modifiers:

> Maria graduated.

We'll add a couple of modifiers in italics:

> *Yesterday* Maria graduated *with honors.*

Positioning modifiers is usually easy, but sometimes they get stranded with nothing to modify—or else they stray off and modify the wrong thing, as in the following examples. The first is from the *Daily Bulletin,* the campus newspaper of the University of Tennessee:

> In 1978, Tennessee became the first state to adopt a child passenger protection law requiring the parents of children under four years of age to be restrained in a child safety seat.

From the *San Bernadino Sun:*

> A mountain lion suspected of killing at least two suburban dogs was shot to death after a state warden spotted it taking a report near the scene of the latest attack.

Repairing Dangling Modifiers

Modifiers that dangle aren't always funny. They can be annoying because they indicate that the writer isn't paying attention, like this:

> Driving through the lush, pine-scented forest, the air was suddenly fouled by the sulphurous belchings of a paper mill.

Clearly the *air* isn't driving though the forest. The opening modifier dangles with nothing in the sentence to modify. You can revise in a couple of ways:

> As we drove through the lush, pine-scented forest, the air was suddenly fouled. . . .

> Driving through the forest, we gasped as the air was suddenly fouled. . . .

To catch wayward modifiers, read your last draft carefully, paying attention to each sentence individually.

Modifiers often dangle in passive constructions, so take special care with the passive voice. The passive voice allows you to omit the person or entity doing the acting, thus positively inviting dangling modifiers:

(faulty)   Knowing that the airliner was off course, only two conclusions can be drawn.

Clearly, it wasn't the "conclusions" that knew the plane was off course. Whoever did the knowing got left out of the sentence entirely. When you revise in active voice, you'll need to supply a subject for the modifier:

(revised)   Knowing that the airliner was off course, *the investigators* could draw only two conclusions.

Moving Misplaced Modifiers

Misplaced modifiers may not be quite as annoying as dangling ones, but they can still mess up the meaning of your sentence, like this:

(faulty)   Once married, the Church considers that a couple has signed a lifelong contract.

It's not the Church that's getting married, so you need to move the modifier:

(revised)   The Church considers that a couple, once married, has signed a lifelong contract.

Sometimes a misplaced modifier can badly skew the meaning of a sentence, as in this example taken from a college newspaper:

(faulty)   DARE is sponsoring a series of presentations on drugs for college students.

That sentence wrongly gives the impression that DARE is in the business of acquainting college students with drugs to use. The meaning is less ambiguous this way:

(revised)   DARE is sponsoring a series of presentations for local college students on the dangers of drug use.

As you revise, check your sentences for lapses in logic caused by misplaced modifiers.

Revising Exercise 14.4

Revise the following sentences to eliminate all misplaced or dangling modifiers. You may need to add information to help some of these make sense.

1. After deciding which section will be sewn first, the material must then be cut.
2. I had been driving for forty years when I fell asleep and had an accident.
3. Otis was robbed at gun point in the elevator where he lives.
4. At college I hope to start singing with a scholarship.
5. A crutch is a device used to take weight off an injured leg by sticking it under the arm and leaning on it.
6. I do not see my Aunt Frieda much in Toronto.
7. With this total lack of responsibility, more and more items were purchased.
8. Consider this letter to the editor of an urban newspaper a few years ago.
9. The poem exemplifies the patriarchal success of the socialization of women.
10. After reading the essays, papers were written discussing the ideas.

Rewriting Exercise 14.5

Explain how the following sentences might be misread. Then rewrite them to make the meaning clear and unambiguous.

1. The company packages natural meals for children that can be shipped anywhere.
2. North Dakota citizens' groups are sending volunteers to help flood relief workers in Manitoba.
3. The Senate plans to resume consideration of legislation to restrict campaign contributions next week.
4. Joel Quenneville signed a $1 million contract to coach the Oilers yesterday.
5. A municipal task force announced its plan to increase parking at a city hall press conference.
6. The plan will increase parking in congested areas.

7. The superintendent called for a meeting to talk about increasing teenage drug use with members of the school board.

8. The passengers wanted their ordeal to end desperately.

9. The Grishams decided their daughter would be a lawyer before she was ten years old.

10. The restaurant had many autographs of celebrities on the walls that had eaten there.

15

A User's Guide to Troublesome Words And Phrases

Usage means the way the language is used. But different people use the language in different ways. And even the same people use the language differently on different occasions. You probably speak one way in the classroom or on the job and another way at a party or a ball game. Good usage, then, is a matter of using language *appropriate* to the occasion.

In this chapter we describe the current usage of terms that are often confused and misunderstood; we also point out when words and expressions are unacceptable or questionable for formal or even informal writing. (To refresh your memory about the characteristics of the various levels of language, see pages 21–24.) In making decisions on usage, we have been guided by *Webster's Dictionary of English Usage; Fowler's Modern English Usage*, 3rd ed.; *The American Heritage Dictionary of the English Language*, 4th ed.; and several popular composition handbooks.

If you are still in doubt about some terms or have questions about words that don't appear in this chapter, consult your trusty collegiate dictionary. But be sure it's a recent one: even the best dictionaries will be out of date on usage within ten years. You may also need to consult Chapter 11 to check pertinent grammatical terms and concepts.

H *azardous Usage*

Standard usage means the language used by educated people, *nonstandard usage* means any language that fails to conform to this accepted standard. Unfortunately, dialectical expressions are considered nonstandard. Some dictionaries label such usage as *illiterate*, which seems harsh, but you should be advised that many people are unalterably opposed to nonstandard English in business and academic writing. Avoid the following words and phrases, or use them only with extreme caution for stylistic effect.

ain't People have been using this word in speech for at least 200 years, but it's still considered nonstandard. Don't use it unless you're writing dialogue or trying to get a laugh. Use *am not, are not (aren't)*, or *is not (isn't)*.

a lot It's still two words: *a* + *lot* (a noun meaning a large extent or amount).

> Your complaints have caused *a lot* of trouble.
>
> We are feeling *a lot* better.

analyzation The standard term is analysis; tacking on extra syllables doesn't make it any grander—only incorrect.

anyways/anywheres These terms are nonstandard. Use *anyway* and *anywhere*.

could of/should of/would of These phrases are nonstandard for *could have, should have, would have.*

enthused Many people prefer that you use enthusiastic.

> (familiar)   The critics were *enthused* about our performance.
>
> (preferred)   The critics were *enthusiastic* about our performance.

etc. This abbreviation means "and so forth." Do not use it just to avoid thinking of good examples, and avoid ending a list with *etc.* unless the other examples are obvious (like large cities: Paris, Rome, London, etc.). Even then, it's usually more effective to end with an example or to use the more graceful phrase *and so on.* Never write *and etc.;* it's redundant.

hardly   This adverb carries a negative meaning, so don't combine it with a negative verb.

(nonstandard)	She *can't hardly* see without her glasses.
(standard)	She *can hardly* see without her glasses.
	She *can't* see without her glasses.

hisself   This word is nonstandard. Use *himself.*

irregardless   Most people still steadfastly refuse to accept irregardless as standard English. Use *regardless* or *nonetheless.*

myself   This word is a reflexive or intensive pronoun; use it only when an antecedent appears in the same sentence: *I cut myself shaving* (reflexive); *I will fix the faucet myself* (intensive). Do not use *myself* in place of *I* (a subject pronoun) or *me* (an object pronoun).

(familiar)	Bertie and *myself* are going to be partners.
(preferred)	Bertie and *I* are going to be partners.
(familiar)	Will you play tennis with Bertie and *myself?*
(preferred)	Will you play tennis with Bertie and *me?*

quote   *Quote* is a verb:

> Leroy quotes Shakespeare in his sleep.

In writing avoid using *quote* or *quotes* as a shortened form of *quotation* or *quotation marks.*

suppose to/use to   These are nonstandard; the correct forms are *supposed to* and *used to.* Be careful to add the *-d* in writing, even though you don't hear it in speech.

theirself/theirselves/themself   These are all nonstandard forms of *themselves.*

D *ouble Trouble: Words That Are Easily Confused*

The English language is filled with words that look alike or sound alike or are alike in meaning, and they cause problems for many writers. The only way to handle these similar terms is to stay alert for them and double-check their every use when you proofread. It's not just a matter of learning how to spell the words correctly; you also have to match the spelling with the meaning. Keeping a list of the ones that give you trouble will increase your awareness and save you time when you edit. And remember: the spell checker on your computer won't help you with these words that sound and look alike.

a/an   Use *a* before words that begin with consonant sounds; use *an* before words that begin with vowel sounds *(a, e, i, o, u).*

a martini	an Irish coffee
a tree toad	an armadillo
a hopeful sign (the *h* is sounded)	an honest decision (the *h* is silent)
a hostile crowd (sounded *h*)	an hour exam (silent *h*)
a one-car accident (*o* sounds like *w*)	an only child
a university (*u* sounds like *y*)	an unusual request

An was once used before unaccented syllables beginning with *h*: *an historian, an hotel.* But that usage has changed; it's now acceptable to write *a historian* or *a hotel.*

accept/except   *Accept,* a verb, means "to receive or to agree with."

> We *accept* your gracious apology.

Except, a preposition, means "other than" or "leaving out."

> He didn't utter a word *except* to complain.

> Everyone will attend the banquet, *except* Alain.

Except isn't used often as a verb, but it means "to exclude."

> Senior citizens are *excepted* from paying full price.

advice/advise   *Advice* is a noun; *advise* is a verb. When you *advise* someone, you are giving *advice.*

> vb.
> We *advise* you to top smoking.

> n.
> Sun-Lee refuses to follow our good *advice.*

affect/effect In general usage the verb *affect* means "to influence," and the noun *effect* means "the result of some influence."

            n.   vb.
The *effect* on my lungs from smoking should *affect* my decision to quit.

                      vb.
Smoking adversely *affects* our health.

                                    n.
Carleton smokes expensive cigars for *effect*.

Just to confuse things further, *effect* can also be a verb meaning "to bring about." And *affect* can be a verb meaning "to put on or simulate" or a noun meaning "emotional response."

            vb.
We need to *effect* [bring about] some changes in the system.

            vb.
He *affects* [puts on] the petulance of a rock star.

                           n.
Psychologists say that inappropriate *affect* [emotional response] is a feature of schizophrenia.

These last three meanings are seldom confused with the more widely used words above. Concentrate on getting those first common meanings straight.

all right/alright Although *alright* is gaining acceptance in the world of advertising, you should stick with *all right* to be safe. *Alright* is definitely not *all right* with everybody yet.

almost/most See *most/almost.*

already/all ready *Already* means "before, previously, or so soon."

    Gabrielle has *already* eaten two cheeseburgers.

All ready means "prepared."

    Pedro is *all ready* to deliver his anti-junk food lecture.

altogether/all together *Altogether* means "entirely, thoroughly."

    Emil's analysis is *altogether* absurd.

All together means "as a group."

Let's sing the last chorus *all together.*

among/between Use *among* when referring to more than two items.

Ashley found it difficult to choose from *among* so many delectable desserts.

Use *between* when referring to only two.

She couldn't decide *between* the raspberry tort and the butterscotch mousse.

anymore/any more Use *any more* if you mean "any additional."

Ashley won't be eating *any more* desserts.

Use *anymore* with negative verbs if you mean "any longer."

She doesn't eat desserts *anymore.*

Don't use *anymore* with positive verbs; use *now* or *nowadays.*

(familiar) All she eats *anymore* is salad and fruit.

(preferred) All she eats *nowadays* is salad and fruit.

apprise/appraise To *apprise* means to "inform or serve notice."

The judge *apprised* the defendant of her right to counsel.

To *appraise* means to "evaluate or judge."

The fugitive *appraised* the situation and caught the next flight to South America.

bad/badly *Bad* is an adjective; use it after linking verbs *(be, feel, seem, appear, look, become, smell, sound, taste).*

We feel *bad* about missing your birthday.

I feel *bad* because I'm coming down with a cold.

Badly is an adverb; use it to modify verbs.

The car is vibrating *badly.*

The car was *badly* damaged.

If you just can't remember these distinctions, choose another word.

> We feel sorry about missing your birthday.
>
> I feel awful because I'm coming down with a cold.
>
> The car is vibrating alarmingly.
>
> The car was seriously damaged.

between/among See *among/between.*

choose/chose *Choose* (rhymes with *ooze*) means a decision is being made now.

> Please *choose* a new lab partner for me.

Chose (rhymes with *toes*) means a choice has already been made.

> The one you *chose* for me last semester was incompetent.

cite/site/sight *Cite*, a verb, means "to quote as an authority or example."

> In her speech Molly Ivins *cited* three passages from the Bill of Rights.

Site, a noun, means "a particular place."

> We found a perfect *site* to hold our rally.

As a verb, *sight* means "to observe or notice."

> Astronomers recently *sighted* a new comet.

As a noun, *sight* means something that is seen or foreseeable or worth seeing.

> There is no end in *sight* to this heat wave.
>
> One of Quebec's most famous *sights* is the Citadel fortress.

compare/contrast These words overlap in meaning. While *compare* generally means to focus on similarities and *contrast* means to focus on differences, you are comparing when you make a contrast.

complement/compliment *Complement* is a verb meaning "to go together with or complete" and a noun meaning "something that completes."

> Aimée's lilac scarf *complements* her lavender sweater.

> The scarf is also a good *complement* to her whole outfit.

Compliment is a verb meaning "to praise or flatter" and a noun meaning "an expression of praise or flattery."

> Many people *complimented* Aimée on her clothes.

> She received many *compliments* on her sense of style.

continual/continuous There is a slight difference between these two words, although many people treat them the same. *Continual* describes an action that is repeated at intervals; its synonyms are *recurrent* or *intermittent*. *Continuous* means something that is extended or prolonged without interruption; its synonyms are *uninterrupted* or *incessant*.

> The *continual* banging of the shutters kept me awake.

> They kept a *continuous* watch for approaching storms.

desert/dessert People who get their just *deserts* are getting what they deserve. People who get *desserts* are eating something like cheesecake or pie with ice cream at the end of a meal.

disinterested/uninterested Although the distinction between these words is important, many people confuse them. *Disinterested* means "impartial or objective."

> You need a totally *disinterested* counselor to help you with your marriage problems.

Uninterested means "not interested."

> Andre is totally *uninterested* in environmental causes.

dominant/dominate *Dominant* is an adjective.

> Luis has a *dominant* personality.

> Brown eyes are genetically *dominant*.

Dominate is a verb.

> Cecil's brothers *dominate* him.

effect/affect   See *affect/effect.*

everyday/every day   Use *everyday* as an adjective to modify a noun.

> Jacques is wearing his *everyday* clothes.

Use *every day* to mean "daily."

> It rains in Juneau almost *every day.*

hung/hanged   These are the alternate past and past participle forms of the verb "to hang." If you are talking about hanging inanimate objects, then *hung* is the correct form:

> The people at the art museum *hung* the pictures upside down.

But if you are referring to executing people by suspending them by the neck, then *hanged* is the one you want.

> They *hanged* the prisoner at dawn.

imply/infer   *Imply* means to state indirectly or throw out a suggestion.

> Theo *implied* that he was a computer expert.

Infer means to draw a conclusion or take in a suggestion.

> The boss *inferred* that Theo had exaggerated his credentials.

its/it's   Do not confuse these two terms. Memorize the two definitions if you have trouble with them, and when you proofread, check to be sure you have not confused them accidentally. *Its* is a possessive pronoun.

> That dog wags *its* tail whenever *its* owner walks into the room.

It's is a contraction of "it is" or "it has."

> *It's* a great day for taking the dog for a walk.

> *It's* been a long time since you walked the dog.

TIP! If you never can keep the two straight, quit using the contraction. Write *it is* or *it has.*

---

lay/lie   To *lay* means to put or place; to *lie* means to recline. Be sure you know the principal forms of each verb; then decide which verb you need:

> (to place)   lay, laid, laid, laying
>
> (to recline)   lie, lay, lain, lying

Remember that *lay* requires a direct object: you always *lay* something. But you never *lie* anything: you just *lie down*, or *lie quietly*, or *lie under a tree*, or *lie on a couch.*

> (no direct object)   Duncan *lies* in the hammock.
>
> (direct object)   Duncan usually *lays* the mail on the hall table.

If you absolutely can't keep these verbs straight in your mind, choose another word.

> Duncan *lounges* in the hammock.
>
> Duncan usually *puts* the mail on the hall table.

lead/led   Pronunciation causes the confusion here.

Lead (rhymes with *bed*), a noun, means "a heavy, grayish metal."

> Our airy hopes sank like *lead.*

Lead (rhymes with *seed*) is the present tense of the verb meaning "to guide."

> He *leads* me beside the still waters.

Led (rhymes with *bed*) is the past tense of the verb *lead.*

> Marcelo *led* the march last year, but he vows he will not *lead* it again.

lose/loose   This is another problem in pronunciation and spelling.

Lose (rhymes with *ooze*) is a verb meaning "to fail to keep something."

> If we *lose* our right to protest, we will ultimately *lose* our freedom.

Loose (rhymes with *goose*) is an adjective meaning "not tight."

The noose is too *loose* on your lasso.

most/almost *Most* is colloquial when used to mean "almost."

(familiar) *Most* everyone in the office took Friday off.

(preferred) *Almost* everyone in the office took Friday off.

prejudice/prejudiced *Prejudice* (without the *-d*) is a noun.

Prejudice remains engrained in our society.

Prejudiced (with the *-d*) is the past participle of the verb *to preju-dice;* it means "affected by prejudice." Do not leave off the *-d* when using this word as an adjective.

adj.   n.
A *prejudiced* person is someone who harbors *prejudice.*

pred. adj.
Our society remains *prejudiced* against minorities.

principal/principle *Principle* means a rule or fundamental truth: a person of high moral *principle,* a primary *principle* of physics, the *principle* of equal justice. You can remember the *-le* spelling by association with the *-le* ending of *rule.* All other uses end with *-al:* a high school *principal,* the *principal* of a loan, a *principal* cause or effect, the *principal* (main character) in a film or play.

probable/probably Both of these words mean "likely." *Probable* (sounds at the end like *capable*) is an adjective, and *probably* (ends with a long *e* sound, like *capably*) is an adverb.

adj.   adv.
The *probable* involvement of the CIA in the uprising *probably* caused the rebels to lose.

quite/quiet *Quite* means "entirely" or "truly"; use it to qualify adjectives and adverbs: *quite* suddenly, *quite* often, *quite* right. *Quiet* means the opposite of "loud."

Carlos was *quite* ready to yell, "Be *quiet,* please!"

raise/rise You never *rise* anything, but you always *raise* something. Prices *rise,* spirits *rise,* curtains *rise,* temperatures *rise,* and the sun *rises;* but you *raise* children, *raise* corn, *raise* prices, *raise* a ruckus, or *raise* the window.

> Taxes are *rising* because Congress has *raised* the defense budget again.

If you cannot keep these verbs straight, avoid them.

> Taxes are going up because Congress has increased the defense budget again.

real/really Do not use *real* as an adverb or qualifier in writing.

> (familiar) Maya saw a *real* interesting movie.
>
> (standard) Maya saw a *really* interesting movie.

rise/raise See *raise/rise.*

sit/set You seldom *sit* anything. You *sit* down or *sit* for a while or *sit* in a chair. One notable exception: *sit* can mean "to cause to be seated." Thus, it's quite correct to write: "The parole officer should *sit* Buffy down and give her a lecture."

But you always set something. You set a glass down or set a time or set the table. Exceptions: in some common phrases *set* does not have an object—the sun *sets,* jello and concrete *set,* and hens *set*—but these uses seldom cause trouble.

than/then See *then/than.*

their/there/they're These words are easy to confuse because they sound exactly alike. But their meanings and uses are quite different.

Their is a possessive modifier or pronoun.

> *Their* dog is friendly. That dog is *theirs.*

There is an adverb or an expletive (a filler word that delays the subject).

> (adverb) Sylvia is over *there.*
>
> (expletive) *There* is no one with her.

They're is a contraction of *they are.*

> *They're* gone now.

then/than These words have quite different meanings. *Then* means "at that time in the past" or "next in time, space, or order."

> We were all much younger *then*.
>
> We watched the late movie and *then* went to bed.

Than is used in comparisons.

> No one talks more *than* Michael does.
>
> Claudia would rather talk *than* eat.

to/too/two *To* is usually a preposition and sometimes an adverb; it also introduces an infinitive.

> *to* the depths, push the door *to*, *to* swing

Too is a qualifier or an adverb meaning "also."

> Don't make *too* much noise. (qualifier of "much")
>
> Clement is going, *too*. (means "also")

Two is the number.

> *two* paychecks, *two* miles

weather/whether *Weather* is what goes on outside; *whether* introduces an alternative. Using the wrong one causes serious misunderstandings.

> We cannot decide *whether* the *weather* will be suitable for a picnic.

who/which/that Use *who* to refer to people (or to animals you are personifying).

> The person *who* lost the car keys. . . .
>
> Lenin, *who* is Susie's cat, . . .

Use *which* to refer to animals and nonliving things.

> The earth, *which* blossoms in the spring, . . .
>
> The cat, *which* is sitting in the window, . . .

Use *that* to refer to either people or things.

The person *that* lost the car keys. . . . *(who* is preferred in formal usage)

The earth *that* blossoms in spring. . . .

The cat *that* is sitting in the window. . . .

your/you're   *Your* is a possessive modifier or pronoun.

Here is *your* book; this book is *yours.*

You're is a contraction of *you are.*

Let me know when *you're* leaving.

Index

for comparison and contrast, 45
for descriptions, 34–35
finding, 6–8
for narratives, 32–33
narrowing, 6–7, 119
for process writing, 38
for research writing, 118–121
to, too, and *two,* 256
Transitions, 58–64
echo, 63–64
listed, 60–61
between paragraphs, 62–64
within paragraphs, 58–62
rhetorical questions as, 59–62
short sentences as, 59–62
Transitive verb, 186–187
Translations, in Works Cited lists (MLA),
168

Underdeveloped paragraphs, 51
Underlining. *See* Italics, use of
uninterested and *disinterested,* 251
Unity, achieving, 58–64
Unnecessary words, 76–77
Unneeded commas, 197–199
Usage, 244–245
Usage levels
familiar writing, 23–24
formal writing, 21–22
informal writing, 23
use to and *suppose to,* 246

Variety, in sentences, 85–91
Verbal phrase fragments, 208–209
Verbs
action, 80–81
agreement between subjects and,
220–228
defined, 184
intransitive, 186
irregular, 228–230
linking, 187
lively, 34, 80–81
regular, 228
singular form of, 220–221
tenses of, 230–232
in thesis, 7
transitive, 186–187
voice of, 77–78
Videotapes, in Works Cited lists (MLA), 171
Voice
active, 77–78
human, writing in a, 18–19
passive, 78–79

we, in formal writing, 19, 21
weather and *whether,* 256
Web pages and sites, 127–129. *See also* World
Wide Web
in Works Cited lists (MLA), 173
whether and *weather,* 256
which, 235, 239, 256
who and *whom,* 238–239
who, which, and *that,* 239, 256–257
Wordiness, 76–77
Word processors
disadvantages of, 100
revising on, 99–100
Words
ambiguities and confusion in, 81–82
biased, avoiding, 27
colloquialisms, 24
definitions of, 81–82
denotative and connotative meanings of,
106
easily confused, 246–257
euphemisms, 28–29
expletives, 223, 225–226
figures of speech, 83–84
gender bias, avoiding, 25–27
jargon, 24–25
lively, 80–81
repetition of, 59, 74, 90–91
slang, 24
specificity and clarity of, 80–83
synonyms, 81–83
unnecessary, 76–77
usage levels of
familiar, 23–24
formal, 21–22
informal, 23
used as words
italicizing of, 218
Working outline, 135–136
Works by the same author
in References lists (APA), 175–176
in Works Cited lists (MLA), 164, 166
Works Cited lists (MLA), 162
sample entries for, 166–173
World Wide Web
advice about using, 130–131
use in research, 125, 126, 127–130
in Works Cited lists (MLA), 173
would of, 245
Writing process, overview of, 3–17
Writing topics. *See* Topics for Writing

you, 19, 23
your and *you're,* 257

Credits

Pages 66–67, 69–70:	Portions of "Overemphasizing Crime," by Anthony Wilson-Smith, August 7, 2000, reprinted courtesy of *Maclean's Magazine*.
Page 124:	"Tennis Technology," © 1998 Time Inc. Reprinted by permission.
Page 128:	Library of Congress Web home page reprinted courtesy of the Library of Congress.
Page 129:	Key word search for "Kwanzaa" page reproduced courtesy of Microsoft. The Amazon.com logo is the registered trademark of Amazon.com, Inc.
Page 150:	"Kwanzaa" reprinted with the permission of Amelia Doggett.

www. Stylewizard.com/cgi-bin/
apawizb.cgi